PORCH TO PULPIT

The Life-Long Search
of a Doorstep Baby

Cover: The photo collage is of the Mission Covenant Church in Helena, Montana where two week old Wesley was left on the porch steps with a note attached.

PORCH
TO
PULPIT

The Life-Long Search
of a Doorstep Baby

Wesley C. Swanson

ACKNOWLEDGEMENTS

I want to especially thank my devoted wife Carolyn, without whose love, encouragement, patience and insightful suggestions this legacy book would not have appeared.

I gratefully acknowledge Linda Larson for all the editing and helpful suggestions and for being my encouraging daughter-in-law.

To Megan Allen, my IT assistant, who guided me through the computer mazes and did final editing.

Special thanks to Sandy Thornton, my publisher who rescued my project and gave me hope when it looked like the project was dead. Thank you dear friend.

To Bob Bach, our good friend from college days, who motivated me to consider writing my life story long before I did.

To Carl H. Johnson, who surprised me at the retired pastor/missionary retreat with the suggested title for my book.

To my sons, step-children and their families who have blessed my life with their friendship, patience and constant love.

I'm eternally grateful for Clarice and Sandy who I loved and lost for a little while, but who modeled how to live in faith and die with hope and now sing with the angels.

To the many friends who so often asked me how my writing was going and prayed for me throughout the process.

I'm so grateful for the congregations that I have been privileged to serve and who showed me what it was like to follow in the footsteps of Jesus and walk by faith and not by sight.

DEDICATED

To my birth mother, who loved me from afar and to my adoptive parents who modeled unconditional love before I could accept it for myself.

CONTENTS

INTRODUCTION

This is a story that begins with fear. It's my life story. I grew up with the fear that I would die young. I even told people that I believed my life would be short. It all began with a fearful lie.

That negative idea, that fear, had slowly worked its way into my mind from childhood fears that my life didn't matter and I was a reject. I'm amazed at the lies I once believed.

But now, as I approach my eightieth birthday, I am glad to say, "I'm still here!" I didn't die young and my life did matter. And now it's time to share my journey from fear and shame to hope. I want to share how I discovered that my life was not worthless and I was not a reject destined to die young. My life has instead been long and rich and blessed by love and grace.

I write this especially for my children and my grandchildren, whom I love dearly, that they may know the fears, the events, the people, the love that marked my life, and mainly the truth that changed my life and gave me hope.

Perhaps, in telling my story, the story of a doorstep baby, you may begin to discover a life free from fear; a life that really matters.

"Jesus said, *'If you hold to my teaching…. Then you will know the truth, and the truth will set you free."* John 8:31-32

CHAPTER 1

THE LIFELONG SEARCH OF A DOORSTEP BABY

ABANDONED ON A DOORSTEP

I never knew my mother. I have no picture of her and no memories of her face. She left no birth certificate with me to give me information about her or even the actual date of my birth. I don't even know her name. Nevertheless, she has always been a significant and formative part of my life and she left me with a lifelong yearning to know my birth mother.

I have never felt the same way about my biological father. I have no compelling desire to know him, though there have been times that I have studied my image in the mirror and wondered if I see a reflection of him in me.

I've puzzled about this strange longing in my soul, this hole in my heart that cries out for my birth mother. I have come to believe this craving is God ordained. The Scriptures affirm repeatedly this bonding of mother and child. Psalm 139:14 and 16 says, "You (Almighty God) knit me together in my mother's womb. I praise you because I am fearfully and wonderfully made...Your eyes saw my unformed body. All the days ordained for me were written in your book before one of them came to be."

Being "knit together" for nine months in a mother's womb brings about an intimate bonding of mother and child that goes deep into the genetic make-up of a person; an inseparable bond. She was the hub of my life as she nursed me at her breast for two and a half weeks. Her arms were my safety-net, my security....and then suddenly she gave me away. She left me on the porch of a church doorstep with no trace of her. She took me from her arms, where I felt safe, and gave me to strangers. And then she disappeared from my world. Abandoned!

Being left on a church doorstep had a profound impact on my life and all of my life relationships. It left me with a hole in my heart and a lifelong fear of rejection and abandonment. And as a grown man I still wrestle with this intense desire to know my mother.

I often wonder about the panic and dread she must have felt as she slipped through the shadows with her baby on that night of June 22, 1938. It was Wednesday Evening Bible Study and prayer meeting night at the Mission Covenant Church in Helena, Montana. Fearing that she might attract attention, or make some noise that would expose her, she must have moved silently toward the church to leave her newborn baby in a basket under the porch covering of the church steps. No one heard her.

In that basket with the baby, she carefully included some well-worn receiving blankets and diapers, some bottles and nipples as well as a note addressed to the church pastor. The note was written on a torn piece of brown grocery bag paper where she wrote that she was "a despondent mother;"

Pastor,
Please give my baby the home I can't.
Don't try to find me.
A despondent mother

The dictionary defines "despondency" as being, "in despair, being disheartened, frustrated, struggling in the face of defeat, having lost hope." I can only guess at her situation, but it must have been one of intense struggle and hopelessness that had left her "despondent." Perhaps her family's poverty at the end of the "Great Depression" did not leave enough food to feed another mouth. She could also have been a young, unmarried girl without the liberty, in that era, to raise her son alone. She had no one else to turn to for help.

I can only make a guess as to her situation, but what *I know* is that *she selected* this young pastor and his wife in Helena, Montana to "give my baby the home I can't."

I've come to believe that my birth mother must have been a courageous and self-sacrificing woman. A part of my yearning to know her is just to say, "Thank you for giving me life and not aborting me. Thank you for giving me to wonderful parents who loved me unconditionally."

I've comforted myself with the hope that she was a believer in Jesus Christ. Otherwise, why would she want me to be raised by a Christian pastor and his wife, and why chose to leave me on the steps of a Christian church unless she wanted her son raised in a faith community?

I look forward to meeting her in heaven someday soon. Until then, I've felt that I needed to respect her request, "Don't try to find me." While many people have urged me over the years to undertake a search for her (especially in this day of DNA tracking), I nevertheless have wanted to honor her request to remain unknown and unsought. But I still cry out for my birth mother.

CELEBRATION IN THE PARSONAGE

On the other side of the church steps, my arrival created quite a stir of excitement; even pandemonium.

Everyone, among the family and friends of Pastor Clarence and Helga Swanson, knew how deeply this young ministry couple longed to start a family of their own. For over eight years of their marriage they had struggled with the pain of infertility. And when Helga had to undergo surgery for a total hysterectomy, they knew the stark reality that they would never conceive a child of their own.

As part of her recovery, Helga traveled with friends in June to Minnesota, where she hoped to recover some strength and begin healing from the physical and emotional pain of infertility. Here they agreed she could spend a quiet month of convalescence at her sister's farm in the northern part of the state, to be joined by her husband during his vacation in July.

In his wife's absence, Pastor Clarence continued serving the church and on a chilly Montana evening in June he welcomed a number of church members to the Wednesday Bible Study and prayer meeting. At the conclusion of the prayer service, as people began to leave, one of the deacons, Mr. Westland, came back into the church and said, "Now that your wife is in Minnesota, did you want our families to wash those sheets and blankets in the wicker basket on the church steps?" The pastor said he knew nothing about a wicker basket with blankets, but thought he better check this out. So, the whole prayer group quickly gathered on the steps of the church as the young pastor examined the contents of the basket. As he lifted sheets and blankets out of the basket he heard a faint cry. With trembling hands, he hurriedly reached to the bottom of the basket, where to his amazement he found a newborn baby wrapped in an old tattered receiving blanket.

The entire prayer group excitedly reassembled inside the church, where upon examining the baby, they found a note from the birth mother attached to the blankets. The note amazingly said this baby was given to the pastor and his wife as she had no home in which to raise her son. With that information from the mother, the prayer group all agreed that the authorities should be called and the baby taken to the Montana Children's Home and Hospital for foundling babies.

While waiting for the authorities to arrive, the pastor suddenly found himself all alone with the baby as church members raced for their cars to get home quickly and tell their families the exciting news of a baby left on the church doorstep. In the absence of any help to change diapers, the pastor did what any man would do, he called his wife and said, "Come home quick, I've just had a baby!"

He called his wife and said, "Come home quick, I've just had a baby!"

After the baby was taken to the foundling hospital, the Sheriff's Department made a careful search for the birth mother but found no one. In the meantime, the Superintendent of the Hospital, Mr. Milo F. Dean, noting the blonde hair and blue eyes of the baby, gave him the Swedish name of Carl Olson. He wrote on the hospital records:

"I, Milo F. Dean, do hereby certify that I am the Superintendent of the Montana Children's Hospital and as such have complete knowledge of the information regarding Carl Olson. I further certify that on June 22, 1938, an infant baby boy of the approximate age of three weeks, was left on the doorstep of Reverend Clarence Swanson. That on the advice of the pediatrician at the hospital, the birth date was established as approximately June 4, 1938. I further certify that no information as to the whereabouts or identity of said parents has been learned, and that an order was made by the District Court of the First Judicial District of the State of Montana, committing the child to the custody and control of the Montana Children's Home and Hospital"
MILO F. DEAN (signed)

Later that week, with the baby now in the care of the hospital, Pastor Clarence sent a letter to his wife in Minnesota, along with a picture of the baby which had been taken by one of the hospital nurses. Helga wrote in her journal:

"When I got the letter from Clarence, I went up to my bedroom at my sister Ethel's home and read it. I just broke down and wept and wept. I had so wanted a baby but for some reason I couldn't have one. And now God, in sending this little one to us, it was such an answer to prayer that it just overwhelmed me. My sister, hearing my crying, wondered what was wrong, so I went downstairs and told her and we rejoiced together."

As soon as Helga returned to Montana, the whole church began celebrating the birth of this little doorstep baby who now lived in the church parsonage. Helga wrote:

"The church members were just as excited about this baby as we were. So the church had a big shower for us and just about everyone gave something to this little son of ours. Even the young men and the Sunday School children gave something. They were all so happy. The church ladies would stop in at the parsonage on Sunday mornings just to get a peek at this baby boy who lay sleeping in a lovely bassinet that our doctor's wife fixed up and let us use as long as we needed it. Wesley was a real joy to me."

Several months later, the pastor and his wife stood before a judge of the District Court in Lewis and Clark County of Montana and adopted that baby. The judge turned to the couple and said, "What name do you want to give this child?" The pastor told the judge, "We want to name him after two great Christian evangelists, John and Charles Wesley. His name will be Wesley Clarence Swanson."

In that Montana courtroom, I began *my new life.* Suddenly, the abandoned baby left on the church doorstep became a *new person.* I received *a new name,* no longer Carl Olson, but now, Wesley Clarence Swanson. I now had *a birth certificate,* I was no longer a non-person, but I had proof of my

At three months, I was happy to be in the bassinet that the Doctor's wife loaned to my parents.

birth. I had *a new date of birth,* approximately June 4, 1938 (actually, my mom Helga picked the date of June 4 to correspond to her birth date of November 4, after the pediatrician said she could set the birth date anytime in the first week of June). And *I had new parents,* Clarence and Helga Swanson, to replace my first parents who gave me away.

Years later, in 2007, I met Helen Sackerson, who knew my birth story. In 1938 she was living in Missoula, Montana and a member of the Mission Covenant Church of Missoula. She was 22 years of age at the time of my adoption and said everyone in Montana was talking about the baby left on the church doorstep in Helena. "Your unique birth story," she said, "created great excitement throughout the state." Then Helen, who was in her late 90's at the time, looked at me and said, "Don't you see the awesome hand of God in your life?"

My Dad was so proud to hold his six month old son.

I was humbled by Helen's insight into the miraculous way God intervened in my life. While my life-story does include the struggle that is typical of an adopted child's journey, it is also a story of God's intervening hand in the life of an abandoned child left on a doorstep.

Oh yes! I do celebrate the fact that I was adopted! And I do understand the joy of my adoption. As an orphan, bereft of my birth parents, I was given to wonderful adoptive parents. I had a blessed childhood. And I was not only given to a loving family, but I was given the added bonus of an extended faith family who blessed me and helped mold me into a man of faith. I want nothing in my story to lessen the joy of my doorstep adoption or the joy of any adopted person. I celebrate the fact that I was adopted for a purpose and that adoption is an experience of grace that taught me some of life's richest and deepest lessons.

But adoption is also a life-long journey of acceptance and taking control of the choices that others made for me as an infant. For those choices, that others made, dramatically changed the course of my life and affected my subsequent perception of myself and my relationship with others.

So, you would think that my story ends like the fairy tale ending, "and they all lived happily ever after." But my story doesn't end there.

When I was left on the doorstep as a foundling child in the late 1930's, it was at a time when adoptive children were not always welcome by extended families and were often held in suspicion. Society, in that era, often looked negatively on adoption and especially the adoption of a baby left on your doorstep. "Be very careful," my parents were told, "you just don't welcome into your home every abandoned kid left on your doorstep." Others said, "He could very well bring you nothing but problems."

As I grew up, everyone in our community knew my story, even the neighborhood bully who would taunt me saying that I was a "throwaway kid, a reject that nobody wanted." And I clearly remember the hurt I felt as a six-year-old, when I came into a room where I heard a favorite aunt say to my parents, "I certainly hope that Wesley doesn't bring bad blood into our family."

It was that negative attitude of society that robbed me, throughout my childhood and youth, of the joy of my adoption. I grew up, as a result, with deep feelings of inferiority, a poor self-image, shame and fear. In my young mind the seeds had been sown that a foundling baby, like me, is a reject who could bring "bad blood" into an adoptive family. To me, it felt like other kids go *first-class* in their birth families, but a foundling child is *second-class*. It was a lie; but I believed it.

At a year and one half. I loved my stuffed elephant toy.

Throughout my childhood, I struggled with tormenting personal question like: "Who am I? Where do I fit in? Who do I really belong to?" But most of all, in dealing with the ever-present fear of rejection, I would ask, "Why did they give me away? Was it my fault? Wasn't I *good enough* for them?" That ever-present fear of

15

rejection and abandonment led me to go to great lengths, throughout my childhood, to be a perfect child. My young mind reasoned that if I got straight A's in school and if I was always obedient at home, then I would *earn* the love of my family and not be in danger of being abandoned again.

While my adoptive parents never, ever, made their love for me conditional upon my good behavior, that's nevertheless what *I believed.* All the while my parents were very patient with me in my struggles. They were always expressing their love for me and affirming that I was "a gift from heaven to them." But I didn't *understand* unconditional love and I continued to believe the fearful lie that if I wasn't perfect, I'd be given away again.

I carried that same idea of perfectionism into my spiritual life. And in the same way that I didn't understand the unconditional love of my parents, I certainly didn't understand the unearned grace of God; grace for even the least and the lowest. I guess I was a very slow learner, because even though I was raised in a pastor's home, and often heard of God's love, I nevertheless grew up thinking that *if I didn't obey all the religious rules* and if I wasn't morally *perfect,* God would hate me and reject me. It all depended on *my performance* and perfect life. And I did try to please God. Oh, how fervently and earnestly I tried to earn His love with a "perfect life." But the more I tried, the more I knew that I fell far short of God's moral perfection, and I lived with overwhelming guilt and a fear of God's rejection.

THE HOLE IN MY HEART

Throughout my childhood, I struggled with these unanswered questions regarding my being abandoned on the church door-step. Many of my most painful questions would *never* be answered as my adoption was a classic example of a "closed adoption." When my birth mother wrote, on the note she left with me, "Don't try to find me," she effectively closed the door for any answers to her person or my birth family or my medical background. The door was firmly closed. It was so final.

I was so young, only a few weeks old, when all this happened on the church steps in Helena, Montana. You'd think I was too young to have any long-term issues causing fear of rejection and abandonment to be a major component in my adoption story. Some people have said, "just get over it, and count your blessings that you were adopted into a loving Christian family." I can only agree. I am so blessed by my mom and dad who loved me and raised me. But it's like I had a major missing puzzle piece in my life. Through no fault of my adoptive parents, I had a hole in my heart that gave me a fear of being rejected, and that hampered my ability to trust any relationship, and prevented me from having good and intimate friendships. That hole in my heart made many differences in how I have lived my life.

- I have grieved over the loss of my birth mother. Her disappearance left a hole in my heart.
- I've struggled to understand the reasons for her desperate actions in giving me away. And in the total absence of any information, I've blamed myself – I must be a reject, "bad blood." It left a hole in my heart.
- The loss of my first family history, my first siblings, my first grandparents, my first extended family; all that loss has left a hole in my heart.
- The loss of my medical health history and genetic history. That loss didn't really hit me until the first time a doctor asked me about my family health history and I said, "I have none, I'm adopted."

I was a very blond and blue eyed little sailor at two years of age.

I was surprised by my feelings of shame over having no family health history. I had a hole in my heart.
- There have been many times in my life when I felt like I was a victim at the time of my birth, of other people's bad choices. It left a hole in my heart.

Today, I no longer see myself as a victim of other people's bad choices.

Today, I no longer see myself as a victim of other people's bad choices. I've found freedom from the fears of rejection and shame. And now, as I write my story, I'm excited to share how I got rid of this negative "victim thinking" that plagued so much of my life since birth. For the remainder of my story is the story of God's love and grace. The rest of my story tells how God's unconditional love, in Jesus Christ, began to remove my victim status and began to fill that hole in my heart with grace and peace and love.

With my parents in another sailor suit at three years of age.

CHAPTER 2

MY JOURNEY WITH MY ADOPTIVE FAMILY

In the midst of my growing childhood fears and emotional struggles, God had amazingly placed me in an adoptive family that had been transformed by God's grace.

My parents were quite literally the children of American pioneers. My father, who was born in a Minnesota log cabin in 1900, grew up helping his father plow fields with teams of oxen, just as the biblical Abraham had done four thousand years before. My mother, likewise, was born in a one room log cabin in northern Minnesota and in her early years grew up in that primitive cabin with ten other siblings.

MY ALCOHOLIC GRANDFATHER – TRANSFORMED BY GRACE

My grandfather, on my dad's side of the family, was Charles Fredrick Swanson, who was born in Kalviks Parish in Småland, Sweden, on August 3, 1870. He came over to America as a young man, "dirt poor," entering this country around 1888, through Castle Garden Immigration Center, before Ellis Island opened. He settled near the central Minnesota town of Foley, where he blazed open a Homestead Farm and married his wife Maria (called Mary), who was born in Varmskog Parish, in Varmland, Sweden.

Charles and Mary had three children; Roy William, who was born in 1894, Silvia Ovidia, who was born in 1898 (she died at age ten from a ruptured appendix), and my dad, Clarence Ragnar, who was born in 1900.

I remember Grandpa Charlie Swanson as a godly man, who loved reading the Bible and singing his faith in all the old Swedish Pietistic revival songs. And I fondly remember, as a six-year-old child, how Grandpa loved to celebrate Christmas with a ten foot Christmas tree in the parlor, all brilliantly adorned with live flaming candles. My young eyes bugged out at the sight of the parlor aglow with the brilliance of dozens of lit candles on the tree. Although, behind the tree was always a pail of water, close at hand, in case the tree caught on fire. It was awesome and scary, all at the same time, to see the tree lit up with live candle flames. I remember thinking that my grandpa really lived on the dangerous edge, because my mother said she would never allow real candles to be lit on a tree in her house.

After Grandma Mary died in 1943, Grandpa Charlie married again, and his new wife, Grandma Augusta Swanson, become the only grand-mother I ever really knew. I spent a lot of time enjoying her cooking and sitting in her simple Swedish kitchen when they lived near us in their retirement in Harris, Minnesota. Grandpa and Grandma Swanson became key parts in the Godly heritage I inherited as an adopted child.

But I was shocked to find out, in later years, that Grandpa Charlie also had a dark side to his life. My parents told me that for many of his early years in America, grandpa had been a hardened alcoholic. When Grandpa was drunk, he would physically abuse his family. My dad and his brother told how they would run and hide when their dad came home drunk, because they knew he would try to catch them and beat them. And he was drunk often. At the same time that Grandpa strug-gled with alcoholism, he also successfully farmed two hundred acres of grain crops, fruit trees and milking cows. He was financially success-ful, but a slave to alcohol. As a successful farmer, Grandpa would often bring his produce and dairy products to markets in the twin cities of Minneapolis and St. Paul. It was often on these trips that he'd get really drunk. One time, in March of 1917, when Grandpa Charlie went to St. Paul to sell his produce and attend a meeting of the Creamery Board, he was stranded in a huge Minnesota snow blizzard which delayed his return home for four days.

While waiting for her husband to return, Grandma Mary had a vision of Charlie down on his knees praying. She insisted that she wasn't asleep, and she wasn't dreaming. She maintained that she had seen a vision of her alcoholic husband praying and crying out to God. Now praying was *definitely out of character* for Charlie. In fact, after being baptized and confirmed in the State Lutheran Church of Sweden, Charlie wanted nothing to do with the church or prayer or anything spiritual. But that night, in the midst of a March blizzard, while Charlie was looking for a tavern to get drunk in, he stumbled across a Swedish gospel service in a Salvation Army Mission, and there, true to Mary's vision, he got down on his knees, a broken man, and turned his life over to Jesus Christ. His life was transformed.

When Grandpa was finally able to get home, through all the snow, instead of being drunk, he burst happily into their home saying, "Mary, you'll never guess what happened to me this week!" Grandma Mary replied, "One thing I know is that you prayed. God showed me that you got down on your knees and prayed." That summer Mary trusted in Jesus Christ for salvation as did their son Roy. But it wasn't until five years later, in December of 1922, that my dad finally surrendered his life to Christ at the little Minnehaha Baptist Church in Minneapolis.

MY PREACHER DAD

It was that humble prayer, by my grandfather at the Salvation Army Mission, that resulted in a new spiritual direction for Charles and Mary Swanson. And that new spiritual foundation in their home had a positive Christian influence on their two sons and in turn gave me a Godly heritage that ultimately gave me hope for my inner healing and spiritual life.

After Dad committed his life to Christ in 1922, he became a member of First Covenant Church in Minneapolis (the old Tabernacle Church). It was here, under the ministry of Rev. Gust F. Johnson, that Dad heard the call of God to enter Christian ministry. To prepare himself for ministry, in 1924 Dad entered the Pastoral Training Department of Moody Bible Institute in Chicago, Illinois, graduating with a major in Biblical Studies in 1927.

As was the case with many pioneer families in the early twentieth century, Dad had to work on the family farm throughout his youth and thus had never finished high school. So, following his graduation from seminary at Moody Bible Institute he enrolled in Minnehaha Academy, the Covenant Church High School in Minneapolis, where he graduated from the Academy in June of 1929. It was at this Christian High School that Dad met, dated and fell in love with Helga Anderson.

Even while attending high school, my dad was serving the Clear Lake Covenant Church in Clayton, Wisconsin, through June of 1929. And then two weeks later, on July 13, 1929, with no money saved, but rich in love, my father married Helga Sophia Anderson at the 25th Avenue Free Church in Minneapolis.

After their marriage, Dad and Mom began their ministry together, serving their Lord in *sixteen churches* over a period of nearly fifty years. Dad felt called to be a church planter (then called a "Home Missions Pastor") and to build and revive struggling smaller churches. Since I was a part of several of these churches that my parents served and they were all significant in my spiritual growth, I will list them here:

Evangelical Community Church, Freedom, MN.	1929 – 1931
Mission Covenant Church, Little Falls, MN.	1931 – 1935
Mission Covenant Church, Culdrum, MN. (circuit)	1931 – 1935
Mission Covenant Church, Darling, MN. (circuit)	1931 – 1935
Lake Jennie Covenant Church, Dassel, MN.	1935 – 1937
Mission Covenant Church, Helena, MT.	1937 – 1943
Mission Covenant Church, Harris, MN.	1943 – 1945
Mission Covenant Church, Rush City, MN. (circuit)	1943 – 1945
Mission Covenant Church, Little Falls, MN.	1945 – 1948
Mission Covenant Church, Poplar, WI.	1948 – 1954
Evangelical Covenant Church, Oberlin, KS.	1954 – 1958
Mission Covenant Church, Shenandoah, IA.	1958 – 1961
Lund Covenant Church, Stockholm, WI.	1961 – 1965
Ben Wade Covenant Church, Lowry, MN.	1965 – 1967
Evangelical Covenant Church, Le Sueur, MN.	1967 – 1970
Lake Jennie Covenant Church, Dassel, MN.	1970 – 1973

I sat under my dad's preaching for over twenty years. He had a deep impact on my life as my father and my pastor. Dad dedicated me to God as an infant in 1939. He confirmed me in faith before the church in 1950. He baptized me, on confession of personal faith, in 1963 and he performed the wedding ceremony in my marriage to Clarice in 1965. It was such a great privilege to have my dad be a part of all those significant events in my life. I was so proud to say, "that's my dad."

And yet, with all those years of pastoral influence on my life, it wasn't Dad's dynamic preaching that had the greatest impact on me. In fact, I'd be hard pressed to remember even one of his sermons. Instead, it was his *example* of the daily living-out of his faith that impacted my life the most. Dad was *dedicated*. He was not a deep theologian but he was a faithful pastor to his flock. He taught God's Word passionately, he prayed unceasingly, he visited the sick, counseling the troubled and built home mission churches. That's what impacted my life. He was faithful.

When Dad and Mom died, they had not one penny left to leave for my brother and me. But they left us something better. They left us a legacy of lives laid down sacrificially in God's service. That's what really impacted me.

Dad was dedicated and faithful.

I'll never forget the example of Dad and Mom's tithing purse. They kept an old leather purse in the top drawer of their bedroom dresser. It held their tithe (ten percent of their salary) for God's work and missions. My parents were poor and served poor churches in farming communities and small villages. They served churches in the Great Depression, and there were some months when the church had no salary to pay their pastor. Nevertheless, whenever my parents did have income, the first ten percent went *gladly* into the tithing purse for God's work. Thanks Dad and Mom for giving to the Lord's work. You impacted my life.

But, in all honesty, I have to say that Dad and I were not really close as father and son. We had very different personalities. Dad was an outdoors-man who loved hunting, fishing and competitive sports. He was in many ways a "Man's Man," who had close hunting buddies and many fishing friends. He loved to golf and an ever-present interest in listening to Minnesota Twins baseball games.

While I occasionally enjoyed fishing and golf, it was never my passion like it was for Dad. And I never liked hunting. I had an absolute revulsion for killing any bird or animal. Mom often read me the bedtime story of "Bambi" the deer, so I remember crying as a kid the first time I shot a Red-Wing Blackbird with the BB gun my dad bought me. He tried so hard to get me interested in hunting. He was absolutely flabbergasted when I froze and couldn't shoot the ten-point buck that had walked right in front of me. I felt I had disappointed him. It added to my fear of rejection.

My dad was more extroverted, outgoing, and even the life of every party. I was more introverted, shy, insecure, more of a "loner" growing up. It was easier to avoid people and close friendships than to risk rejection. So, I enjoyed doing things alone, like hobbies, art and music. And while I did enjoy playing football and swimming as a kid, I was for the most part fearfully turned off by organized competitive sports in school. What I really feared was rejection when team sides were chosen and I was the last to be chosen. I knew that in some sports, like basketball, I seemed to be awkward, even uncoordinated, and there were good reasons why I was the last to be chosen. Mom said my awkwardness was the after-effects of a childhood bout with crippling Polio. Nevertheless, when I was the last to be chosen for a team, my heart ached and my fears of rejection sky-rocketed.

Dad and I never once spoke about my being an adopted, doorstep-baby. It seemed like it wasn't a safe subject to bring up. My parents always wanted to focus on the positive blessings of adoption; I was God's answer to their prayer. So, for me to even suggest that I struggled with mixed feelings of gratitude for my adoptive family, but also painful fears over abandonment and longings for my birth mother, would only have brought hurt to my dad. So, I struggled silently through all my growing years with fears of rejection and abandonment.

But for all of our differences, I truly loved and admired my dad. He was my dependable, encouraging father-figure, who modeled a strong and yet a caring man who loved me. He was there for me. He never abandoned me. I am so thankful for the Godly heritage that my father and grandfather gave to me. These men, struggling and rough-hewn men, were models of saving grace that gave me hope. God gave me a glimpse of Himself and His grace through them.

MY MOM – "AN ANGEL IN WORK GLOVES"

It was my mom, Helga Sophia Swanson, who embodied unconditional love and gave me the promise of acceptance and hope in the midst of my fears of rejection.

William Shakespeare, in *Measure for Measure* says, "The miserable have no other medicine; but only hope." Mom's early life was definitely miserable, but never lacked hope. She was born November 4, 1905 in a primitive, one-room log cabin in Roseau County, Minnesota. Helga somehow survived her first eight years of life, living with her parents and ten other children in that tiny cabin.

Helga was born to a Swedish immigrant father, Alfred Nicoloi Anderson who was born in Oslo, Norway on January 27, 1867. While Grandpa Alfred was born to Swedish parents working in Norway, his education was all in Norwegian and thus he spoke a mixture of Swedish and Norwegian that everyone had difficulty understanding. He emigrated to America in 1884.

Helga's mother was Clara Hanson Anderson born in Foglavik, Sweden on April 10, 1867. She emigrated to America in 1884 and following the death of her first husband was married to Alfred Anderson in 1895. Clara bore eleven children including: Fred, Ethel, Edwin,

Jennie (She died in the 1918 flu epidemic), William, Agnes, Mable, Helga, Clark and twin girls, Netti and Julia who died in infancy. Clara was the loving, sacrificing mother of faith that every child would wish for. Helga was very close to her mother and found in her mother's arms the refuge she longed for in those miserable times.

Helga and all her siblings had to work long hours each day to help their father raise the crops and tend the sheep and cattle on the swampy, stony land of their small homestead farm in northern Minnesota. There was very little time for any schooling and Helga only spoke Swedish as a child.

Then in 1914, after seventeen years of back-breaking farm work, Grandpa Anderson sold the farm and bought a hotel in Graettinger, Iowa. Here again they all worked hard, but barely eked out a living, running the hotel. Many of the traveling salesmen would sneak out of the hotel without ever paying them for their board and room. And then, to top off their miserable childhood, her father sold the hotel in 1918 and moved the whole family to land he had *never seen*, near Jacksonville, Florida. The land turned out to be *one huge swamp* with not even a shack for the family to live in. Grandpa had been swindled.

The family moved back to Minnesota in miserable poverty. But, while living in cramped quarters with relatives in Minneapolis, Helga was able to finish the eighth grade in school, and at age 16 was working full time in a laundry to help support her family and save enough money to go to high school.

It was also at age 16 that Helga and her family began attending the little 17th Avenue, Salem Evangelical Church in Minneapolis. Here it was that Helga heard the gospel of salvation by grace, and she began a personal relationship with God by faith in Jesus Christ. Her faith became the bedrock of her hope in the midst of abject poverty. She now began to use her musical skills with the guitar to sing of her faith on gospel teams and to direct church choirs.

Helga was resilient and determined, in the face of tremendous odds, to continue her education. Using her own savings from working in the laundry, she enrolled in Minnehaha Academy, a Christian high school in south Minneapolis. She graduated in 1927 from the school's Business/Secretarial course as Valedictorian. Here it was that she met, dated and fell in love with Clarence Swanson.

Mom and Dad were married on July 13, 1929 at the 25th Avenue Free Church in Minneapolis. They began their honeymoon and married life with a net worth of $130, all of which they had received as wedding gifts. So even on their honeymoon Dad would preach in little country churches to earn enough money to get them back to their first church in Minnesota. They reported that the collection each evening was about $2.50.

Following their honeymoon, Mom and Dad began their ministry together, eventually serving 16 churches. Mom was a model pastor's wife, who felt personally called to ministry and thus served faithfully, alongside her husband, in all 16 of those churches. In nine of those churches she directed both adult and children's choirs. She was the director of Christian education in most of the churches, serving as Sunday School Superintendent, Vacation Bible School and Children's Church Organizer as well as a Sunday school teacher and often a leader of the Women's Auxiliary. Mom had the gift of hospitality as she happily housed and entertained *hundreds* of itinerant missionaries, evangelists and visitors to the church, all of whom were invited to the parsonage for her wonderful Sunday chicken dinners.

Even in retirement, Mom continued showing her servant-heart of ministry. She was always a "Doer;" I called her my "Angel in Work Gloves". At age 92, she was still entertaining by inviting all the new residents at her Covenant Manor Retirement Center to come to her apartment for Swedish pancake breakfasts. She served food to the homeless each week at First Covenant Church, sang in the Covenant Manor choir, knit afghan blankets and sewed patchwork quilts for scores of friends and missionaries and was always baking cookies and her delicious Swedish rye bread and giving them away to encourage family members and neighbors.

I was very close to my mom. She was the "safe person" in my life that I could talk with and share my honest feelings. Though I know there were times that she felt uncomfortable when I would speak of my birth mother, she nevertheless understood my mixed feelings over my adoption as a door-step baby and she was always there to listen to me and encourage me.

Ultimately my healing came from the grace of God, but He used my mom to show me what unconditional love is like.

MY SIX FOOT-FOUR "LITTLE BROTHER"

When my parents moved to Poplar, Wisconsin in 1948, they decided to apply to the State Child Welfare Department and open their home for foster-child care. In October of 1950, a 15-month-old baby boy (born July 11, 1949) by the name of John Robert, was placed in our home as a foster child. John was in the Foster Care system because both of his parents were in prison for counterfeiting currency.

I was 12-years-old at the time and remember how excited and happy we all were to have this baby come to our home. But, our excitement was short lived when this baby arrived at our home screaming and kicking and refusing to be held by anyone. The lady from the Welfare Department explained that John was an abused child who had been beaten and neglected by female relatives who had been assigned to care for him after his parent's incarceration.

John was petrified to go to sleep. Mom would spend all night comforting this terrified baby.

We can only speculate as to the abuse that John had endured as a baby, but the result was that he came to us *a very angry child*, often explosive in his behavior and terrified of all women. John would scream whenever a woman, even my mother, would come close to him. He would only allow my dad and me to feed him, hold him, and change his diaper.

John had terrible sleeping habits. Every night, for months, it was a dreadful ordeal of listening to a screaming baby who was petrified to go to sleep. Dad and I would take turns holding him and rocking him in our arms, sometime through the entire night, only to have him awaken, screaming, the moment we laid him in his crib. Weeks later, he slowly began to accept my mom's loving care and then she would spend all night sitting beside his crib to comfort him and stroke his back until he went back to sleep. Mom wrote in her journal, "I lost 16 pounds through those months of spending all night comforting this terrified baby."

The early pattern of angry and explosive behavior continued as John grew into a kid who would throw temper tantrums by lying on the floor and screaming. In later years, medical professionals told us that there was a very real possibility that John suffered from Fetal Alcohol Syndrome. His early explosive behavior as a baby, his sudden irritation with others, his poor sleep habits and his rapidly changing moods were all symptoms of FAS in infants and became his pattern in his growing years.

My parents were good and patient Christian people who were committed to hopefully making a loving difference in John's life. We all assumed that we would only have John in our foster home for a few years at most. Thus, I remember well the day in 1951, when John's birth mother came to our home, accompanied by a prison guard, to ask if

My brother John is three in this family photo which was taken following his adoption in 1952.

our family would consider adopting John. There were tears in all our eyes as she explained that she would not be free for many years to care for her son and she felt that our home would be a safe and loving home in which he could grow up.

While I knew first-hand of John's explosive behavior I nevertheless was delighted to have a little brother and so joined in celebration on October 28, 1952 when we adopted him into our family as John Robert Swanson.

Because my brother was eleven-years younger than I, it didn't give us much time together in our growing-up years. I was a senior in high-school when he was just starting first-grade. I know that I didn't always handle his temper tantrums well, but I still loved my little brother and remember many enjoyable experiences we had together. One such experience was in 1959 when the two of us had a fun and adventuresome car trip to Mexico City. He was just 10-years-old and I was 21, and we had a blast tenting and camping throughout the United States and Mexico. But the fact was, that when I left home for college in 1956, our relationship became even more distant and our contact infrequent.

Because of Dad's ministry assignments, John grew up in five different communities and in four different school systems. Certainly, all those changes of schools and friends were not good for him. After graduating from high-school in Minnesota in 1967, he quit junior college after trying it for only a few months and enlisted in the U.S. Army. John did very well in the discipline of the Army where he became a sergeant in the Motor Transport Unit. But, I believe it was also in the Army that he began to drink heavily and he began smoking marijuana which eventually introduced him to other drugs. My brother struggled with drug and alcohol addiction for over thirty-five years.

In February of 1993 I was startled awake at 2:30 a.m. by a telephone call from John asking if he could come from Florida and stay with us in Colorado for a short time. He said that he had not been paying his drug debts and that the Miami Mafia was after him and would harm him. I was really disturbed by this news, but not surprised. I said he would be welcome in our home as long as he agreed to not having or using any drugs while living in our home. He agreed.

John's first weeks in our home were difficult and awkward, as he slept off his addiction, spending most of his time sleeping in our guest room or watching T.V. This was especially difficult for my wife, Sandy, who had my brother constantly under foot, hanging around the house all day, while I was at work. I was not sensitive as to why this situation was so difficult for her, only to discover some months later, that she was very ill all this time with colon cancer. Later on, when I learned of her serious illness, I held her close in my arms as I apologized for the difficult situation that I had put her into.

After those early weeks of John hanging around the house, I sat him down and said he had to find some employment and couldn't just be sitting around all day. Because John had skills in carpentry and some past experience in framing homes, I offered to set him up with all the tools he would need to find work with a contractor in framing houses in Denver. I paid for all his equipment, his skill-saws, nail-guns and compressors. Within a week, he had a job.

It was in May of 1993, during John's stay in our home, that we received the shocking news that my wife Sandy had colon cancer. Subsequent surgery revealed that the tumor had metastasized to her lungs and liver and she only had months to live. We were devastated. We asked John to move into my son Mark's condominium in Denver, so as to make our guest-room available to Sandy's visiting relatives. But it was while John lived in the spare bedroom at Mark's home that he began to fall back into his old habits with drugs and alcohol. Finally, Mark had to ask his uncle to leave his home and find other living arrangements.

John found an apartment of his own and a new girlfriend to share it with him, but their drug/alcohol lifestyle soon became unsustainable. Shortly after they began living together, I began receiving notices from pawn shops that the tools I had purchased for his work were being pawned off for cash. John was back into alcohol and cocaine, only now he needed money to pay drug bills for two people.

As Sandy's health worsened, we saw less and less of John. He and his girlfriend were preoccupied with partying and paying for their drug bills, so we didn't see John until Sandy's death and funeral on April 14, 1994. And then following the funeral he suddenly he disappeared from

Denver and that was the last I saw him for eleven years. I learned weeks later that he and his girlfriend had returned to Florida without telling us. Years later he wrote to me to explain,

"When I met Jill, the partying started again. I quit going to A.A. and N.A. but, I had never really bought into them. I thought of them as weak people, a bunch of losers. But because of our partying we backed ourselves into a financial corner and so took off for Florida."

During that eleven-year absence, our mom's health steadily declined. When Mom lost her eyesight, due to macular degeneration, I moved her to Colorado so I could help care for her in her last years. I kept John informed of his mom's condition, and asked him to please call or write to her on her birthday or on Mother's Day. It was like Mom was hanging on and waiting for that letter or a final visit with her younger son. She thought that his silence meant that she had done something to alienate him. But then, to our delight, in June of 2005, John sent a five-page letter on legal size paper telling mom that, "He was sorry that he had not been a better son to her and that she was the best mom he could ever have had." She had me read that line to her over and over again.

It was the following August of 2005, that we received an unexpected phone call from John saying that he was coming for the celebration of Mom's one hundredth birthday, on November 4. He also informed us that, after eleven years of absence, he wanted to stay with us for a week. When we met him at the airport, we cautioned him not to expect too much from Mom, as she was very weak and hadn't spoken for several days. But when we walked into her room at the nursing home, and they embraced in tears, she talked with him for two hours. It was a *sweet reconciliation*. Mom had held on for that reunion and birthday celebration. She died, peacefully, one month later, on December 7, 2005.

Life really changes when you are dealing with the drug or alcohol addiction of a family member. I've struggled over the years, to find a balance in our support and help for my brother's recovery from addictions, without enabling his addiction or covering-up, for his addictions. I've tried to be supportive and loving to my brother, without being codependent in his struggle with drugs. But I'm afraid that's just what I've become, weak and codependent in his battle with addiction. So again, in 2010, I struggled with my response to his homelessness. Do I send him money to buy a mobile home in a Florida trailer park, or do I say "No," and let him come to terms with the consequences of his addictions? I ended up sending him the money he requested when no one else would help.

I have often said that I don't always like the way John treated his family and I definitely don't support his life-style choices, but I nevertheless love him and pray for him daily. I don't have to like everything he did and I'll not shield him from the consequences of his addiction, but I can still love him and care about him. So, I celebrated with him when he wrote to me in 2010 saying:

> *"I've found a new N.A. group here in Florida and a wonderful sponsor. I'm working the 12 Step Program and I have faith that I will continue my program. It's not so much about John quitting drugs, but about John changing his life. Every morning I pray, 'God take my will and my life, guide me in my recovery, show me how to live."*

This was a joyous turning point in John's life. I responded with affirmation and praise for his new insight and the amazing progress made in dealing with his addictions. And I believe that our parents say "Amen" in heaven for the answer to their prayers for their son.

FOOTNOTE TO "A GODLY HERITAGE"

After 45 years of ministry, Mom and Dad retired in March 1967. While their years of ministry had many joys, it also had many challenges. Certainly, one of the challenges was that their ministry in small town and start-up churches often provided them with little or no income. This meant that when the folks retired they had no savings, and in order to supplement their small pension and Social Security, they both needed to continue working. For nine years of their retirement Mom worked as a cook in the Dassel Minnesota Nursing Home and Dad ministered for five years at the Lake Jenny Covenant Church where he had previously served in 1935 – 1937.

Throughout their entire ministry, the folks had lived in church parsonages. But at their retirement my brother-in-law, Ken Olson, offered to sell them the Olson family farmhouse and two acres of land for $5,000. They received that offer of a home as a gift from God and for the first time in their married lives were home-owners. Mom wrote in her journal:

> *"I was so happy to move into a home of our own. I remember going out into the yard, raising my arms to heaven and saying, 'Thank you*

*Lord for this home. It's our home and no one can tell us you can't do this, or tell us you can't do that. It is **our home!**"*

During the 14 years that my folks lived on the Dassel farm, Dad began having seizures, which resulted in his having brain surgery in 1977 for a benign tumor. Once, while preaching at the Trimont Covenant Church in Minnesota, he had a grand mal seizure and fell backward, pulling the pulpit over on top of him. After the startled ushers, in panic thinking he was dead, pulled the pulpit off of him he revived, got up and insisted that he finish his sermon sitting down on a chair. You can bet that while that congregation may not have remembered the content of that sermon, they would never forget the drama of that Sunday or the dedication of this man of God.

As Dad's health worsened, they found it necessary to sell the farm home in 1981 and move into the newly built Covenant Manor Retirement Village in Minneapolis. But just five months after their move, Dad's tumor had grown back so significantly that he became belligerent, even violent at times, so that Mom was physically unable to care for him. Dad was placed in the Alzheimer's Care Unit of the retirement home and it was here that he died in June, 1982. Dad was buried in the little cemetery in Lake Jenny, Minnesota, near the church which he had loved and served for so many years.

At first, after Dad's death, Mom struggled with negative feelings of guilt and remorse, blaming herself for putting Dad in the Alzheimer's

Unit and not trying to care for him at home. This grief struggle continued with her for some months until God gave her a vision. As Mom told it, she was sitting in her apartment when she saw Dad in a vision in which he was riding in a parade in heaven. She said Dad was riding in

Mom was 95 in this photo – still playing her guitar and singing her songs of faith.

something that looked like a big white Cadillac convertible and that he waved at mom in the crowd and said, "Holly (Mom's nickname), it's O.K. now." That was all he said, but it was enough to give Mom peace that Dad was O.K. and at peace now in heaven.

With the assuaging of the grief and guilt surrounding Dad's death, Mom seemed to flourish in her spirit and person. She made many new friends at the retirement village and even had a "special" boyfriend. Mom said these were the best years of her life. She said she felt like a queen in her lovely apartment and enjoyed entertaining family and friends in the beautiful village dining room.

Mom always had a good sense of humor, but it seemed to especially flourish in retirement. She relaxed and began having fun in her later years. She often had a quick quip in response to people's comments. Once, at age 98, she surprised me when a nurse complemented her on her pretty blouse and she quipped, "Well you can't have it."

Mom lived to the ripe old age of 100 and joked that she was, "hanging on," to get the Centenarian Greeting from President George W. Bush, for whom she had twice voted and prayed for daily.

We buried Mom on December 12, 2005 at the Lake Jenny Covenant Church, next to Dad, and with a great Christmas celebration of thanksgiving to God for a life well lived. She was my "Angel in Work Gloves" and my model of unconditional love.

CHAPTER 3

PLUCKED FROM CLOSE CALLS WITH DEATH

RESCUED FROM CRIPPLING POLIO

When I was 4-years-old I was diagnosed with crippling polio also known as Infantile Paralysis. In the 1940's and 50's polio was one of the most widespread and dreadful childhood diseases in the world. Polio is a virus that can cause nerve damage in the brain-stem or spinal-cord, resulting in paralysis in the patient's arms, legs, torso or lungs. I was paralyzed for weeks in my arms and legs due to this illness.

The day I became ill, I had been with my folks to the Masonic Home in the Helena Valley, where dad would hold religious services once a month. The elderly people there would give me hand-made gifts and I enjoyed entertaining them by jumping, running and talking with them. They loved to egg me on to greater heights in jumping. Mom wrote in her journal:

> "When we got home, Wesley said, 'I don't feel good Mama.' And as I laid him down on a cot, he immediately spewed up everything in his stomach with such force that it was like a jet-stream. Right away I called our baby doctor, Dr. Moore, and when I explained it to him he said he'd be right over. He put Wesley through some simple exercises, like touching his chin to his knees, and Wesley just couldn't do it. Dr. Moore had him in the hospital as soon as he could. They took a spinal test and it came back, Bulbar Polio."

The next day I was moved out of the General Hospital and into the Helena Children's Hospital, where I was placed in a glassed-in isolation room. Dr. Moore asked my parents if they would approve my being treated with a new treatment for polio patients called the "Sister Kenny Treatment." This treatment was introduced in America in 1940 by an Australian nurse named Elizabeth Kenny. She was a pioneer in Physical Therapy in which she used hot wet towels (a form of hydro-therapy) and gentle exercise to break the hold of the paralysis, instead of braces which were used by most doctors to keep the limbs rigid. Mom again wrote in her journal:

> "As this treatment had not been used in Helena before, the hospital had no equipment for this procedure. So, Dr. Moore brought in a wash-tub and an old-type hand-wringer fixed on the wash-tub. They used large wooden sticks to lift the hot towels out of the boiling water and after putting them through the wringer, they would wrap these hot cloths around Wesley. There were several other young polio patients in the hospital, but none of them had the Sister Kenny Treatment. Some of the nurses were fearful of taking care of Wesley and Dr. Moore had to give them a real lecture as to why they became nurses. Wesley was wrapped from head to toe with hot cloths and these wrappings were changed every fifteen minutes."

I remember, as a 4-year-old, crying as the hot towels were wrapped around me, "hot, hot, too hot!" I cried. But the treatment was meant to use moist heat to break the hold of the paralysis, so there was no stopping the treatment because I was crying. The treatment continued around the clock, and so did the paralysis. The treatment apparently was making no difference.

All over the city and state people were earnestly praying for my recovery. The little church in Helena, that my folks served, held special times of prayer for the "doorstep-baby" who was now crippled with polio. My dad called Dr. T.W. Anderson, the president of the national church body, to ask for denominational-wide prayer for my healing. As the denomination was holding its national "Annual Meeting" at the historic Tabernacle Covenant Church in Minneapolis, President Anderson interrupted the meeting on Friday, June 19, to ask the assembly to unite in prayer for me. The Year Book minutes of the 1942 Annual Meeting read as follows:

> "Special acknowledgment was given to the greeting from Pastor C.R. Swanson, whose son was ill with Infantile Paralysis. The Conference united in earnest prayer for the restoration to health of this son, and for the bestowment of God's sustaining grace to his parents."

It was around noon, Central Standard Time, that the National Covenant Meeting in Minneapolis united in "earnest prayer" for my healing. A thousand miles away in Helena, on that same day at 11:00 a.m.

in the Mountain Time Zone, Dr. Moore and his nurse came running down the hospital hallway, almost shouting to my parents, "Something wonderful has just happened to Wesley! He has suddenly turned for the better." Just days later I walked out of the hospital, holding my dad's hand, totally free from the paralysis of polio.

At age four, I'm standing at a mountain cabin just two months after my healing from Polio.

MOUNTAIN MOVING PRAYER

I have no doubt that my life was touched by a miracle. In an instant I was changed from a paralyzed child to a healed and normal little boy. It sends shivers down my spine when I realize that the Creator of the World, the King of the Universe, interrupted the crippling process of disease and supernaturally healed a stricken 4-year-old boy, the little door-step baby, in answer to the mountain-moving prayer of faith by God's people.

Jesus said, "I tell you the truth, if you have faith and do not doubt… you can say to this mountain, 'Go, throw yourself into the sea,' and it will be done. If you believe, you will receive whatever you ask for in prayer." (Matthew 21:21-22)

My crippling disease of polio was an enormous mountain. According to the laws of nature, and medical treatment at that time, I should never have walked again in my life. But, it was when people of faith, focused not on the mountain of my disease, but focused on *the Mountain Mover Himself* - His faithfulness, His authority, His sufficiency - that the mountain of disease in my life was miraculously moved and God healed me.

Dr. Moore, my pediatrician, only confirmed that supernatural intervention when he said to my parents, *"I don't understand everything that happened in Wesley's recovery, but one thing I do know is that your prayers have done more than my work."*

I have learned, over the years, that not every prayer is answered as we ask, and not every answered prayer is a miraculous interruption of the laws of nature. But Jesus did say in Matthew 21:22, that a believer can be confident in prayer and that, "whatever you ask for in prayer," will be heard in heaven and answered. Sometimes the answer is "yes;" Sometimes the answer is "no;" Sometimes the answer is "wait." But God always answers! And in my life, as a young child crippled by polio, God answered miraculously and healed me completely. My mom wrote at that time in her journal:

"God surely answered prayer. So many were praying, all our loved ones and friends throughout the nation, and we knew it was God's will that our little son should be healed. Physical healing is not always God's plan, but this time it was. God had greater plans for Wesley. Satan tried to get rid of him. But our God is greater and more powerful, and Satan lost out. Praise the Lord."

My entire life has been impacted by that miraculous, mountain-moving answer to prayer.

A SHATTERED SKULL

Just one year after my battle with polio, I suffered a skull fracture that shattered the left side of my skull in a school play-ground accident. It was a life-threatening accident.

In 1943, when I was 5-years-old, my parents had moved from Helena, Montana to serve a Covenant Church in Harris, Minnesota. This new assignment actually included serving a circuit of two small churches that were five miles apart, in a ministry to both the Swedish Mission Church of Harris and the Mission Covenant Church of Rush City, Minnesota.

Shortly after moving to Minnesota, these two churches both held their annual Vacation Bible School the same week in June. My dad was in charge of the school in Rush City and my mom was in charge of the school in Harris. The Harris Bible School was held in the local elementary school where I attended.

I remember that the accident happened during recess as I was running across the school playground with a small frog cupped in my hands. I had found the frog in a ditch and I was running to show it to some friends. Being distracted by the frog, I hadn't noticed that I was running directly into the path of two boys who were pumping themselves high and crooked on a playground swing. The swing was held up by chains that were attached to iron hooks which were screwed into the wooden seat of the swing. The force of the swing hit the left side of my head and crushed my skull. I was 5-years-old and bleeding to death. My mom wrote in her journal:

"While the children were all out for recess I was getting the next lesson ready when one of the children came running in to me saying, 'Wesley is lying on the ground and can't get up.' I rushed out and found him, all bloody, trying to raise his head, but he fell right back down on the ground. I almost froze with panic, but I picked him up in my arms, breathing a prayer for strength, and carried him to the home of a neighbor. He was bleeding a lot. He had been struck by the swing on the left side of his head and it had crushed the side of his head so deeply that I could lay the palm of my hand into the depressed hole."
"I got someone to take me to our doctor in North Branch. He took a couple of x-rays, and after studying them he said, 'I don't dare touch this. I'll call the head brain specialist at University Hospital in Minneapolis and ask him to make this his special case.' I called Clarence and told him what had happened and we arranged to drive down to Minneapolis. Clarence drove like a crazy man and I had to tell him to slow down because the doctor had said we shouldn't jar his head at all. When we got to the city limits, Clarence saw a motorcycle cop and he stopped him and asked if he would lead us to the hospital. He took one look in the back seat and saw Wesley's bloody head, and that he was unconscious, and he just said, 'Follow me.' The patrolman turned on his siren and we took off fast. Clarence had a hard time following him so fast in the city, but we did have a clear way."

After the initial emergency room treatment, I had to wait a week in the hospital before I could have surgery, as they wanted to stop the bleeding and wait for the depression on the side of my head to return to normal. On the day of surgery, they shaved my head, which embarrassed me terribly,

I was five years old and just out of the hospital after surgery for a skull fracture.

and the brain surgeon, Dr. Peyton, found that a part of my skull had been cracked into four pieces with one of the pieces shattered into tiny bits. The surgeon picked out all those crushed pieces and moved the remaining three pieces of skull around to fill in the empty space. He said, in time, I would grow new bone and those spaces would be closed. One week later I was released and walked out of the hospital holding my mother's hand.

GOD STILL ANSWERS PRAYER

Is it even conceivable that the Creator of the Universe, once again, heard and answered prayer for the deliverance and healing of a little 5-year-old boy with a skull fracture, who just the year before was miraculously delivered from crippling polio?

Scoffers tell us that we live in a "closed universe" and that prayer makes no difference. There are those who say that, if we believe in a God of Love who allows bad things to happen to innocent people, then God must be either uncaring or powerless. For them prayer is useless in the face of tragedy, sickness and injustice.

"It seemed to me, that it was like the devil was doing his best to get rid of our little boy."

But I can't live that way. I can't live in a "closed universe" that tries to shut out the incarnational God who comes among us in Jesus the Messiah. My heart holds firmly on to Jesus who is called "Immanuel' - which means, 'God with us" (Matthew 1:23). So, I am certainly convinced, that once again my life was touched and preserved by a powerful answer to prayer. God was with us! My mother certainly believed that when she wrote in her journal:

> *"It seemed to me, that it was like the devil was doing his best to get rid of our little boy, and get him out of this world. Satan knew what plans God had for him, I'm sure, but our God is greater than Satan who is our enemy.... So, in just two weeks after the accident, Wesley came home with me, healed and recovered from a skull fracture that could have taken his life. How we did thank our Lord, once again, for answered prayer."*

I've learned that I must pray simply like a little child. I pray with childlike trust, even when life is dark. Jesus taught us to approach God as, "Our Father in heaven." (Matthew 6:9). And he said that our Father in heaven longs to hear and answer the prayers of His children.

That's what Jesus said in Matthew 7:7-11:

> *"Ask and it will be given you; seek and you will find; knock and the door will be opened for you.... Which of you, if his son asks for bread, will give him a stone? Or if he asks for a fish, will give him a snake? If you then, though you are evil, know how to give good gifts to your children, how much more will your Father in heaven give good gifts to those who ask him!"*

I love the *"how much more"* part of these verses. It speaks of the abundant generosity of God who longs to "give good gifts to those who ask him." Even in the darkest hours of my life, especially those awful days in 1984, when my wife Clarice was dying from a brain tumor, I cried out in faith to my Heavenly Father, like a wounded child. Jesus said it's alright to pray like a child: "Let the little children come to me" (Matthew 10:14). And then again, ten years later, when my second wife, Sandy, was dying from colon cancer, I cried out in the agony of my soul to the Heavenly Father who "cares for you" (I Peter 5:7). And to our shattered spirits, the God who "cares" brought a calming to our confused minds and a peace that passes understanding (John 14:27). Where else can you go to find that deep peace in your soul in life's darkest hours? And to top it off, He brought an abundance of other believers who cared for us, loved us, and wept with us in prayer. Oh yes! I do believe God still answers prayer! I've witnessed it myself.

CHAPTER 4

GROWING UP IN THE PARSONAGE

The dictionary defines a parsonage as, "a church house provided for a parson." In my childhood and youth, I lived in eight different parsonages that churches provided for my parents as part of their call to serve the church. Most of the parsonages were very old, very large, and some even had no indoor plumbing or bathrooms. But Mom always made those parsonages warm and homey.

HELENA, MONTANA 1938 - 1943

The parsonage in Helena was unique in that the church building housed both the sanctuary upstairs with the parsonage and Sunday school rooms downstairs. The doors to the church opened to a turreted tower with stairs leading up to the sanctuary. It's on those outside steps, in front of the church doors, that I was left in a basket at two weeks of age.

HARRIS, MINNESOTA 1943 – 1945

In 1943, my parents moved to the small Minnesota village of Harris with a population of about 600. Harris is located 50 miles north of Minneapolis. Here my dad served two churches in a circuit ministry that included both Harris and Rush City. Just weeks after moving to Minnesota I suffered the skull fracture which I've already described.

Our family lived in the old two-story parsonage in Harris, which was located directly across the street from the church. While the parsonage did have electricity, it did not have in-door plumbing or central heating. Our toilet was a one seat, wood framed, outdoor toilet located about 25 feet from the back door of our house. In the summer our "out-house" was hot and smelly and in the winter, it was freezing cold to sit in. Without an indoor bathroom, our Saturday night bath was always in a big, galvanized, tub that Mom filled with water in the kitchen. The only heat in the house was the wood-burning, cooking stove in the kitchen, and the oil-burning heater in the dining room. The upstairs was always freezing-cold in the winter and stuffy-hot in the summer.

Immediately behind the house was the outdoor water pump, painted "firehouse red," from which we pumped all our drinking water, cooking and bathing water. Mom would heat all the water we used as a family on the wood-burning cooking stove in the kitchen. As a kid, I was expected to help pump pails of water and bring them into the house, where we had a small "dipper," to dip out cups of water from the pail for drinking or cooking.

My mom did have an electric washing machine, which looked like a large, metal barrel on rollers. The clothes were washed in the gyrating, hot water of the machine and then rinsed, by hand, in a galvanized tub that sat on the floor. Next, Mom would insert the clothes between two rubber, wringer-rollers that were attached to the top of the washing machine. The clothes would move slowly through the rubber wringers, which would squeeze out some of the water, before Mom would take them outside and hang them to dry on the clothesline.

I remember once, as a very young boy, that I was so intrigued by the rollers on Mom's washing machine, that I climbed up on a stool, and stuck my hand into the rollers while they were still rolling. To my horror, I found that the rollers grabbed my hand and I couldn't get it out. Slowly the rollers pulled my hand and then my whole arm into the machine. My arm was pulled in all the way to my shoulder when Mom finally heard my cries and came in from hanging clothes outside and turned off the ringers. I got scolded. But I was thankful to still have an arm.

With the entry of the United States into the Second World War, after Pearl Harbor in 1941, I grew up in a period of American history that was dominated by war. Even though I was a young boy, living in a small Minnesota town, I was still very aware of the fact that our nation was at war. I remember sitting with my dad, beside our 1939 RCA Victor upright radio, listening to the broadcast of the D-Day Invasion of Normandy in June 1944. And I remember the frightening news reports of the power and devastation of the atomic bomb that was dropped on Hiroshima, Japan in August, 1945. It was a fearful time for a little boy and I remember the heartfelt prayers of my folks for our nation and for the young men of our church and family who were serving on the battle fields of Europe and Japan. All my toys, growing up, had to do with our country's war effort; my lead soldiers and sailors, my silk parachute soldier and the cardboard fighter airplanes which hung by a string from the ceiling of my bedroom. These cardboard model planes were offered by Wheaties Cereal in 1944, which I would cut out and assemble, including an American P- 510 Mustang and an American Thunderbolt P-47.

While 1944 was a very serious time to begin first grade, it was also a very exciting time in America, as our country rallied around an all-out war effort. And our family was no exception. To aid in the war effort our family had a large "Victory Garden" in the back of the Harris parsonage. The U.S. Government in 1941, began to encourage American families to plant gardens as a patriotic contribution that citizens could make by

I had just turned six years old and I was participating in a community patriotic event in 1944.

growing their own food. By 1943, there were 18 million Victory Gardens in the United States, which freed-up more food for our troops as well as our European allies who were under attack. I remember, as a young boy, planting seeds and pulling weeds in our family Victory Garden. Better yet, I remember enjoying eating fresh sweet peas from the pods as I worked beside my parents in our garden.

Each Friday, along with my G.I. Joe lunch box, I remember bringing ten cents to school to buy War Bond Stamps, which the government encouraged as our patriotic duty and to help finance the tremendous costs of the war. Because food was in short supply, every American family was issued a series of rationing books during the war, beginning in 1942. Every rationing book contained removable stamps that were good for certain rationed items and you could not buy any of those items without giving the grocer the right ration stamps. The rationed items included, gasoline, sugar, coffee, nylons (modern day panty hose), meat, cooking oil, canned goods, shoes, car tires and much more. I remember how my parents would agonize over their rationing book as they planned family menus, so as not to use up their allotted stamps before the month was up. Once, Dad blew out two tires on his old 1935 Chevrolet and he had to receive special permission from the local rationing board to buy two new tires. He was granted the new tires because he was a minister. To conserve gas the speed limit in 1943 was 35 MPH and gas cost 20 cents per gallon.

While we had no kindergarten in 1943, my experience in first grade in the Harris Elementary School, was generally happy. I can remember how much I enjoyed learning to read in my, "Dick and Jane" and "See Spot Run," basic readers. And I loved art projects and recess. I walked about two miles to school and had to cross a busy highway and two railroad tracks. But I always walked with Bezzy, my best friend and neighbor. We both loved my two dogs, Duke (Dad's hunting dog) and Tippy my mutt. We also enjoyed building forts together and sledding down the nearby hills in the long Minnesota winters.

But it was also in elementary school that I began to wake up to the fact that some people thought of an adopted kid as strange, even weird. Like when a classmate said, "Your parents gave you away because nobody wanted you," I felt like a reject. Other kids came "first class" into their families; I was "second class."

The final straw to my poor self-esteem came at age 6, when I over-heard a dearly loved aunt say to my parents, "I certainly hope that Wesley doesn't bring bad blood into our family." My young mind struggled to understand the meaning of "bad blood." Whatever it meant to others, I certainly understood that I was regarded as potentially a "bad boy" for my family. Like many adoptees, I developed antennae that could sense rejection a mile away. The seeds of my fear of rejection were sown at a very young age and continued to grow as the years went by.

LITTLE FALLS, MINNESOTA – 1945 – 1948

After I attended only the first grade in Harris, my father, in 1945, accepted a ministry call to serve the Mission Covenant Church of Little Falls, Minnesota. This was the second time my folks had served the church in that city (he also served it in 1931-1935), and now he was called back to help resolve some divisions in the church. We hadn't even lived a full two years in Harris and here we were, already moving. I was basically a shy child, and I remember how difficult it was for me to be uprooted and find new friends, a new school, a new church. But relocating was to be the customary routine for our family and it only increased my fear of rejection.

Our family moved into the old, two-story, church parsonage located on 2nd Street NE in Little Falls. My bedroom was squeezed into my dad's study, in-between all his books and desk. And once each year, I shared that room with my maternal grandfather, Alfred Anderson, who came to live with us for several months annually after Grandma Clara's death.

It was Christmas Eve 1948 and Dad and I are reading the Christmas story from the Bible before opening Christmas gifts.

The city of Little Falls was named after the waterfalls and dam that were located on the Mississippi River which flowed through the heart of the city. Here is where I learned to swim at the public beach on the river. My neighbor and buddy, Douglas Larson, would be with me at the beach most every summer day of the week. We both loved to swim and took great pride when we qualified each summer to swim out to the big raft and diving board in the middle of the river. Because the river was deep and the current swift, the city life-guard always gave us a swimming test to see if we were good enough to swim out to the big raft. I remember the pride I felt when I first successfully proved I could swim that far.

I attended school, from the second grade to the fifth grade, at the old Washington Elementary School, which has since been torn down. At that time, the school was very run-down and very crowded. When I was in the fifth-grade, my teacher served as both our classroom teacher and the school principal in a small room that was crowded with 35 students.

I remember when I was in the fourth grade, that there was an older boy who got his enjoyment from bullying and beating-up the younger children. He would follow us home after school and try to catch us and push us down and do his worst. When my dad learned of the situation, he began to come to school at the end of classes and walk with us home. When the bully saw my big, 6'2" dad walking with us, he didn't bother us anymore. I was so proud of my dad.

But my dad didn't stop with just his protection of me. He also enrolled me in boxing lessons being offered at the community recreation classes at the nearby high school. He wanted me to learn to protect myself. But I was such a skinny kid, and somewhat timid, and I never did use my new boxing skills against that bully.

I always liked school, but was pretty much a non-achiever in the lower grades. It wasn't until high-school that I began to really study and develop some leadership skills. My grades in elementary school were very average and I still can remember feeling "dumb" in the fourth grade when I had difficulty understanding long division, while most of my class-mates had already mastered the skill. It was a young student-teacher, who was a temporary aid in our class, who sat down with me person-

ally and helped me to finally get a grasp on long division. I remember, to this day, that it was like a light went off in my brain and I suddenly understood that math process. I didn't feel "dumb" anymore. And I remember feeling so grateful to that student-teacher for taking the time to help me. A teacher's personal attention is what my heart and mind needed all the time.

Our family life centered around the Mission Covenant Church where my dad served as Pastor. The church was a simple, white frame building, that seated about 120 people and was located across the street from our home. It was just assumed

Getting ready to race with my friends at my ninth birthday party celebrated at Pine Grove Park in Little Falls.

that I would attend Sunday school as well as both the morning and evening preaching services along with the Wednesday night Bible Study meeting. I can never remember objecting to all that church attendance, but I did understand that our family had different priorities than most of my Roman Catholic friends who went to their church only occasionally.

My two favorite parks in Little Falls were the Pine Grove City Park and the Charles A. Lindbergh State Park. I often wanted my birthday's celebrated at Pine Grove Park, with its magnificent stand of huge white pine trees (the last standing grove of white pine in the state), and its ample room for boys to run and play.

But Little Falls was also famous for being the location of the boy-hood home of Charles A. Lindbergh Jr., who in 1927 made the first trans-Atlantic, non-stop flight from New York to Paris. His home was part of the five-hundred acre, Lindbergh State Park, which included endless hiking trails and streams. My favorite part was the old, swinging, cable-bridge. We kids loved to make it jump and swing when little girls were on it so they'd all scream. As a child, I mistakenly thought that the Lindbergh home in the park was the place where the Lindbergh baby had, in 1932, been kidnapped and murdered. It was a big and scary thing in my mind and I thought that maybe I'd be kidnapped too. When I later learned that this, "crime of the century" had occurred in New Jersey and not in Minnesota, I was greatly relieved of my fears of being kidnapped in Little Falls.

In 1947, when I was 9 years old, my folks helped me enter a Wheat-ies cereal contest sponsored by General Mills. The contest offered 1000 Columbia bicycles to the winners of the, "WHEATIES NAME YOUR BIKE CONTEST". I collected many Wheaties box-tops to submit with my entries of possible bike names. One of the bike names that I sub-mitted and especially liked, was "Whiz."

Not long after, I got a letter from Jack Armstrong, "the All-American Boy", who was the radio-star promoting the contest. The letter said that my entry of "Whiz" had won and I was soon to be the owner of a brand-new Columbia bike. Wow, I was thrilled beyond words. Not only did I win a bike, but I actually got a letter from Jack Armstrong whose radio adventure series were almost as popular, in my mind, as "The Lone Ranger and Tonto."

After receiving the letter, I waited impatiently for several weeks for my bike to arrive. That wonderful day finally came, my mom got a call from our friend, Mr. J.O. Johnson at the railroad freight office, telling us that my bike had arrived. I was so excited, jumping up and down, I could hardly wait for dad to get home so we could go and pick up my prize-winning bike. It seemed like all the kids from our neighborhood flooded our front yard as dad helped me unpack the crate holding my bike. After we all admired the bike, I suddenly realized that I had never ridden a two-wheel bike before and had no idea what to do next! Finally, my dad helped me climb on and sit on the bike. He gave it a big push and I was off. After peddling around the block, to the cheers of neighborhood kids, I now realized I had no idea how to stop and get off the bike! Finally, I just fell with my bike on the grass. It wasn't graceful but it worked and I learned later how to stop a bike and get off. That bike lasted me 10 years.

I suddenly realized that I had never ridden a two-wheel bike before and had no idea what to do next!

In 1946, while living in Little Falls, my grandfather gave my folks some money to buy 23 acres of lake-shore property on Lake Kabekona, near Walker, Minnesota. The folks also bought, and remodeled, an old one room C.C.C. cabin (Civilian Conservation Corps) which they had moved onto their lake property and it became our lake cabin. Dad later added a screened-in porch, which doubled as a bedroom for my brother, John and me. This rustic cabin became a place of exciting adventure for me, every summer, for the next 12 years. It made no difference to me that our cabin had no electricity or indoor plumbing. I was always excited to light the kerosene lamps at night, warm myself each morning by the wood-burning stove and traveling each week to the Benedict General Store to get ice for the old-fashioned ice-box in the kitchen nook. I still catch myself, as an adult, calling a refrigerator an "ice box." We also had

I was a proud nine-year-old when I caught 20 Sunfish and Perch while fishing off my raft on the lake at our cabin in Minnesota.

a two-seater outdoor toilet, which mom christened, by writing on the door, "the dew-drop-in."

Lake Kabekona, is about four miles long and one half-mile-wide, reaching a depth of 133 feet and with ten miles of shoreline. The lake is the second clearest lake in Minnesota with crystal clear water that is the habitat for its large Loon birdlife. But our lake was small compared to the nearby Leech Lake, to which we were connected by a small creek. I would love our family trips down that creek, where we would drift in the wooden boat that Dad had built, seeing the large walleye and northern pike swimming along-side our boat. Dad also built a long dock off our beach with a live-fish box at the end of the dock. He also built a big, floating raft which became my favorite fishing spot. Once, in just one hour of fishing off the raft, I caught 20 perch and sunfish.

While I often got poison-ivy at the cabin and we all suffered from the swarms of mosquitoes each evening, I nevertheless have so many wonderful memories from our fun times there. I was always busy building my tree-house forts, creating big sand castles in the white beach sand, picking wild blueberries with my folks for Mom's sweet blueberry pies, and traveling to Bemidji to see the big Paul Bunyan and Blue Ox statues. The cabin was my Disneyland.

But in 1959, some drunken and angry Indians from the Leech Lake Indian Reservation, destroyed many cabins along the lake, including ours. They took an ax to just about everything, smashing windows, doors, furniture and breaking all the dishes and pot and pans. They were eventually arrested but the destruction of the cabin broke my parents heart, and fearing the violence of the area, they sold the land in 1971 to a resort developer.

POPLAR, WISCONSIN – 1948-1954

By the time I was ten years old, our family had moved four times and our latest move was in 1948 to the small dairy farming community of Poplar, Wisconsin. This little village of 400 people was located in the far northern part of Wisconsin, about 20 miles from the Great Lake port cities of Superior, Wisconsin and Duluth, Minnesota.

We enjoyed our new home in Poplar, which was located in this idyllic farming village nestled in the hardwood maple and evergreen-pine forests of Northern Wisconsin. The gravel roads of the community crossed the railroad tracks which ran through the middle of the town. The daily whistle from the steam engines that chugged down these tracks was my introduction to the awesome joy of railroad trains. I spent many hours as a youth, sitting by the village depot and marveling at these enormous steam engines that shook the ground as they rumbled through town, or stopped to thirstily take on water. This is where I developed my interest in model trains, a hobby that would last a lifetime.

Our small village had two flourishing churches, the Lutheran Church and the Mission Covenant Church, which were located almost next to each other. The Covenant Church, which my dad served, was built in the classic Mission Friend style with a tall tower entrance and a sanctuary that seated about 200. But this Covenant Church was unique in that the sanctuary had two beautiful stained glass windows. The large window at the front of the church and just behind the choir loft depicted the Biblical scene of Christ knocking at the door from Revelation 3:20. As a boy, I studied that window every Sunday. I saw that the door latch was on the inside and Christ was outside patiently knocking and waiting for the person on the inside to open the door. It was here that I began to understand that I needed to make a decision to open my heart's door to Jesus.

In addition to the churches, our little village had a bank, a hardware store, an auto repair garage and an old-fashioned grocery store where Burt Peterson, the owner, would wait on you from behind the counter and personally fill your paper bag with the grocery items on your list. In the back of the grocery store was the U. S. Post Office where I would go after school to get our family mail. Here again we got personal attention, as the Post Master would hand me our mail from the family box.

Our home in Poplar was located about five blocks from the church and was another big, three-bedroom house with a large indoor bathroom and linen closet all located upstairs. The downstairs featured a large kitchen and breakfast nook with a walk-in pantry, a big living room, dining room, and a study for my dad. This house also had a full basement with a huge coal burning furnace and an area where I built my first HO-gauge train set. My folks had given me the train set as a Christmas gift in 1950 and Dad and I built the set, on plywood sheets, complete with papier mache mountains and tunnels, cities and farms.

One fun feature of our Poplar home was the party-line, hand crank telephone that sat on the kitchen counter next to the sink. I especially remember it as a fun feature because I was just getting old enough to start using it often to call friends. The party-line was always an exciting opportunity to listen-in to other people's conversations, which I did often. To use the phone, you would turn the hand crank and ring a sequence of long and short rings. Our phone number was one long and two short rings. When we heard our own ring, we would answer the call but anyone else on our party-line could also listen in to the conversation. That was the way community news and personal gossip got passed around in our town.

I'm often amazed by the fact that I have lived to see such fantastic technical developments; from the primitive hand-crank phone to advanced cell phones with all their apps. I was actually twelve years old when I saw my first television set, which was at our neighbors home next door. They had one of the first TV sets in town which was a small 15", black and white set that had only one channel. The only shows to be seen were Saturday Night Wrestling with Gorgeous George, "I Love Lucy", and "Dragnet". Today we have a 42 inch T.V. set with over 500 channels and that size T.V. seems small compared to some.

The village of Poplar was somewhat famous as the hometown of Major Richard Ira Bong, who in World War II shot down some 40 Japanese aircraft and was honored throughout America as "The Ace of Ace's". His life story, as a "Poplar boy," was proudly taught in our elementary school, where a life-size model of his twin-engine P-38 Lightning aircraft was mounted on steel beams next to our school ball-field. Each year the school had all the students board buses and travel to the Major Richard Bong State Forest, where we'd spend a day planting seedling pine trees. It was our annual lesson in conservation and civic pride.

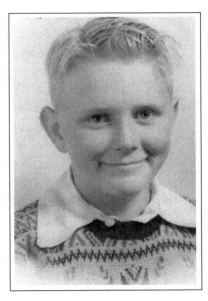

Our elementary school was very old with outdated equipment, cracked blackboards and overworked teachers who each taught two classes in the four rooms of the school. My fifth and sixth grade teacher was Elsie Holms who was a good teacher, but when she ran out of patience with an unruly student, she would take them in the coat-room and paddle them with a wooden stick. This form of discipline would never be tolerated now, but today's lack of classroom discipline could well account for the terrible disrespect of teachers and the high drop-out rates in public schools.

I was eleven years old and in the sixth grade in the Poplar, Wisconsin grade school.

In the sixth-grade I had a secret girlfriend. It was so secret that even she didn't know that I was sweet on her. In my eleven-year-old mind I was certain that God meant for us to be together because our initials matched each other's. I thought we'd get married, and go to Africa as missionaries. But my dreams were dashed when I learned she already had a boyfriend.

My seventh and eighth grade teacher was Mrs. Peterson who was quite strict and often frustrated with our class. I remember her telling our entire eighth grade, that we were all failures in Algebra and she didn't think that one of us would ever graduate from high school. That comment certainly didn't help with my self-esteem and I long remember her negative opinion of our class.

In the 40's, small town elementary schools in Wisconsin had no sports programs, no physical education teachers, no music or art programs and not even a school principal to support the teachers. Recess was often a bedlam of activities, all organized by what the students could come up with – usually either softball or jump-rope. In the winter, we'd bring our sleds and skis from home and slide down the big hill behind the school.

Perhaps the best part of school was the hot-lunch program, which cost a child ten-cents each day and included home-made bread, home-canned peaches, pears and vegetables that the school cooks canned each summer to reduce the cost of school lunches. I always smiled pleasantly at the cooks who scooped me up big portions of the lunch of the day.

America in 1948 was making a difficult transition from the war years to peace time. Growing up in this era of American history was filled with anxiety over issues like "the Cold War," with the Soviet Union, the "Atomic Age," with the threat of an A-bomb destroying entire nations and the "Hot War" in 1950, with American troops in Korea. Listening to the news at the breakfast table was unnerving. In school, we often discussed what we'd do if Russia fired an atomic bomb at our town. It was all serious business for a child to grasp.

South of Poplar was a town called Maple, where it was reported that a lot of the Finnish emigrants who had moved in there were communists. Local gossips said that there were political fist-fights at the Maple town-hall meetings. This only supported the contention of our state senator, Joe McCarthy, who was holding hearings in Washington and accusing people everywhere of being Communists; in government, in Hollywood, in the universities and even among the clergy. This was very alarming for a kid. The whole country seemed to be hunting Communists and everyone was suspect. I was so concerned that I remember asking my dad if he was afraid of being investigated as a Communist sympathizer because he'd voted for F.D.R. He calmly said he had nothing to fear and that he'd gladly testify in Washington if Senator Joe subpoenaed him. Joe never called.

Economic recovery, from both the war years and the Great Depression, was slow in coming to small Midwest communities like ours. And while my dad, as a pastor, was recognized as a community leader, it was not reflected in his salary. My folks were very poor. There were times that Dad couldn't afford to have a car, so we walked everywhere. Mom sold greeting cards from our home so she could have a little extra cash, especially at Christmas time. I was often embarrassed as a kid that some of my clothes were hand-me-downs from relatives or came plucked from the church, second-hand, missionary clothing-barrel, before being sent off to missionaries in Africa. Once a kid in church recognized the shirt I was wearing as his old shirt that his mom had put in the missionary barrel.

On the positive side, our home was always filled with love, good humor and lots of family and friends who came over for Mom's chicken dinners. I grew up with very caring parents who held me accountable, but always allowed me to have plenty of time to just be a kid. Summers were spent with my friends, swimming in the town pond, building forts in the woods or playing back-yard football. Winters offered all kinds of fun and adventure in Wisconsin's abundant snow and ice. But my constant companion growing up was my springer spaniel dog named, Trixie. I loved that dog. Where I went, Trixie went. But one day, as Trixie and I were walking in the deep snow ruts of our road, a speeding car ran over my dog and killed her. I saw the whole thing happen right in front of me. I ran to her, in the road, and as she died in my arms she licked my cheek with a parting kiss. I cried for two days. On Sunday, my folks allowed me to stay home from church because my eyes were all red and swollen from crying.

Since the public schools offered very little in extracurricular activities for youth, it was the churches and community youth organizations like 4-H Clubs, where we pledged our "heads, hearts, hands and health to better service." It was those organizations that filled the gap and offered positive programs for youth.

In 1949, I joined our local 4-H Club and raised chickens as my service project. Each spring I ordered my chickens from the hatchery and four boxes of baby chicks would arrive through the post-office. Since it was too cold in the spring for the baby chicks to be outside, we put newspapers on the floor of my mom's large kitchen pantry and all 100 baby chicks spent their first weeks of life cozy and warm inside our house walk-in pantry. When the chicks grew into pullets, I would put a plank down the steps from the outside pantry door to an area I'd fenced-in outside so the pullets could run and enjoy the grass. Later that summer, Dad and I built a chicken coop in our back-yard with a much larger fenced-in area. For five years, I enjoyed raising 100 happy, egg laying, free-range chickens.

I named my prize rooster "King" that I raised along with 99 other chickens for my 4-H project in 1952.

Each month my mom would go with me to the feed store and help me pick up chicken-feed. In those years, chicken feed came in brightly patterned cotton sacks and Mom would use the empty sacks to sew everyday dresses for herself. Her dresses were always colorful and well-made from patterns she bought at J.C. Penney. I never considered it odd that my mom made dresses from chicken-feed sacks. We were poor and our great depression mind-set taught us that everything had a useful purpose and nothing was thrown away.

As a part of my 4-H experience I would annually go to the Tri-State Fair in Superior, Wisconsin. There I would give my "chicken speech" and demonstrate how to cut up a chicken for freezing. In addition to learning at 4-H how to speak publicly I also, as a 12-year-old, was earning $1.00 a dozen by selling eggs.

One negative aspect of my chicken project was that we could only keep 25 chickens over the winter in our small chicken coop. That meant that every fall I had to cut the heads off of at least 75 chickens. After a year of feeding, watering and collecting eggs from 100 chickens, I had become attached to them and even gave some of them names. It was painful for me to cut off the heads of my chicken friends. But Mom and Dad would always help in both the killing, plucking and cutting up the chickens for freezing. We ate a lot of chicken in my growing-up years.

My dad confirmed me in the Christian faith, along with four other boys, on October 19, 1952. The five of us; Bob Bergstien, Nils Herse, Bob Abell, Larry Borg and myself, had to stand before the entire congregation on Confirmation Sunday and be prepared to answer any question from Luther's Catechism. I was sweating the whole time, hoping that Dad would have mercy on his son and ask easy questions of me.

In retrospect, I think confirmation, while being a good introduction to faith, was more of a nerve-racking experience for me than a spiritual high. Although there were times of significant spiritual commitment in my youth, particularly at Covenant Park Bible Camp, in the final analysis, it was my parents love for Christ and their example of godly living that drew me to take my first steps of faith. "Faith," it is said, "is more caught than taught," and my folks example of faith was more of a love relationship with God than a negative demand to follow legalistic rules. And so, I caught and loyally confessed my parent's faith on Confirmation Sunday. But it was not yet a firsthand faith in Jesus Christ as Savior.

In the fall of 1952, I entered my freshman year of high-school at Northwestern Consolidated High School in nearby Maple, Wisconsin. Because it was only the fourth year of classes for this newly consolidated school, we had a rocky beginning to the year. The senior class decided that the school needed some initiation-week traditions, so they required that all the freshmen boys dress like girls and all the freshmen girls dress like boys for a day. I was humiliated. But I guess that's what the upperclassmen wanted, to remind the freshmen of their lowly position.

High school classes included all the basics of English, taught by Miss Virginia Tarter; Algebra, taught by Mr. Kortesma; Biology, taught by Mr. Flechelkotter; Typing, taught by Mrs. Doris Anderson; Physical Education, taught by Mr. Lucas; and Wood Shop, taught by Mr. Christianson. I remember botching my project in wood shop so that the fancy corner shelf (my plan A) became the roof for a bird house (my plan B). But my very favorite class in high school was playing the baritone horn in Mr. John Watkins' high school band. I was not very good at playing that instrument, but I had lots of fun and laughs in marching band. I must have come out of my shell in high school and loosened up from my shy, introverted self. I can remember thinking how good it was to have a fresh-start in high school, where no one knew that I was a rejected, doorstep-baby. So, my year-book was full of autographs from classmates who said I was a funny kid and full of fun:

- *"I'll never forget the fun we had with you in band." – Shirley*
- *"Best wishes to a musician that's always laughing and blowing hot air, just like the Democrats." - Barbara*

- "I must say that I've enjoyed your cute remarks and humor all year. Just find someone else to be the victim of your pranks." - Al

My high school years were a mixture of joy and pain. I truly enjoyed growing up in Poplar where the slow, dependable cadence of family life, friends, school and church gave me some confidence. But then in the spring of 1954, Dad resigned from the church and announced that we were moving to Kansas. It was my fifth move in 14 years. I was devastated. The thought of being uprooted in my junior year of high school and leaving all my friends to start another new school seemed so unfair and it renewed all my old fears of abandonment. But Dad was confident that God was calling him to start a new Covenant Church in Kansas, so in June 1954 we packed up and moved again.

OBERLIN, KANSAS – 1954 – 1958

I was 16 in 1954 and enrolled as a Junior in Decatur Community High School in Oberlin, Kansas.

Oberlin, Kansas, in the year 1954, was a small city of 2200 people located in Northwest Kansas at the intersection of U.S. Highway 36 and 83. The city is surrounded by the rolling hills and wheat fields of western Kansas, some 230 miles east of Denver, Colorado. The whole region is a semi-arid climate zone, very hot and dry, with miles and miles of flat land filled with wheat and milo fields. It was 105 degrees on that June day that we moved into town.

Our family temporarily moved into a very small, run down, five-room rented house with one tiny bathroom, and where my brother and I shared a bunkbed that was squeezed into a little 6'X6' bedroom. Two years later, the church bought a newer home as their parsonage. It had three bedrooms, two bathrooms and, I think the previous owner had rented out both levels of this home to separate families, as each level had its own kitchen, living room and dining room. It was the nicest home of my entire childhood.

This move to Oberlin in my junior year of high-school was really tough on me. I realized from my very first day, in this new school, that I was the outsider in a closely-knit group of school mates who had grown up together, played sports together and now were dating one another. In addition, I was not a part of the 'In Crowd,' where alcohol was often a part of the party life. I, by conviction and family training, abstained from all alcohol. It was amazing to me that more of the students didn't abstain from alcohol, as the summer before our move, three of our classmates were killed while driving under the influence of alcohol. In addition, they smashed into another car killing both parents of my friend Dallas Musgrave.

I was elected as Prom King in my Senior year of High School.

But in many ways, the school situation in Oberlin was a vast improvement over the new and untested high school in Wisconsin. Decatur Community High School in Kansas had high academic expectations for their students and the school was much more college preparatory. Here we had an excellent teacher in English/Literature in the young and vibrant Dean Coughenour. We were challenged in U.S. history and U.S. government classes with Charley Lyons and I studied two years of Spanish with Patsy Hagemeister and a year of bookkeeping with Mildred Agnew. But it was our journalism/speech teacher, Gertrude Railsback, who took a personal interest in me; coaching me in state-wide speech competition, encouraging me to be editor of the school paper and yearbook and advising me as a member of the school debate team. She became my favorite high school teacher and had a deep impact on my life.

I flourished in my studies in Oberlin and was recognized by my classmates as a leader. For two years, I was elected to the student council and then elected as the prom king in my senior year. I became Editor of the school paper and the year book, as well as Spiritual Chaplain of the school Hi-Y club. I sang in the mixed choir and Boy's Glee Club, acted in the school play, was a member of the debate team, participated in state speech competition for original oration and elected as vice-president of my senior class. I know there were other students far more qualified for election to these positions, but I came to realize that I was respected in the school for my moral and spiritual convictions.

Church involvement was also a big part of my life in Oberlin. My dad had been called to plant a new church in the city with a small group of people who had been meeting in home Bible studies, but they now began meeting on Sundays in the rented Seventh Day Adventist Church. Once again, while Dad preached, Mom led the choir and I taught the junior boys Sunday school class.

Within two years, this young congregation had grown enough to begin building their own church facility on property they purchased directly across from the city hospital. My dad was deeply involved in the church construction, almost to the point of acting as the general contractor. I was really proud of his leadership when this new church was dedicated in February, 1956, with Dr. T. W. Anderson, president of the denomination, preaching the dedication sermon.

In my junior year of high school, I realized that my parents had very little money to help me go to college and I needed a job to start saving money. My first job at age 15, was working after school at the local Safeway store, where I stocked shelves with canned goods and carried grocery bags to customers' cars. I learned early, that my back was not strong (perhaps from my bout with Polio) and I injured my back further by bending and lifting heavy boxes at work.

While I was in severe pain from that back injury, my dad took me to the local chiropractor for a back treatment. To my utter shock, this chiropractor exposed himself while I laid on the treatment table and tried to molest me. I jumped off of the table and ran out to the lobby where my dad was waiting and shouted, "I don't want a back treatment and I never want to come back to that doctor again." Dad thought that the doctor had somehow hurt me physically in the treatment. But I felt betrayed and embarrassed by that doctor's advances. And I was angry. He didn't care about my back pain or have any intention of treating me as a patient. I was just his victim and he made me feel like a nobody, like my life didn't matter. He abandoned me when I had trusted him for help and all my old fears of rejection swept over me. But the shock of that doctor's actions left me so traumatized that I was unable to ever tell my dad what the doctor had done. I learned some years later that the doctor was sent to prison for

My high school class picture sporting my "flat top" haircut.

child molestation and I was sad that I hadn't blown the whistle on him before he abused others.

Being unable to handle the heavy work at the Safeway store, I got another job working with the local funeral director, Mr. Griffith, who embalmed bodies in the basement of his furniture store. I worked for Mr. Griffith after school and on weekends, in both the furniture store and the funeral parlor. Once, when he was away for a few hours, I got curious about what it would feel like to lie in one of the coffins on display in the basement. I crawled into a coffin and found that it was soft and cushy and I even contemplated taking a nap, until I heard Mr. Griffith return unexpectedly upstairs. He never knew that I was trying-out his caskets and I sure didn't tell him. But it did occur to me that I was really testing out what I would look like in a casket since I was convinced that I would die young. And now the negative experience I'd had with the attempted abuse by the chiropractor only enforced my feelings of rejection and worthlessness, which convinced me I would die young.

CHAPTER 5

CHICAGO AND COLLEGE

I graduated from Decatur Community High School on May 17, 1956, as part of a class of 42 members. That spring I applied to several state colleges in Kansas, as well as to our church college (now North Park University) in Chicago, Illinois. This school, on the north side of Chicago, had been a junior college for 65 years and now was transitioning to a four-year school and enrolling their first four-year class. I chose to attend North Park College because of the encouragement of Dr. T. W. Anderson, then President of the Covenant Denomination, in a personal letter he wrote, urging me to be part of this first class.

"Dear Wesley,
In the thoughtful Christmas greeting from your parents, a reference was made to the fact that you are now a senior in high school and that you may possibly come to North Park in the fall. Your parents are both my former students at Minnehaha Academy, whose friendship I have valued through the years. I have also known you from your very infancy in Helena, Montana.
Possibly you don't know that the class that enters North Park next fall will undoubtedly be the first class to graduate from our four year course with a B.A. degree in 1960. I earnestly hope that you will be in this historic class. I know you will enjoy the fine Christian fellowship and excellent education that our own school offers."
Faithfully, Theodore W. Anderson, President

Going to Chicago for college was really a huge stretch for me for several reasons:

- I was basically a shy homebody who was frightened at the thought of traveling 1000 miles from my small town in Kansas to the second largest city in the United States, with a population, in 1956, of three million.
- The city of Chicago, in addition to its size, was not only known as the "Windy City," but also the "City of Gangsters." Very terrifying to contemplate.
- But my main obstacle was a financial one. My family couldn't afford to send me to a private school so far from home. My folks scraped together about $500 from their small income (Dad cashed in a small life insurance policy he had) and they promised to send a little each September. But tuition, room and board was $1,000 a year. I also had my savings of about $300 from my two years of part-time work and a scholarship of $245 from the local Order of the Eastern Star. But that was all I had for four years of college. So, finances were a real stretch.
- I knew that I would have to work after school and on weekends, almost full time, in order to pay for four years of college. But I had no prospect of a job in Chicago.

All of these reasons gave me very little hope of ever going to college in Chicago. But my folks and I prayed earnestly for a James 1:5 kind of wisdom from God, to make the right decision. God gave us a peace that He would make it possible. In the spring of 1956, the North Park acceptance letter was the awesome confirmation that I was going to North Park.

Standing with my family as a high school senior outside of our new home in Oberlin, Kansas.

Still, it was a scary time that fall, when my folks loaded their car with my clothes and we made the long, one thousand-mile, trip to Chicago. Upon our arrival, I rendezvoused with my new roommate, John Simonson, who was also from northwest Kansas. And then I said a tearful goodbye to my parents. When they left, I struggled with dark feeling of loneliness and even abandonment. My roommate also battled with homesickness and he left college and returned home to Kansas after one semester.

THE NEW NORTH PARK UNIVERSITY

In 1956, North Park College was going through a major transition from a small Junior College to a fully accredited four-year university, offering Bachelor and Master degrees.

The school, at that time, still had much of the old junior college, Christian flavor with evening devotions in the dining hall, prayer before some classes, gospel songfests (called "singspirations") on the back campus on Sunday evenings and required chapel services each week. A number of my classes were still held in the limited facilities of Old Main, which was built in 1893, and aging rapidly. This old building housed our college library, which was located way up on third floor and there was no elevator. As a result, I didn't use the library very much. In 1958, I was a part of an assembly-line of students and teachers who helped move the entire library from the third floor of Old Main to the newly built Wallgren Library.

While science classes were held in the 55-year-old building called Wilson Hall and music classes were held in Hanson Hall, the majority of our classes were held in the basement of the large seminary building called, Nyvall Hall. We joked that North Park was the largest college of underground education in the nation. So, I attended "underground" college with classes in English literature from E. Gustav Johnson, biology from Carroll Peterson, Bible survey and philosophy classes from Elder Lindahl and Mel Soneson, political science classes from Robert Byrd, Spanish classes from Bonevive Farsj, speech classes from Margaret Peterson and a wide range of history classes (my major) from Zenos Hawkinson, Earland Carlson, Ernest Sandeen and Karl Olsson.

My home away from home was the men's dormitory on campus, room number 411 in J. Fred Berg Hall. When I moved into that dorm in 1956 it was a spanking-new building that housed 200 men. I can hardly believe that I have grandsons who are now living in that same dormitory over 60 years later. I remember that day in September, 1956 when the school dedicated the building in honor of Dr. J. Fred Berg, then Vice President of the school. At that dedication, Dr. Berg said, "I want you to remember that this building was dedicated in my honor, not in my memory – I'm not dead yet."

The rooms in Burg Hall were spartan and very small with minimal space for two beds, two desks and two dressers with clothes closets. But most of us got really creative in arranging the room, with some beds hanging from the ceiling, thus allowing more room for boys to wrestle on the floor.

While the rooms were small, it was the fellowship and fun of 200 men living in that building that made Burg Hall an exciting place in which to be residing. As it turned out, there were eleven guys from Kansas, all

Photo taken for my college graduation in 1960

living on the fourth floor of the dorm. We became good friends, some of whom I still correspond with 60 years later. There was always laughter, excitement and pranks whenever we got together for bull-sessions or Bible studies.

Our Kansas guys formed our own Bible Study, meeting each week with seminarian David Larsen as our teacher. David is the brother of Paul Larsen who served as president of our denomination and was a wonderful caring mentor to our group of young Kansas guys who all lived near his fourth-floor dorm room. David was often into eschatology and the study of the Biblical book of Revelation, which he chose to teach our group of Kansas freshmen. Sometimes when our freshman brains couldn't handle any more dispensational theory we would spice-up the Bible study by playing some pranks on David. I remember one time when we really embarrassed him by hiding five wine bottles under his bed pillow. I have no idea where we found those five wine bottles, but you could hear his explosive reaction throughout the building when he pulled back his bed covers at night and found those bottles. He tried to retaliate by slinging the bottles down the hall and into our rooms. We would sling them right back into his room. Suddenly, Professor Carroll Peterson, the dorm Resident Counselor showed up on our floor just as David was holding all five bottles ready to sling them down the hallway. The embarrassed expression on David's face was worth a year's tuition.

Since the majority of students living on campus were from Evangelical Covenant Church backgrounds I felt that I had found both my spiritual and intellectual home. But not everyone among the student body felt as comfortable as I did. Some were in open rebellion to faith, while others were carefully examining their childhood faith to see if there was any substance to what they had been taught in their home churches. And then there were those who were deeply committed to Christ and consistent in their Christian walk and testimony. I thought that I was a part of this latter group of committed Christians, but in fact I was very legalistic and believed that it was my rigid performance of church attendance and good works that obligated God to love me. My religion was more about me than it was of God. And my number one pet-peeve was these angry and rebellious fellow students.

But God was stirring in my heart, helping me to see that the real issue was me.

Some of the students who were in open rebellion to their childhood faith were especially critical of the school's policy of required weekly chapel attendance. They felt that the "new North Park," the "more sophisticated and intellectual" four-year school, gave them the freedom to disrupt Chapel for everyone, with their pranks. Once, a group of students took all the chapel metal chairs in a midnight raid and threw them all into the school swimming pool in the basement of the Chapel. It resulted in Chapel being canceled that day but the oil from the chairs also ruined the school swimming pool forever. It made me mad.

On another occasion, students hid alarm clocks under many of the chapel chairs all set to go off with loud alarms during the visiting pastor's message. It seemed childish to me, which it was, and drove me deeper into my legalism. I was very judgmental, even angry with these students, but I was afraid to confront them for fear they'd reject me. So, I just kept quiet and let the anger simmer inside. But God was stirring in my heart, helping me to see that the real issue was me, my rigidness and anger, not those students.

MY ENCOUNTER WITH HOLOCAUSTS SURVIVORS

My judgmental attitude was also being stretched at my employment off- campus. Within two weeks following my arrival at the campus, I got a job at the Jewell Grocery Store on Bryn Mawr Avenue, in Chicago. I was hired to manage the dairy section of the store, which meant rotating all the merchandise and stocking the cooler with milk, cream, cottage-cheese and dozens of varieties of cheese. The manager of the store was Harry Wiese, a kind-hearted Jew, who always guaranteed me a job each fall when I returned for classes. I walked 14 blocks each way after classes, walking through a predominately Orthodox Jewish neighborhood, which included many recent Jewish emigrants from Europe. I remember the shock I felt the first time I saw a customer at the store with tattooed numbers on her arm. They were the terrible numbers of the Holocaust when she had been a prisoner in a Nazi Concentration Camp. Over the years of working there I saw many other Jewish customers with the tattooed numbers on their arms. It was a soul stretching experience for me.

I had come to college totally naive and sheltered from the horror of the Jewish Holocaust. I was seven years old when the Second World War was over and I cannot remember *even hearing* of the Holocaust until I was a student in college. But now, my workplace included people who were a living example of the suffering of the Jewish people, the genocide of six-million Jews under Adolf Hitler's Nazi Germany.

For all the anti-Semitic propaganda being spread in the world at that time, I did not grow up in an anti-Semitic home or church. My parents taught me to love the Jewish people. And I grew up in an Evangelical Christian Church which taught me to respect and support Israel. I remember how we celebrated the establishment of the State of Israel in 1948 as the fulfillment of prophecy. I was taught that the Jewish people were "God's chosen people." I was taught that we, as Christians, owed a debt to Israel who was blessed to have the patriarchs of faith, the Covenants of promise, the temple worship, the prophets who foretold, in specific detail the coming of Messiah in Jesus, who is Immanuel, "meaning God is with us" (Matthew 1:23).

Above all else, I fervently believed that Jesus the Messiah had come to restore all nations to God and make us one people. "There is neither Jew nor Greek, slave nor free, male nor female, for you are all one in Christ Jesus" (Galatians 3:23). I believed that Jesus the Messiah, the Son of God, took our sins upon Himself, fulfilling the prophecy of Isaiah, "He was pierced for our transgressions, He was crushed for our iniquities; the punishment that brought us peace was upon Him, and by His wounds we are healed" (Isaiah 53:5). "But God has raised this Jesus to life, and we are all witnesses of the fact" (Acts 2:32). The death and resurrection of Jesus, the Messiah, is the very heart and core of my faith. But now I worked daily with people who, for the most part, didn't believe in Jesus as the promised Messiah and who blamed Christians for the genocide of Jews worldwide. For the first time in my life I worked and studied with people who didn't believe as I did. It was a time of intense personal struggle.

How can I hold to my core beliefs and still love those who bug me at school and disagree with me at work? My rigid, performance-based faith didn't allow it. My struggle to be religiously perfect and thus avoid rejection by God didn't allow it. This was an intense time of intellectual and spiritual struggle in my life. God was stretching my heart and my mind. I was beginning to learn how vital it is to love and respect all people, even those whose beliefs were different from mine. It was Martin Luther King Jr. who said, "We must learn to live together as brothers or we will perish together as fools." By working in this Jewish community, God was using my new Jewish friends to open my eyes to my brothers and sisters in a suffering and unjust world and to break down some of my prejudiced and judgmental attitudes so I wouldn't perish as a fool.

A BLEEDING STOMACH ULCER

In the fall of 1959, these intellectual and emotional events were moving rapidly toward a physical and spiritual crisis in my life. That fall I began to have burning, acidic pain, in my stomach. It was especially painful after eating meals and in bed at night. I became alarmed when I discovered red blood in my stools and I went to the school nurse. The nurse sent me immediately to the school doctor who ordered an X-ray at Swedish Covenant Hospital. The X-ray revealed a bleeding peptic stomach ulcer. I was hospitalized for a period of two weeks.

It was depressing for me to be hospitalized. It wasn't so much the pain of the ulcer, or the medical treatment, or the bland hospital meals that bothered me, but rather the emotional stress of missing two weeks of college classes. And, not only was I hopelessly behind in my classes but I was unable to work and earn the money needed for my college tuition, room and board. I felt I would have to drop out of school and return to Kansas in defeat.

A little glimmer of hope slipped into my hospital room as friends came to visit me, some bringing class notes and assignments to try to help me keep up with my studies. And I was especially blessed by visits from Professor Bonnie Farsje and Zenos Hawkinson who came to the hospital to encourage me and pray with me. Then to my total surprise, the College Business Manager, Mr. Nate Pohl, adjusted my financial payment schedule so I could temporarily reduce the amount of tuition I paid each month.

After those two weeks of hospitalization I came back to my dorm room very weak, wanting to sleep all the time and struggling with self-pity. Eventually I did have to drop two college courses and I had my work hours at the Jewell Store reduced and this only depressed me further. Added to all those struggles was the humiliation of having to stand outside of the school cafeteria and wait for Miss Growth, head of Food Services, to arrange for my nightly meal of two hard-boiled eggs, plain mashed potatoes without gravy and milk – lots of milk.

"You have never come to terms with your adoption as a foundling baby."

The college required that I begin counseling appointments with one of the school psychologists to see if I could understand what caused this ulcer at such a young age. After my second visit with the psychologist he said, "It seems obvious, from what you've shared, that you have never come to terms with your adoption as a foundling baby." That's all he said, but it was an eye-opening, epiphany moment for me. "Yes," I said, "that's me." I had sudden insight into all those years of struggling with the fears of rejection and abandonment. It was certainly true that I had also burned-out myself in college by taking a full-load of college classes while at the same time working almost full time. But the real cause of my health crisis was my life-long struggle with the emotional fear of rejection related to my feelings of abandonment on the church steps by my birth-mother.

All of this personal adoption history was no big deal for me in my earliest years of life. It was just a part of my life story that people everywhere seemed to know and tell others: "That's the boy who was left on the church door-step." Early on it seemed to even give me some prideful notoriety. I was unique, even special. But sometime around first grade, the neighborhood kids and bullies started teasing me. "You don't have real parents," they teased, "You don't even know who your parents are." And most hurtful was the taunt, "Nobody wanted you, so they gave you away." Even though my adoptive parents loved me unconditionally and always affirmed me, the put-down by playground bullies began to take its toll on me emotionally. And then at age six when I overheard my aunt say, "I certainly hope that Wesley doesn't bring bad-blood into our family," I couldn't get it out of my head. And I started to believe the lie, "I am bad blood, bad from birth and worthy of rejection." This lie had followed me throughout my childhood and youth, affecting my sense of self-worth, infecting my personal relationships, including my relationship with God.

MY PRODIGAL PRAYER

During the same week that I was released from the hospital, there was a series of religious meetings held on campus called Christian Life Emphasis Week. The guest speaker for the week was Dr. Sam Shoemaker, a Holy Spirit filled Episcopal Priest from Calvary Episcopal Church in Pittsburgh. He was a breath of fresh-air as he communicated the gracious message of Jesus Christ each evening. My roommate, noticing my struggle with depression, said, "Wes, you look so wiped out, why don't we go to the campus meetings tonight?" I went, but reluctantly, not expecting anything to lift my discouraged heart. It turned out to be a life changing night.

But the father had never stopped loving his wayward son.

Dr. Shoemaker spoke that night on the Prodigal Son from Luke, chapter 15. He described the self-loathing of the young son as he wasted his life to the point of feeling totally worthless – "I am no longer worthy to be called your son." The son didn't understand the unconditional love of his father. Nor did I understand my Heavenly Father's unconditional love. But when the son "came to his senses," he returned to the father, asking only to be a servant in the home since he felt that he wasn't worthy to be a son. But the father had *never stopped loving* his wayward son. He had been faithfully waiting, longing for his son to return home. And when the broken son appeared, there was no rejection by the father, no condemnation, not even a lecture from the father regarding the son's failures. Rather, the father embraced his son in love and forgiveness and totally without merit on his son's part, he welcomed him home with all the rights of a son restored to him. What grace the father showed to his lost son! Jesus said, this is the way God, our heavenly father, welcomes home his lost children.

Throughout my youth, I had often heard of God's love for the lost. But I was convinced that God's unmerited love was not meant for a reject like me. I had built a counterfeit religion that was based on *my own legalistic efforts* to earn God's love. It was a religion of my own good works, my own doing. I did believe in God. I had a head knowledge about God and I was even zealous for our family's church tradition. But *I had never,* by a free act of my own will, put my faith in Jesus Christ *alone* to save me. It had always been Jesus *plus* my good works, Jesus *plus* my baptism and confirmation, Jesus *plus* my church attendance and faithful Bible reading in order to be saved. But all my "pluses," all my religious performance was never good enough to give me the peace that I could ever earn God's love. I thought it was all about me. I had put my faith in myself and not in the saving grace of Jesus the Messiah. I didn't understand that salvation was by *faith alone*, in Jesus Christ *alone*, and all through God's grace *alone*. The Apostle Paul made that clear in Ephesians 2:8-9:

> *"For it is by grace that you have been saved, through faith – and this is not from yourselves, it is the gift of God – not by works, so that no one can boast."*

That night, when I was at the absolute end of my own resources, my own doing, I bowed in that chapel, a broken young man and I prayed the prayer of a prodigal son: "Father, I have sinned. I feel so empty, so unworthy to be called your son. For so long I have doubted and rejected your unconditional love for me in Jesus, who died for me. I confess that I am spiritually bankrupt in my own efforts. But, tonight I heard that you love me as I am and you unconditionally welcome me home. I'm coming home tonight. I humbly receive the embrace of your forgiveness and your saving love in Jesus. Thank you, Father. Amen."

TWICE ADOPTED, TWICE LOVED

That night I realized that I had been adopted a second time. I was first adopted by the Swanson family who so lovingly welcomed me into their home when I was left on their door-step. And now, by faith alone in Christ alone, I was *amazingly adopted* by my Heavenly Father, who loved this prodigal son unconditionally and welcomed me with the full rights of a son into the Father's faith family. I was twice adopted and twice loved. I was doubly blessed.

My heavenly papa, my Abba will never abandon me.

I was overwhelmed with joy that night when I realized that God, my loving Heavenly Father, would never abandon or reject me. I remembered a Bible promise where God says, "Never will I leave you; never will I forsake you. So, we can say with confidence, "the Lord is my helper; I will not be afraid" (Hebrews 13:5-6). Amazing! My heavenly papa, my Abba will *never abandon me.*

Later that night I knelt before God in my room and I wept as I realized that I had been *fully forgiven through faith alone*, in Jesus alone, who died in my place on the cross. God's love through the sacrifice of Jesus, the lamb of God, had paid it all. I died that night to Wes Swanson's legalistic religious effort to try and please God and I invited the risen Christ to live in me. The Christian life is no longer about me, but rather it's about the risen Christ living in and through me. That's what Paul the Apostle said in Galatians 2:20, "I have been crucified with Christ and I no longer live, but Christ lives in me. The life I live in the body, I live by faith in the Son of God, who loved me and gave himself for me." I wept with joy as I realized that I was free, *totally free,* from the need to *perform* in order to earn God's love and acceptance. The risen Christ lives in me. I was no longer a slave to fear, because my Abba loves me and I am his child. I felt like my heart was floating with a new freedom, a new awareness of forgiveness and a new certainty that I would never be forsaken or abandoned by my Heavenly Father. This night was indeed a life changer. I'm not saying that I was instantly healed of all my fears of rejection. I had spent a lifetime, up to that point, tortured by feelings of unworthiness, inferiority and fears of abandonment. It takes time and grace to rewrite the tapes that had so long been playing those lies in my mind. But it was a beginning, a wonderful beginning of a new life, a new peace with God, a new freedom to accept God's unconditional love for me. It was the beginning of freedom from fear as "perfect love drives out fear" (I John 4:18). It was also the beginning of a new relationship with God the Holy Spirit, changing me from within.

GRADUATION CELEBRATION

It was Monday morning June 13, 1960 and the new gymnasium on campus was packed with a sea of faces watching me as I walked up to the stage to receive my college diploma. I remember that my hands were sweaty and trembling as Dr. Karl Olsson, President of North Park College, handed me my diploma and shook my wet hand. I could hardly believe that after all the hard work, all the health set-backs, all the financial struggles and all the fears that I had wrestled with, I had now achieved my goal of a college education.

As I turned on stage to face the school photographer, I caught sight of my parents who had traveled from their new parish in Iowa to attend my graduation. They were standing and applauding for me – Dad with a big proud grin on his face and Mom with tears streaming down her cheeks. I was the first member of the Swanson family to graduate from college and it was my parents love, prayers and sacrifice that made it possible. The encouraging letter from Dr. T. W. Anderson, sent to me four years before I graduated and challenging me to be part of that historic class, had paid off.

The theme of our graduation was inscribed in the school motto: "In Thy Light, we shall see Light." That had certainly been true in my life. The light of God's truth had set me free from fear to live a full and abundant life in God's love. And it set me on a whole new course for my future career and ministry. Jesus had made that very promise when he said, "If you hold to my teaching, then you will know the truth, and the truth will set you free" (John 8:31-32). Our graduation ceremony concluded with the entire assembly singing a great hymn of faith by Hugh Kerr. It summed up my years at North Park and the awesome sense of God's leading through it all. I could hardly sing the hymn for the tears in my eyes and the lump in my throat:

"God of our life, through all the circling years,
we trust in Thee;
In all the past, through all our hopes and fears,
Thy hand we see."

CHAPTER SIX

CALLED TO MINISTRY

When I was about twelve years old, a little old Swedish lady in my dad's church in Wisconsin said to me, "Oh Vesley, wouldn't it be vonderful if you'd become a preacher like your papa." I was surprised by her suggestion and I was almost rude when I responded by saying, "Yuck no, I'm no preacher, I thought you had to be called by God to be a preacher, not just following in your dad's footsteps." She must have thought me to be impertinent as she walked away looking puzzled. But she actually planted a seed in my heart that came to flower some ten years later when God did call me to be a preacher.

MY CALL

Following my prodigal prayer in the fall of 1959, I knew that God was calling me to Christian ministry as a preacher of the gospel. My call was certainly not by my hearing the audible voice of God, like God's audible calling of the Biblical Samuel in the night. Nor was it a sudden emotional response to a stirring sermon that motivated me to yield my life to the Lord's service. Rather, it was a growing internal conviction and a deep desire to share the liberating Gospel of Jesus Christ who had set me free. It was like a fire in my soul that I could not shake off or keep to myself. God's call on my life was a burning passion in my heart to share with others how Christ had liberated me from a life of fear and given me the assurance of God's love and peace. My daily study and reading of God's Word was also stoking the fires of this passion.

It was like a fire in my soul that I could not shake off.

But it was not just an inner spiritual conviction that convinced me of God's call on my life. It was also the confirmation I received from other

Christian's and church leaders who told me that they affirmed God's call on my life and they saw God's gifts for ministry in my life. Amazingly, I discovered that I loved to preach. Though I am by nature a more quiet and introverted person, my great joy and privilege has nevertheless been to stand before the great congregation of God's people and proclaim the life-giving Word of God. And whenever someone would say to me, "I heard God speak to my heart today through your preaching," I was humbled, but also confirmed in the call of God on my life.

In retrospect, I see the awesome hand of God working through the struggles of my life to mold me for ministry. I believe I am who I am today because of my abandonment on the church step and my adoption. God was involved in the whole process, bringing something good out of my brokenness and strife. And if I had not been left on the church door-step and adopted, I would be a very different person today. While I might very well be serving God, it would not be with the same joy and passion that I have today in preaching the Gospel of the grace of Jesus Christ. Paul the Apostle says it best, "In all things God works for the good of those who love Him, who have been called according to His purpose" (Romans 8:28). I say Amen to that.

SEMINARY

In the winter of 1959, I received the letter of acceptance into North Park Theological Seminary and I prepared immediately to enter the seminary in the fall of 1960.

I was blessed to begin my seminary studies under the administrative leadership of Dean Eric Hawkinson who retired the next year after 27 years of teaching and administrating the seminary. I benefited greatly from his wise teaching of the first-year homiletics class, as well as his godly example and grace in dealing with students, faculty and denominational issues.

The next year, Donald C. Frisk became Dean of the seminary and led the school to boldly implement the Master of Divinity (M-Div.) degree program. In addition, I grew by leaps-and-bounds under the teaching of Dr. Frank Neuberg, who made the Old Testament come alive. He spoke and read 23 ancient languages and it was rather intimidating when he said, at our first class, that he never gives an "A" to any student and the only person in history who should have gotten an "A" was Plato in Platonic studies. I was happy with a "B" in his class. I was enriched by my New Testament studies under Henry Gustafson and loved the

Preaching and Practicum classes taught by Wesley Nelson and Dr. Earl Dahlstrom. I was also really stretched in Church History classes with Dr. Karl Olsson and Dr. F. Burton Nelson and challenged by New Testament Greek classes. But my favorite classes were in homiletics or the "Art of Preaching."

It was in high school debate competition I had discovered that I really enjoyed public speaking. It was exciting for me to be able to lay out my debate position and while commanding the attention of a room full of people I could influence and even sway their opinion. I also discovered that I had a good voice. From somewhere in my gene pool I inherited a strong and commanding voice that I used effectively in my seminary preaching classes. Class evaluations of my preaching often included compliments on the strength and versatility of my voice. That is, all except for one young seminarian who always tried to ridicule my preaching and poke fun at my voice. He would mock my voice in class, saying I was purposely contorting my voice to sound like Billy Graham. I would respond to his criticism by saying that I had a fire in my heart to preach the gospel of Christ and I used the voice God gave me to proclaim it with passion. I suspected, at the time, that he was tearing me down to build himself up, as he was a very insecure young man and left the seminary after his second year of study.

I also discovered in seminary, that while I loved to preach the gospel of Christ, the challenge of standing before a large audience left me an emotional wreck. There were times that I would be so nervous before preaching that I would go into the bathroom and vomit. I felt defeated by my overwrought nerves until an old pastor told me, "Don't worry about being nervous before preaching. Instead, you should worry about the day you feel so self-confident that you feel no nervousness before preaching God's word." I've always been thankful for that wise word. Preaching is not about me, it's about declaring God's Word.

I was very grateful for the outstanding seminary training I received at North Park Seminary. Those years gave me tools for life-long learning from God's Word. And it was here that I determined, above all else, to be a preacher of the authoritative and reliable Word of God. The Bible is a product of God Himself. The Bible describes itself as, "God breathed," (2 Timothy 3:16). Everything in it is written by men who, "Spoke from God as they were carried along by the Holy Spirit," (I Peter 1:21). The Bible is a reliable book and it is to God's Word that I have turned, for seven decades, to learn dependable truths about God, about the person and work of Jesus the Messiah, about the path to salvation and our life after death. Historically, as Covenanters, we were called "a People of the Book." And in our Catechism we confess, "That the Holy Scriptures, both the Old and New Testament, are the Word of God and the only perfect rule for faith, doctrine and conduct." A "perfect rule" means that the Bible is an authoritative rule, an unerring and absolute truth in all the that it affirms concerning matters of faith, doctrine and conduct. I am a man of God's authoritative Word. And it was that passionate declaration of God's absolute truth that, over the next 40 years, I would see lives transformed, my congregations grow and believers built-up in faith. But I was also greatly influenced by the powerful Biblical preaching that I, as a young seminary student, heard each Sunday from Pastor Douglas Cederleaf at North Park Covenant Church in Chicago. His preaching kept stoking the fires of my passion for preaching the Word of God and my ongoing conviction in God's call to Pastoral Ministry.

SUMMER ASSIGNMENT – DASSEL, MINNESOTA

In the spring of 1961, Dean Eric Hawkinson asked me to consider serving a summer ministry assignment in Dassel, Minnesota where Pastor Clarence D. Anderson was suffering with some ministry exhaustion and needed a summer assistant to help in the pastoral work of the church.

The Dassel Mission Covenant Church was located about 65 miles west of Minneapolis, Minnesota and was a healthy small town/country church of about 300 members. It was a kind and loving church and a good match for me to get first-hand experience in preaching, visitation, teaching Confirmation classes and leading youth ministries. They were patient with me as a first-year seminary student.

Not only did I confirm my call to ministry that summer but I also met Clarice Olson, the youngest daughter of Oscar and Madge Olson, who were active members of the church. Clarice and her sister Marilyn came home each summer from teaching elementary education in Minneapolis. Their mother Madge must have seen that this young pastor was potential son-in-law material as she started inviting me to weekly Sunday meals at the Olson home where Clarice so beautifully helped to serve those bountiful meals to this hungry young pastor. Clarice certainly got my attention during that first summer in Dassel. But it was in 1964, when I was invited back by the church for a second summer, that the love-fires really started burning in my heart. Fortunately, the invitations to the Olson home continued.

DULUTH INTERNSHIP 1962 - 1963

In a February 1962 meeting with the Regional Conference Superintendents of the Covenant Church, I was asked to consider a year of Seminary Internship at First Covenant Church in Duluth, Minnesota under the mentoring of their pastor, Rev. Earl Van Der Veer. Internship is meant to put some "flesh on the bones" of classroom theories by having each seminarian serve a year in a local church and also give a student time to further clarify their call to ministry. Since I had long admired the leadership and ministry of Pastor Van Der Veer and I had personally known his wife Dorothy from my childhood, I jumped at the opportunity to serve my internship in Duluth, which I did from the spring of 1962 to the fall of 1963.

Duluth is a seaport city of about 100,000 people and is located along the steep hillsides surrounding Lake Superior, which is the largest fresh water lake in the world. Because of its location next to this big body of water, Duluth is known as, "the air-conditioned city," which makes it cool all summer and very cold and snowy all winter. I shouldn't have been surprised by the cold weather as I had grown up on the nearby Wisconsin side of Lake Superior, just 30 miles from Duluth. But it still took some adjustment on my part to acclimate myself to over 50 days a year of -20 degree Fahrenheit, weather.

I had an awesome internship experience at First Covenant Church, grew to love the congregation and especially enjoyed serving the church youth. I had many memorable experiences in my time of intern ministry but I primarily remember two experiences, one was traumatic and the other somewhat humorous.

While serving my internship program I had my first car accident in my beloved 56 Chevrolet Bel Air two-door sedan. I had taken a group of Hi-League youth to summer camp at Covenant Park Bible Camp in Mahtowa, Minnesota. While serving as a counselor there, I was asked by the camp director to use my car to take a group of campers on a tour of a nearby paper mill. While traveling on dirt roads, one of the young girls jokingly yelled that we had missed the turnoff for the mill. I instinctively hit my brakes and another car from the camp, that was following too closely behind us, crashed into the back of my car, causing $548 worth of damage to my car. Fortunately, no one was injured, but I learned the hard lesson of always avoiding any sudden distraction while driving youth in my car. And I learned about the high cost of car repair on a youth pastor's salary.

I had a more humorous, if not personally embarrassing experience shortly after arriving at my internship church in Duluth. The pastor of the nearby Salem Covenant Church had called to ask if I would preach in his church one Sunday while he was on vacation. Since I was unfamiliar with the location of his church I asked for directions and he said, "You can't miss finding the church. It's a large, brown, stucco church on 59th Avenue in West Duluth."

On the Sunday I was to preach, I had to first teach my Hi-League Sunday School class at my church and I was thus pressed for time to drive across the city and find Salem Covenant Church. I felt relieved when I pulled up alongside of the brown, stucco church with still a few minutes to spare before the 11:00 a.m. service. I saw through an open door at the back of the church that robed choir members were filing in to the sanctuary. Naturally, I thought that was where I would meet the worship leader and so I fell into line with the choir. Suddenly a man, not in a robe, stopped me and asked what I was doing by following the choir! I explained that I had been asked to preach there on that Sunday and he said, "That's strange, because I'm the pastor here and I intend to be preaching today." When I protested that I had also been asked to preach he said, "Who asked you to preach here?" I said, "It was Pastor Ken from Salem Covenant." He laughed and said, "This is Bethel Baptist Church. Salem Covenant is across the street just kitty-corner from us." I had the wrong church. I quickly looked down the street and there it was, a similar brown, stucco church with a large sign that said, "Salem Covenant Church." My face was beet-red as I apologized to the pastor and ran across the street to meet the anxious church chairman who was feverishly looking for the lost preacher of the morning.

VIGIL FOR THE 1964 CIVIL RIGHTS ACT

I returned to Chicago from my seminary internship in the fall of 1963. It was a time of great racial unrest and national tragedy following the assassination of President John F. Kennedy. It was also a time in my personal life that my eyes were really beginning to be opened to the disastrous impact of racial discrimination and injustice in our nation.

I had grown up in "lily-white" communities in the Midwest United States and had never, ever talked to a person of color until I was in college. It was like we lived in a white bubble that excluded people of color and we were content to ignore the racial segregation and strife that was tearing at the heart of our nation.

In my home, while I never heard my dad preach from the pulpit on the moral implications of American racial injustice, I also never heard him speak despairingly of other races. Both Dad and Mom taught us to be respectful of all races and to their credit, they were very supportive of the integration of all races into the church, as seen by their welcome of African American families into the membership of the Helena, Montana congregation in the 1940's.

But it was when I left for college and moved to Chicago in 1956, that I experienced living in a racially diverse city that was also rigidly segregated at that time. In my class studies and by interacting with black churches in Chicago, I became personally aware of the great moral tragedy of racial discrimination that was eating at the very heart of our nation.

It was also in Chicago that I was privileged to hear Dr. Martin Luther King Jr. speak at the Chicago Sunday Evening Club in January, 1963. Sitting close to the front of Orchestra Hall, a group of us from seminary heard Dr. King Jr. speak on the theme, "Paul's letter to American Christians." I was deeply convicted over the silence of American Evangelicals in the face of such racial injustice. My conscience was further disturbed in 1963, following a series of protests from the African American community in the south, most notably being the Birmingham Campaign in Alabama (sometimes called the "Children's Campaign") in which children and students endured attacks by police dogs and high pressure water hoses during their peaceful sit-ins and protests against segregation. Then in September of 1963, our nation was shaken to the core as four young black girls were killed when a bomb ripped apart the 16th Street Baptist Church in Birmingham.

Equality and racial justice.

In the light of these national events, I began asking myself how I might impact my pastoral ministry and churches for racial justice and equality for people of color. So, in the Spring of 1964, I was thrilled when I was privileged to travel with five other North Park Seminarians to Washington D.C. where we participated in the Theological Students 24 Hour Vigil for the Civil Rights Bill. The vigil was to continue around the clock until the Civil Rights Bill was passed by Congress. Protestant, Catholic and Jewish Seminarians from throughout the nation volunteered to take their turn at the vigil. The six of us from North Park Theological Seminary, were assigned to take the week of May 4-8, to stand before the Lincoln Memorial in silence and prayerful support of the Civil Rights Bill.

The Civil Rights Act of 1964 outlawed discrimination based on race, color, religion, sex, or national origin. It gave all Americans the right to be served in facilities which are open to the public, including hotels, theaters, retail stores and lunch counters. It also gave protection for the right to vote and ended racial segregation in schools and the workplace.

You could feel the tension in Washington as the debates were held in congress over the Civil Rights Bill. It was almost palpable when we visited our congressmen to urge their support for the bill. There was a desperateness on the part of some state delegations to filibuster the Civil Rights Bill to death thus preventing it from going to a vote in Congress. Each day that we seminarians stood in prayer at the vigil site, the American Nazi Party, with their commander George Lincoln Rockwell, would stand with a group of Nazi protesters not more than 50 feet from us, with signs that read: "Nazi Party Vigil on behalf of the white Christian majority which oppose minority tyranny." The Nazi group glared angrily at us and I believe they would have attacked us were it not for the police officers standing nearby at the Lincoln Memorial.

Standing at the Civil Rights Vigil in Washington, D.C. with my fellow seminarians from North Park.

I made several visits to Capitol Hill that week to urge congressmen in both the House of Representatives and the Senate to vote in favor of the Civil Rights Bill. Since I was a resident of the northern state of Wisconsin, I met no opposition to my request for a favorable vote. In fact, I got an invitation to have lunch in the House of Representatives dining room from my Representative, Vernon Thomson, who later became Governor of the state of Wisconsin. He even had a picture taken of the two of us standing on the steps of the Capitol.

The impact of that week in Washington D. C. did more to infuse my years of ministry with compassion, mercy and justice than any classroom lecture or book assignment could accomplish. I found in myself a new longing for compassion and justice in our nation that was now a passion in my ministry. I realize now that this passion was really the by-product of God's mercy and grace which had been poured out to me in Christ.

My ministry approach to "proclaiming justice in the land" was not to substitute the saving Gospel of Jesus Christ with a social gospel, or to fling angry stones of sermonic condemnation at the congregation for their unbiblical prejudices. But rather, my approach was to boldly proclaim the love and grace and compassion of Jesus Christ for *all the lost,* including me. And then to open the eyes of our church family to the great spiritual and social needs of our community and world inviting them, in the spirit of repentance and humility, to bring Jesus's love to our spiritually broken nation. I know that the task of government is to "bear the sword…as an agent of wrath to bring punishment on the wrongdoer." (Romans 13:4) But for the believing church,

Standing on the Capitol steps in 1964 with my representative Vernon Thompson from Wisconsin.

who has been "washed…sanctified…justified in the name of the Lord Jesus" (1Corinthians 6: 11), our task is not to shout "Stop in the name of the law!" but to whisper, "There's hope and grace for you at the foot of the cross." Here is where we see lives and homes and churches changed from the inside-out.

I'm sure that others have found many good ways of working through the local church to bring about compassion, mercy and justice. But I praise God for the transformation of lives and entire congregations that a bold proclamation of the grace of God in Jesus Christ brings to a church. In my 42 years of ministry, I have constantly rejoiced to see hearts opening to a fresh vision of compassion and service based upon *Jesus grace alone.* It was often then that the lay membership, who had been transformed by grace, would step up to the plate and blaze the trail to organize "gospel centered" social action. Throughout my ministry, as we developed our local church ministries of compassion, we saw hundreds of members dedicate themselves to bringing compassionate change to our communities through a wonderful variety of outreach programs. They staffed our church foodbank ministry, opened our church facilities each month to provide shelter and meals for homeless families, organized Christian pre-schools for the community in our Christian education wing, offered spiritual 12-Step Programs to addicts, sponsored cancer support groups and grief support groups as well as E.S.L. classes for recent immigrants. We organized Spanish language ministries in our churches and prison ministries to those incarcerated as well as those being released from prison. We emphasized prayer for healing in our church and throughout our wounded communities. We organized after-school tutoring programs for latch-key kids and helped our community establish a Neighborhood Watch Program in our drug and gang-infested community.

In the wider community, our churches reached out with health clinics and health fairs to neighbors without health insurance. We clothed and fed hundreds of homeless and disadvantaged people with Thanksgiving meals and clothing drives. We constructed and remodeled homes for inner-city families. We reached out to unwed teen-moms with pregnancy support and a permanent home and training center for these young moms. We sponsored a county wide ministry to foster home children and teens called Royal Family Kid's Camp. We organized medical, educational and construction projects in Uganda (dental work with AIDs children), Romania (AIDs children), Honduras, Ecuador, Mexico and Alaska (Alaska Christian College). Our members caught the vision and organized our church sponsorship of scores of refugees from Vietnam, Ethiopia, the Hmong of Laos and Thailand, as well as merciful ministries to undocumented Mexicans and Hispanic refugees. We reached out to African American and Hispanic pastors with supportive ministries to their churches and in their communities. At the same time, we continued to be dedicated and sacrificial in our support for Covenant World Mission and Covenant World Relief. All this was the direct result of churches *transformed by the grace* of the Lord Jesus Christ and then, touching their world with that same grace.

SEMINARY GRADUATION AND ENGAGEMENT

In the spring of 1965, the rapid events that were occurring in my life left me out of breath. First of all, in addition to working many hours each week as a church custodian and a volunteer youth worker, I was feverously trying to complete all my seminary papers and assignments, as well as preparing for final exams.

But on the first of April, 1965 I had also driven to Minnesota to preach as a candidate for the position of pastor of the Mission Covenant Church of Little Falls. In making my plans for the trip to Minnesota, I had called and asked Clarice Olson if she would travel with me to Little

Falls for this weekend of candidacy. We had been writing to each other and seeing each other for over a year now and we were in love. I told her that I'd like her to go with me to see where I had lived as a child. But I really wanted her with me so the congregation could meet my future wife. Some of the older ladies in the church prematurely introduced her as "Mrs. Swanson." It was a little early, as we weren't even engaged yet, but I liked the sound of it. By April 25, I had accepted the church's Letter of Call to become their pastor, following my graduation. It all left me a little winded and out of breath.

I really wanted her with me so the congregation could meet my future wife.

When seminary graduation came on June 12 – 15, 1965, Clarice came down by train to be with me for the exciting events of that week. She stayed with her friend, Nony Bengtson and joined me on Saturday night, June 12 as my date at the Seminary Senior Banquet, held at the Pantry Restaurant in Park Ridge.

My folks were in the middle of moving that week to a new parish in Lowry, Minnesota and so were unable to attend my seminary graduation. It was therefore doubly special to have Clarice with me as my family representative at the Sunday morning Baccalaureate Service, on June 13 and that evening at the Seminary Consecration Service. That evening, following the service, I asked Clarice to marry me and offered her a diamond ring. She said "yes," and I was thrilled and even more breathless.

The next morning, June 14, the graduation ceremony was held in the school gymnasium and, as a newly engaged man, I was especially proud to accept my Masters of Divinity Degree, or "M-Div. Degree" from Dean Donald Frisk. I can still feel the afterglow of that day.

Clarice and I made the announcement of our engagement and set the date of August 14, 1965 for our wedding at the Dassel Covenant Church, just two months after our engagement. All these momentous events left me panting for breath but also incredibly blessed.

CHAPTER 7

LOVE AND MARRIAGE

Whenever I think of my life as symbolized by a cup of blessing, I never think of it as a half empty cup, or even a half full cup, but rather a cup full and running over with blessings. Yes, there have been many losses, enormous sorrows and griefs, but my life experiences have taught me that, "In everything God is working for the good of those who love Him" (Romans 8:28). I clearly saw this in the blessings of love and marriage.

FALLING IN LOVE WITH CLARICE

I had dated very little in college. My life was consumed with work and studies, not with finding a partner in life. I had a simple faith that God was saving a special woman to be my mate and I also knew that I was basically a romantic at heart and I could prematurely fall in love with a woman who showed me special attention. So, I kept my eyes on the goal before me. I agreed with the counsel of Proverbs 4: 23 & 25, "Above all else, guard you heart for it is the wellspring of life. Let your eyes look straight ahead, fix your gaze directly before you." Now, as I began my senior year of Seminary, it was like my heart was free from that single-minded gaze and I began seriously praying for God's specific leading in my relationship with Clarice Olson who I first met in June 1961, when I served as a summer Youth Pastor assignment in her home church of Dassel.

Clarice had graduated from St. Cloud State University with a B. S. Degree in Elementary Education and had received certification for teaching special education from the University of Minnesota. She taught special education for eight years in the Hopkins and Columbia

Heights school districts in the suburbs of Minneapolis and each summer she, together with her sister Marilyn, returned to Dassel to live at home with their parents. I hadn't been serving at the church in Dassel for more than a week, when suddenly there she was, sitting right in front of me in the soprano section of the church choir. I stood in the bass section next to Wayne Paulson who immediately started kidding me about the cute teacher who was going to be home in Dassel all summer.

Shortly after learning to know Clarice in the church choir I started getting invitations from her mother to come to the Olson home for Sunday dinner. I didn't think much about it at first, but then came a second, third and fourth invitation to their home and Clarice was always the focus of my attention, as she helped her mother prepare the meal and set the table. I definitely began to take note and show interest in this beautiful woman. Once, when I overheard her brother whisper to her to, "Go on out there and sit next to Wes, let him know you're interested in him," I knew that the whole family was involved in the plan and thought she would make a perfect pastor's wife.

Toward the end of that summer I decided to ask Clarice to attend a national youth rally in Minneapolis with me. I thought that the trip into the city would give the two of us lots of time to get acquainted. But plans changed quickly when three high-school youth from the church called and asked if they could ride with us to the rally. Clarice ended up sitting in the back seat with two teen-age boys. It was the date that never happened.

We had little contact with each other for the next two years as I served my seminary internship in Duluth Minnesota from 1962-1963 and she returned to teaching in Minneapolis. Aside from writing her a few letters, there was no time to get to know each other until the spring of 1964, when the Dassel Church invited me to serve a second summer as their youth pastor. I was really looking forward to another term of service in Dassel and especially excited about having an entire summer to get acquainted with Clarice. But after arriving at the church, I learned that Clarice had decided to travel most of the summer on an extended trip to Scandinavia and Europe. My heart sank. I hardly knew her but I already missed her.

I was smitten and I knew I was in love with her.

At the very end of that long summer, Clarice returned from her trip and my heart did a flip-flop when I saw her again. Just before she returned to her teaching position in Minneapolis, she invited all the church youth over to her parent's home for a party. She was radiant that night as she served snacks to everyone, dressed in a new, flowing dress with her hair swept back to feature her lovely face. I was smitten and I knew I was in love with her.

Clarice was a year and six months older than I, which I found intriguing. She lived in a far more mature and grown-up world of teachers and professional young adults. And when we were together, in those last days of the summer of 1964, we talked and talked, adult type talk, about life goals and values, family and growth in faith, travel dreams and things that made life rich and blessed. When I returned to seminary that fall, I began seriously courting her through letters, phone calls and planning trips for her to come to Chicago for special weekends.

The trips that Clarice made to be with me were really exciting. She always came by train and stayed with Dassel friends living near the campus. I arranged my work schedule so that we could have uninterrupted time to be together and planned dates to really impress her with my knowledge of Chicago and my fondness for her. We enjoyed visiting the Chicago Art Institute, the Conservatory at Lincoln Park, a symphony concert at Orchestra Hall, a wonderful meal at the Kungsholm Scandinavian Restaurant, with its miniature opera theater and worshipping together at Fourth Presbyterian Church.

Once we went by elevated train and subway to have dinner together at the fabulous George Diamond's Steak House in the Chicago Loop. But we were not alone. We laughed all the way down as we tried to shake-off two of the guys from my resident counseling group at the dorm who were following us to see if we were holding hands and kissing. They couldn't believe that their resident counselor was in love.

I had been quietly pricing diamond rings that spring. There was an old Swedish Jeweler at Erickson Jewelers, on Clark Street in Andersonville, who always gave a good deal to seminary students. I made repeated trips to the store to study the rings and settings before finally settling on a round diamond in a solitaire setting that I could afford. My problem was that I didn't know Clarice's ring size and I had to take a guess at that size when I ordered the ring. The store called just before graduation to tell me that the ring was ready. I was so nervous and certain it wouldn't fit her finger.

On June 13, 1965, after the Sunday evening Seminary Consecration Service, Clarice and I went for a ride in my 56 Chevy. I wanted this to be the perfect night to ask her to marry me, so I headed the car toward the romantic Edgewater Beach on Lake Michigan. But I was so nervous in driving us to my romantic spot that I drove through a red stop light and got pulled over by a Chicago traffic cop. He asked what my work was and I told him that I was a seminary student. He said, "ok Father, I'll let you go this time, but be more careful when you're driving the Sister home from Mass." I said a very humble, "Thank you Officer," and then drove instead to the less romantic and closer spot at the North Park Athletic Field, where I asked Clarice to marry me. Amazingly she said "yes," in spite of my embarrassment over the traffic stop, and wonder of wonders, the ring fit her perfectly! Time seemed to fly that night as we spent hours talking about our future together and setting the date for our wedding on August 14, 1965. With a kiss, I took her back to her apartment where there were lots of cheers and hugs and congratulations from all the girls who lived there. And even though it was a late hour, we called her parents to share the happy news. The next morning the girls in the apartment served a fun breakfast to Clarice in bed and I went to call my parents and share the exciting news.

I had said very little to my folks about my relationship and growing love for Clarice. I still had some latent fears of rejection and felt that if things didn't work out between us, nobody was going to know it. So, when I called to tell my parents of my engagement to Clarice, they were surprised. My mother was even shocked. I felt badly that I hadn't kept them more in the loop, but they got over their surprise and learned to love Clarice like a daughter.

It was after 1:00 a.m. when I got back to my room on the night of my engagement. I was so high emotionally that I couldn't sleep, so I did something that was totally out of character for me. I had been given a big blue cigar that one of my seminary friends had handed out at the birth of his son and I went walking along the north branch of the Chicago river smoking that cigar. It made me a little ill, but at the time it seemed like an appropriate way to celebrate my engagement.

"I'M GETTING MARRIED IN THE MORNING"

Since I was serving a small church in Park Falls, Wisconsin all summer (some 250 miles from Dassel), it meant that all the details in arranging our wedding fell into Clarice's lap. In just two months of time she reserved the church, ordered and sent invitations, planned the reception, ordered flowers, arranged music and bought a wedding dress for herself and dresses for all the bridesmaids. We talked daily on the phone and I learned to say simply, "Yes dear, you're doing everything great."

As our wedding day approached, it seemed that every radio station was playing the hit song from the musical My Fair Lady. The memorable line was:

I'm getting married in the morning!
Ding dong! The bells are gonna chime.
But get me to the church on time!

I certainly wasn't like the drunken and roguish Alfred P. Doolittle who sang the hit song in the musical, but I still couldn't get it out of my mind and as I drove I sang it constantly, at the top of my lungs, all the way from Wisconsin to my wedding ceremony in Minnesota.

I wasn't late for our wedding and everything came together so beautifully, on that night of August 14 as nearly 400 guests gathered in the Dassel Covenant Church for our wedding. The Chancel of the church was aglow with tall cathedral candelabras surrounded by huge palm branches and big bouquets of white gladiolus flowers.

Clarice was stunning in her full-length wedding gown that had a beautiful lace covering and a veil that fell below her shoulders. She wore a single strand of pearls that I had given her and carried a white Bible covered with pink roses. I wore a traditional tuxedo with a boutonniere on my lapel.

It was a very hot August Saturday evening as our wedding party entered the packed church. Everyone was perspiring and I was amazed that no one in our wedding party fainted. Standing up beside Clarice was her sister Marilyn as her maid of honor, her sister-in-law Ruth and

Our wedding party on August 14, 1965.

her teacher-friend Jean Erickson. Clarice's niece, Sheryl Tengwall, stood as our junior bridesmaid and little Lori Olson was our flower girl. I had asked my college and seminary friend, Ralph Sturdy to be my best man together with another seminary friend, LeRoy Carlson and my brother, John Swanson to be groomsmen. Clarice's nephew, Keith Olson, was the junior groomsman and her brothers, a brother-in-law and cousin, were ushers.

We were married in the church that we both loved. Clarice had grown up and been confirmed in faith in the Dassel Covenant Church and I had been privileged to serve this church for two summers as their youth pastor. Here we made sacred vows before Almighty God, which my father read as the officiant of the ceremony, and we repeated: "I do promise and covenant; Before God and these witnesses; To be your loving and faithful husband/wife; In plenty and in want; In joy and in sorrow; In sickness and in health; For as long as we both shall live." We sealed our wedded love with golden wedding bands, (though her hands were sweaty and swollen and I couldn't get the ring all the way on her finger). Then with a tender kiss we began our married life together. We kept those promises faithfully for the next 19 years and 4 days, through all the circumstances of life and love, sickness and death – "for as long as we both shall live."

HAPPY DAYS

After the wedding reception, with all the hugs and congratulations of 400 guests, we drove 60 miles to our honeymoon motel in New Ulm, Minnesota. It was a happy and good wedding night.

We awoke surprisingly early the next morning and decided that on our first full day of married life we would begin by worshipping God at the First Methodist Church of New Ulm. We both agreed that this was a great way to begin our marriage, especially for a fledgling pastor and his wife.

The next five days of our honeymoon were spent at the Mount Rushmore Memorial in South Dakota, with lots of hiking, picnics in the forests and fun side trips to the Black Hills Passion Play in Spearfish and the Thunderhead Underground Falls. We were so in love and we must have radiated happiness as several people commented, "You two seem so happy, are you on your honeymoon?" We blushed and said a happy, "Yes!"

On Friday of our honeymoon week, we drove from South Dakota to our first home in Little Falls, Minnesota where I would begin my pastoral ministry that next Sunday. The church parsonage was located directly behind the church at 206 N.E. 4th Avenue and was built so close to the church that I could reach out the side window of the attached garage and touch the back of the church.

We were laughing when we entered our home for the first time, as I attempted to lift my bride and carry her across the threshold, only to discover the sunday school superintendent was inside the house laying kitchen flooring and laughing at us. I was shocked to see him and while I didn't drop my bride, I did lose my enthusiasm for this intimate moment of honeymoon love as embarrassment took over.

Though our congregation was very small, they had an abundance of love for their newly married pastor and wife. Following my installation as their pastor, on the next Sunday, they had a welcome reception and pantry shower for us with gifts of everything from a dozen eggs, five pounds of flour, measuring cups for baking and an electric frying pan. We were so privileged to serve that loving congregation which my folks had served twice in years past.

These were happy years, though not without challenges. Because my total pastoral income was $250 a month, or $3,000 per year, Clarice felt that she should teach school in order to supplement our income and pay off some of our wedding and first furniture debt. The job that the Little Falls School District offered her was to teach their fledgling special education program at the junior high level. Unfortunately, that job brought many tears to Clarice as the other teachers would dump unruly students, even violent students, into her classroom just to get rid of them, expecting her to teach 30-plus wild kids. She lasted just two years in that job.

Our first year of ministry was definitely exciting, but also exhausting. Just eight months after our arrival, the congregation voted to sell the old church building and begin construction on a new church and parsonage, on land they owned north of the city. So, in addition to preaching (three times each week), teaching confirmation classes, visiting the sick and acting as the church custodian and office secretary, I was also meeting weekly with architects and contractors, organizing the church's 75th anniversary celebration, while completing my ordination paper and requirements for ordination the next summer. To top it off, we became proud parents of our first son less than two years after our arrival. We dedicated the new church in November, 1967 and celebrated the birth of our second son who was born just 20 months after our first child. Did I say we were living in the "fast track" while serving our first Church?

After five happy and growing years in Little Falls, I submitted my resignation to the congregation and accepted a call to pastor a young, newly organized congregation in Northbrook, Illinois. It was difficult to leave

Little Falls, but with the strong encouragement of our denominational leaders and a growing sense of God's leading, we accepted their letter of call and our family moved to this growing Chicago suburb in July 1970.

In 1970, our family moved to North-brook, Illinois when Paul was three and Mark was 16 months.

The Northbrook Evangelical Covenant Church was an exciting part of a planned development by our denomination in which that church was to be the spiritual center of a large Covenant retirement village. Our ministry in Northbrook began immediately with a rapid pace of growth and expansion. Within 18 months of our arrival, we had raised $230,000 to launch us into a $750,000 building program, which gave us an expanded sanctuary seating 500 people and tripled our Sunday school facilities.

We were very happy in our Northbrook home and church ministry and now our family was complete with the birth of our third son. But we were stretched and exhausted, both physically and mentally. By the spring of 1975, both Clarice and I really needed a vacation break.

LIVING WITH A THIEF – CANCER

As we prepared to leave for several weeks of family vacation that spring, I began to be concerned for Clarice's health. She seemed at times to be so tired that she couldn't gather her thoughts and was often distracted from the task at hand. Sometimes she just sat on a chair with a blank look on her face. When I would ask, "Is anything wrong Hon?" she would respond in her chipper voice, "I'm fine, just catching my breath." She had good reason to be out of breath with three young sons, ages 2, 6 and 8. We were both tired. So, I would chalk it up to our active lifestyle and not voice my concerns to anyone.

But when we arrived in Minnesota for vacation that summer, her sisters noticed immediately that something was very wrong with Clarice's health. I shared my concerns and that I had found it necessary to take on more and more responsibility for preparing family meals, cleaning the house and caring for the boys, as she seemed to be constantly exhausted.

We agreed that this vacation was very important and our hope was that it would give her needed rest and recovery. And we did have a great vacation that summer. We spent much of our time at my folks Lake Erie cabin, just 12 miles from our family in Dassel. Clarice was more relaxed, laughing and enjoying the warmth and love of being with family and friends. I spent most of my time keeping the boys busy with fishing, swimming and boating so Clarice could rest.

We got back to our home in Northbrook, Illinois just in time to celebrate our oldest son, Paul's 8th birthday. The birthday invitations were sent to five of Paul's friends and included the information that we would be going to a nearby amusement park called Santa's Village. Clarice was excited to celebrate her son's birthday, but when his friends arrived to go to the amusement park she said, "I just can't go, I'm

Our family Christmas picture in 1973. Paul is six, Mark is four and Luke is six months.

so tired, I really need a nap." Now I knew that something was wrong and when we returned three hours later I was really alarmed to discover her still in bed, fast asleep.

The next day, I stayed home from work so Clarice could rest and I cleaned up from the party and cared for the boys. But I had a pre-marital counseling appointment with a young couple at church that evening. I felt good about keeping the appointment because Clarice was in bed resting and the boys were all playing with friends next door. Around 7:00 p.m. Clarice got up from bed and wandered around the house in a stupor-like condition. She picked up our two-year-old son, Luke, and continued wandering aimlessly around the house in this trance-like state. She was unable to speak. Mark, age 6, kept asking, "Mom, what's the matter?" And when she couldn't answer he asked, "Should I call 911?" After repeatedly asking her that question, she finally nodded a "Yes." But before he could call, Paul, now turned 8, came home from a bike ride with his friend Tommy Mackie. Suddenly, Clarice walked out of our house, holding a crying Luke and walked over to our neighbors, the Boyle's home directly across the street. The Boyle family had all gone out to eat, but had left the side door to their home unlocked. Clarice walked in their home without knocking and wandered silently around, still holding her crying two-year-old son. The older boys followed behind Clarice as she wandered through the neighbor's home. In her incapacitated state, she evidently sensed her desperate need for medical help and was probably looking for Peg Boyle who was a nurse. When Clarice couldn't find anyone in the Boyle home, she walked out of their house and headed across the street to our house where she fell, at our front door-step and suffered a grand mal seizure. The boys were our heroes in this crisis. Realizing that their mother needed medical help immediately, Mark stayed with his mom, while Paul and Tommy ran two blocks over to get Tommy's mother, Penna Mackie, who was also a nurse. Penna called 911.

The boys were our heroes!

I was just getting well into the counseling session at church, when I received an urgent phone call from Jim Aspegren, the administrator of Covenant Village, telling me to get home immediately as an ambulance, police and fire trucks were at our home. The young couple that I was counseling said that my face turned "chalk white" as I quickly excused myself and drove rapidly home. As I drove those eight blocks, my mind was dark with confusion and I was crying out to God, "Oh God help us. What's happened? Have the boy's been hurt? Is it Clarice? Help us Father!"

I couldn't park in front of our house as the street was filled with emergency and police vehicles, all with their lights blazing. I ran down the street, my heart pounding like a drum in my chest and I spotted my three sons standing in front of the house with neighbors huddled around them. The paramedics had, by this time, pried Luke from his mother's rigid arms and moved her inside our home to continue working with her. The police would not allow me to go into our home, so I gathered the boys in my arms and we circled together in prayer, "Oh God help us now. Jesus, be with Mommy. Help her we pray." As we prayed, the entire church was being called to pray for us. The darkness was being driven away.

It seemed like hours before they brought Clarice out of the house on a stretcher and placed her in the ambulance to take her to Highland Park Hospital. By this time, several members from our church had arrived, including the Larsons, who offered to stay with the boys so I could follow Clarice to the hospital. After arriving at the ER waiting room, I nervously waited for over an hour before a nurse said I could go in to see my wife. She cautioned, "Don't stay long, she's very exhausted."

The ER Room was dimly lit and as I pulled the curtains aside to her cubicle, I hardly recognized Clarice. Her face was ashen, her eyes were glassy and expressionless and she was clutching her tennis shoes tightly to herself, almost as if she was still holding on to Luke. She was very confused and had no memory of what had happened. I just held her and wept. She said nothing. After an hour together, I kissed her and left to get home to our boys.

Early the next morning, I returned to find Clarice somewhat improved and I immediately looked up the young resident doctor who had treated her the night before. He looked me straight in the eye and announced his professional diagnosis: "Your wife will be fine," he said, "She has nothing more than an overly emotional religious syndrome." He had seen on the hospital records that I was a minister and he figured that he hit the nail on the head with his speedy diagnosis of religious emotionalism. We were very suspicious of this diagnosis, so we quickly checked out of that hospital and had Clarice admitted instead to Swedish Covenant Hospital in Chicago.

After several days of testing and x-rays at Swedish Hospital, the head of neurosurgery met with us and in a somber, scarcely audible voice while avoiding all eye contact with us, he whispered, "Your wife has a very large brain tumor that will probably take her life within four months." I gasped. It was extremely hot in the windowless consultation room, but I felt a sudden chill surge through my body. Clarice said nothing. It was like she never heard what the doctor had said. I began trembling as I silently prayed, "Oh God, help us. The boys need their mother, give us hope!"

Chicago friends rallied around us and caused medical doors to be opened for further tests at Northwestern University Hospital in Evanston and at Rush Memorial Hospital in Chicago. Clarice was at four different hospitals in four months and was given *four different diagnoses* in those months. The doctors at Northwestern University Hospital said that it was likely old calcium deposits on the brain from a past head injury and could be successfully treated. Rush Memorial doctors said it was possibly encephalitis, inflammation of the brain. The young doctor at Highland Park Hospital said she was suffering from religious emotionalism. But it was the old brain surgeon at Swedish Hospital, with the bad bedside manners, who got it right. It proved to indeed be a malignant brain tumor. But he was wrong about the "four months to live" prognosis. Clarice had, by the grace of God, nine years to live and many of them were good years in which she had time to love her sons and help them to grow up into the godly men they are today. God is ultimately in control.

Clarice was 38 years old when she was diagnosed with a malignant brain tumor and then told she had four months to live. I was a total mess.

I felt like I had all the wind knocked out of me. I constantly walked on pins and needles waiting for the next seizure, the next crisis. But, by God's grace and the marvels of modern medicine, Clarice slowly regained strength, the seizures were fairly well controlled and we began to resume a somewhat normal life.

If you can call "normal life" the housing and feeding of 500 pastors and delegates from around the nation, which our young congregation in Northbrook was asked by our denomination to hold in our newly dedicated facilities. This huge event, of the Midwinter Pastor's Conference of the Evangelical Covenant Church, was held in our church on February 9-13, 1976, just six months after Clarice's diagnosis of cancer. And I had the responsibility of being the host pastor for that entire event.

Following the Midwinter Conference I was exhausted and close to burnout. I began to suffer from a stress-related form of angina with its painful spasms around my chest, shoulders and arms. While my doctor assured me that my heart was strong and I was not having a heart attack, I nevertheless knew I had to make some changes to relieve this high level of stress in my life. So, in the fall of 1976, I notified the church leadership that I was resigning and accepting the call to be the lead pastor of a well-established, one-hundred-year-old church, in Grand Rapids, Michigan.

By the time we moved to Michigan, Clarice had been encouraged by a year-and-one-half of fairly good health. She was on a heavy dose of daily seizure medication and had to take things much more slowly. But we had adjusted to her new energy-level and lived by the dictum, "Take it slower, one day at a time." She seemed to handle the move very well and the boys were flourishing in their new neighborhood and school. But with the fall of 1979, things changed drastically.

A family picture taken in 1976, a year after Clarice's grand mal seizure.

In September of that year, Clarice began falling again. She fell four times in our home and two times while walking on nearby sidewalks. Her falls came suddenly and without warning. Once she fell down the entire length of our second-floor stairway. And then she began to have seizures again, often multiple seizures in a day. Some seizures would sweep over her, like wave after wave, sometimes lasting for 24 hours at a time. It would take her a week to recover from the exhaustion of these multiple seizures. Medication could no longer control them. It was a very dark time. In January of 1980 I wrote in my journal:

"Has God forsaken us? Is He punishing me for some sin in my life, some unfaithfulness? Would my loving God ever plant cancer in my beloved wife to consume her brain? Is disease and death God's ally? NO! NO! My God is on the side of life and love and forgiveness and peace and healing and salvation. He is never in alliance with disease and death. They are the enemies of God which he has declared He will defeat and destroy (Revelation 21:4). The Apostle Paul says in Romans 8:31, 'Since God is for us, who can be against us.' Oh yes, the God I serve is FOR US! He's is on our side! I remember weeping the first time I heard the Covenant Pastors chorus sing the spiritual:

'If it had not been, that the Lord was on my side,
Tell me where would I be? Where would I be?"

As I sit through the long hours, holding Clarice's head in the midst of those wrenching seizures, I'm praying, "Lord, stay close to our side in this fiery furnace. Oh, stay close."

Our surgeon, Dr. Hedeman, scheduled brain surgery for February 4, 1980. He was a very frank man. He laid it on the line with us. "I know," he said, "That you have elected to go ahead with surgery, but I want you to understand that the results could be disastrous for Clarice. It could severely affect her memory, her speech, her ability to function." And then looking directly at Clarice he said, "It could make you a vegetable." Clarice said nothing. It was like she never even heard the doctor. And when I asked her later about the doctor's conversation, she remembered nothing of it. I held her close to me and wiped tears away, tears that were flowing from my eyes. I was shaken to the core.

My life verse is from Proverbs 3:5-6, "Trust in the Lord with all your heart; Lean not on your own understanding. In all your ways acknowledge Him, and He will direct your paths." I understand that God has never promised us a continually rosy path in life. But He did promise to direct and guide us through all the events and storms of life (Psalm 23). The journey of faith is not just wearing rose-colored glasses and thinking positively in the calamities of life, but it's trusting and obeying God, even when all is dark. So, I earnestly prayed, "Dear Lord, this is a dark time in our journey. But our focus is on you. Though you take Clarice away, I will still trust in you." And God gave to both of us peace in that horrible storm.

It's trusting and obeying God, even when all is dark.

On February 4, our surgeon removed a large tumor that was located in the right frontal lobe of Clarice's brain. It was the size of a tennis ball and it was malignant. But amazingly, just 18 hours after surgery, Clarice was up and walking around with no apparent speech or memory loss. All body and mental functions seemed normal and Clarice's beautiful smile and personality were back. The telephone lines were hot as we called family and friends throughout the nation to tell them the good news. The boys hugged their mother tightly and we prayed together: "Thank you Father, thank you."

After seven days of recovery in the hospital, the doctors began six and one half weeks of outpatient, daily radiation. The radiation department at Butterworth Hospital was located in the dark and depressing basement of the hospital. But Clarice was "Mrs. Sunshine" in the midst of the gloom of so many seriously ill patients. She amazed me over the next months, as she circulated throughout the waiting room, greeting every patient and caregiver by name, encouraging them with hugs and prayers and often giving them some of her homemade cookies. In the midst of her own crisis, she concentrated on loving and caring for others.

And how joyously she plunged in anew to loving and caring for her three sons and myself as her husband. I was so deeply touched when she wrote to me on that Valentine's Day, *"I couldn't find a card that said how thankful I am for a husband like you Wes. I'm thankful for your love, that you're my husband and for our three boys. I'm thankful for the trust and confidence I know in our love. I'm thankful for your acceptance of me, your patience and understanding and encouragement when I've been so weak and ill. And I'm thankful that we share our faith and that God is the center of our lives."* She wrote this two weeks after brain surgery.

Within two months, Clarice returned to attending church and so enjoyed being back with the dear faith family that had surrounded her in prayer. By this time, she had lost all of her hair in radiation and she wore a wig. But the wig was no big deal to her until the Sunday that June Bjorklund hugged her too enthusiastically and knocked the wig off in church. Clarice felt more concern for June, who was mortified, so she quickly plopped it back on her head as if nothing had happened. It was a little off center, but I was *so proud* of the inner beauty of Clarice which filled our lives with sunshine.

After weeks of radiation treatment, Clarice regained strength and it seemed that our family returned to normal again. Besides being a wife and mother, she managed to organize our church ladies Bible study, she served on the Women's Ministry Board, she was the room-mother for Luke's school classroom, she taught a fifth-grade Sunday School class, she took a class in the Swedish language and she regularly entertained friends and church groups in our home. For the next three years following surgery, Clarice was enjoying life and it breathed fresh air into our family life.

Once again, summer travel became an option for our family. In 1981, we made a family trip to Washington D.C., visiting the Capitol, the White House, the Smithsonian Museums, Mount Vernon and eating wonderful meals at Williamsburg. The boys were so excited to see their mother active again.

In the summer of 1982, we spent six weeks of my sabbatical, with the five of us squeezed into our family car, making a 6,000-mile round trip through Mexico. I was, at that time, chairman of the Covenant Board of World Mission and so we were led in our travels by veteran Covenant missionary Jerry Reed, who guided our study of the Mexico mission. This sabbatical study, included preaching and teaching in all three regions of Mexico. And Clarice was well enough to enjoy teaching several groups of women in the churches around Mitla and Tlacolula, in the south of Mexico. We also had many exciting adventures exploring Mexico City, Oaxaca and Acapulco. We concluded our sabbatical travels with *The boys were so excited to see their mother active again.* two weeks of vacation in Colorado where Clarice joined our boys on a five-mile hike in the Wild Basin Forest. God was so good to give us this vacation of a life-time, with happy memories to last just as long.

But by the winter of 1982, the old symptoms of seizures and falling began to appear once again. Our surgeon, Dr. Hedeman, told us that the tumor was growing rapidly. He called it a glioblastoma, a type of tumor that grows very fast and would certainly take her life in the next months. The three wonderful years that we had with our darling Clarice, since her last surgery in 1980, were now coming to a heart-breaking close.

For eight years, the specter of cancer had hovered, menacingly, over our home and the life of my wife and our boy's mother. The long winter of 1982 – 1983 saw her undergo many difficult chemotherapy treatments.

But we saw no improvement and observed only negative changes in her health. And the seizures continued. I wrote in my journal on January 14, 1983:

> *"I must deal with my sense of doom and despondency. Simply because a doctor said the tumor will kill Clarice in a few months doesn't mean that God concurs. After all, the doctors told us last year that, 'She should have been history long ago.' All the doctors are mystified that she has lived with such advanced cancer for these three years.*
>
> *How good our Lord has been to give us these three miracle years. Clarice has been so strong, so happy, so positive and felt so good until this past fall. We've seen daily reminders that God is in control.*
>
> *So, I will continue to rest in God. We have this day to love each other and claim the grace that's sufficient for this hour. I was so encouraged to read God's promise for today in I Peter 5:7,*
> *'Cast all your anxiety on Him because He cares for you.'*
>
> *The Swedish hymn writer pens our faith,*
> **'Though He giveth, or He taketh,**
> **God his children ne'er forsaketh."**

Our life together seemed so very fragile. We could never let Clarice be alone or drive a car or walk down the stairs alone, as the seizures came frequently and without warning. Our church family had been so loving and supportive. The women of the church had been wonderful to come and be with her for hours, sometimes reading a book to her or just sitting quietly beside her, holding her hand. The boys were very aware of the acute seriousness of their mother's life-and-death struggle. It pained me to see them so hurt. I felt caught in the middle as I tried to meet all of Clarice's medical needs and doctor appointments, and at the same time keep the boy's life as stable as possible. I tried daily to affirm each of the boys in their sports, music, and school studies. I made it a priority to be at all of their sports events. I had a "Help our Family Thrive" chart in the kitchen to help the boy's see how important they each were to their mother and to our family. They each had daily tasks to help care for their mother, feed her, talk with her (even when she no longer responded) and just love her. I wanted them to know how important their love and participation was in making our family work. We made our dinner table a fun and happy place at meal time, with a joke of the day by each boy, good food served "family style" and always prayer for each other after eating. But, for all our united efforts, Clarice's health continued to decline. I wrote in my journal on January 25:

> "We met with Dr. Hedeman again yesterday and he said that Clarice has only six months to live. Clarice doesn't seem to understand how critical her situation is. It just doesn't seem to register with her. She is very lethargic and just sits, staring, for long periods of time. When I asked her if she understands what the doctor said, she replied, "Well, yes and no. I just can't remember what he said." Then she said, "Don't you think it's just that I'm getting old? I feel so old."
>
> Sometimes when I hold her in my arms she doesn't feel like a 45-year-old woman at all, but rather like a helpless and lost little girl. I want, with all I have within me, to love and protect her from this thief, cancer, that has invaded our home. I hold her close and pray, "O God, help us be strong."

Someone has said that when we work, WE work, but when we pray, GOD WORKS. Over those years, I have fled daily to my Abba, my heavenly daddy and cried out my anguish in simple, childlike prayers, "Oh Jesus, have mercy on us and save us." Over and over I would pray that prayer. It spoke peace to my soul. And God answered, with a brief respite. I wrote on February 23 in my journal:

> "In the past several days, we've seen a real improvement in Clarice's condition. The chemotherapy seems to be working. She is more alert and has even wanted to help prepare some meals. What a joy to see her more like her sunny self. Still, there are definite personality changes that especially trouble the boys. Clarice will laugh at times, almost uncontrollably, especially when she can't think of how to finish her sentence. And then she will sing, over and over, all the old songs like, "Ruben, Ruben, I've been thinking, what a grand world this would be, if all the boys were all transported far beyond the northern sea." But her favorite gospel song is, "Oh, what a wonderful, wonderful day, day I will never forget..." and then she will forget the rest of the song. I feel that by singing those old songs, she's trying to reassure herself that she won't forget everything. It hurts to see her struggling, but I'm so proud of her that she is fighting against the enemy of cancer with song and laughter and faith. My reading for today included Psalm 17:22,

> "A cheerful heart is good medicine."

By May of 1983 the chemotherapy treatment is no longer effective and Clarice began falling all the time. The tumor had grown so markedly that the doctors told us that there is no further medical treatment available for her. Our doctors were very compassionate men, but they told us frankly that time had run out and Clarice had only weeks to live. Somewhere in those discussions with our doctors, the question of a second brain tumor surgery came up. They were reluctant to offer a second surgery and warned us that while it might give her a few extra months of life, it could be disastrous for her, both mentally and physically.

I wrote in my journal on May 5,

> *"I feel numb most of the time now. It feels like the weight of the world has been dumped on my shoulders. What are we to do? What does Clarice want the doctors to do? She is now totally unable to talk about it, much less make a decision. I don't know her wishes. 'Oh God, help us!'*
>
> *I called her sisters tonight and we agreed that the doctor's prognosis was not good at the time of her first surgery. They warned us then of dire consequences. But God has given her three good years of life. We'll never regret the decision for that first surgery.*
>
> *So, the decision is made tonight to go ahead with the second brain surgery."*

In the midst of these very dark days before surgery, God gave us a wonderful word of assurance that we were not forsaken or forgotten by Him. The same day that the hospital called to set the date of May 17, for the second brain surgery, we received a phone call from Ralph Sturdy who was the best man in our wedding. Ralph called to ask us how it was going with Clarice's health. He said that in his prayer time that week God had been nudging him, "Pray for Clarice, pray for Clarice." But he said, "I don't know what's happening, how should I be praying for you?" I was amazed and humbled by God's ever-present care for us. Here, when we were struggling, feeling all alone in the battle, our caring God was nudging another believer, hundreds of miles away from us, to remember us, pray for us and reach out to us. I recalled my Bible reading that morning from the Psalms and I wept with joy as I read it, remembering that God has never forgotten us:

> *"I am poor and needy;*
> *Yet the Lord thinks of me.*
> *You are my help and my deliverer;*
> *O my God, do not delay."* Psalm 40:17

Following the second surgery, our surgeon said that he was able to remove 98% of the malignant tumor, but it was a very invasive surgery and significant damage was done to the brain structures. It had many negative consequences for Clarice's ability to speak, walk and care for herself. Her recovery was further complicated by a staph infection, in both the brain and the surgical wound and she was losing vast amounts of brain fluid through her nose. She remained in the hospital for 39 days, with constant injections of antibiotics.

Each day, as I drove up to Butterworth Hospital, I sang through my tears, at the top of my voice, the old country western song that Johnny Cash revived, *"You are my sunshine, my only sunshine. You make me happy when skies are grey. You'll never know Dear how much I love you. Please don't take my sunshine away."*

On June 29, after 40 days in the hospital, I took Clarice back to our home. She was very weak, unable to walk and extremely limited in what she could do for herself. Dr. Hedeman warned me that I would never be able to care for her at home. He said, "You'll never make it through one day of care for her at home." But home is where she wanted to be and so we turned our main-floor dining room into her hospice room with a hospital bed and a Hoyer Lift to get her up and out of bed and into the wheelchair or on the bedside commode. We also contracted with a home nursing care agency to help care for her each day from 8:00 a.m. to 4:00 p.m. The boys and I cared for her each afternoon and through the night. We were so privileged to love and care for Clarice, in our home, over the next 16 months.

I never regretted the decision to go ahead with the second surgery. It gave us precious time to hold each other and weep, time to speak words of love and time to get ready to let go. As a believer, I hold fast to the Biblical definition of human life as a triumvirate of body, mind and spirit. So, while some friends would lament that she had no "quality of physical life," I would remind them that she is still rich in heart and spirit and she still loves her family deeply, prays and worships daily and is a testimony to everyone of a vital and living faith. She gave her three sons the finest gift that any mother could give. She lived with daily faith and died with eternal hope. Just before her death in August 1984, I wrote in my journal:

> *"A couple from church said to me today that they could never come and visit Clarice, as it was just too difficult to see her so sick. Admittedly, it isn't easy to see her so ill. She can no longer speak words, her*

face is swollen with the "moon-face affect" from heavy doses of steroid medication, she has lost all her hair from radiation and has two ominous scars on her head from brain surgeries.

But for me, she couldn't be **more beautiful**. Her eyes are windows to her soul and they continually communicate love and welcome and tenderness and warmth of heart. She communicates volumes with a wink or a raised eyebrow and her face is constantly aglow with a mother's love for her boys, a wife's companionship with her husband and a living faith in God. Even her scars are beautiful. As her badge of courage, they testify to her tenacious and faith-filled spirit, that won the battle. How I love this beautiful woman who is the victor over cancer."

The boys were remarkable in their tender love and care for their mother. They were never ashamed of her physical appearance, but always invited their friends into our home to visit with her. They lay in bed with her after school and ate snacks and told her all about their day's activities. I wrote in my journal:

"The boys are always willing to work with me in caring for their mother. They wash her hands and face before feeding her in the mornings and get her up in the Hoyer lift each evening so she can join us at the dinner table in her wheelchair. I see no anger or rebellion or unwillingness to help. How could they have such a loving and cooperative spirit, were it not for the Holy Spirit in their lives and in answer to prayer.

Tilly Van Gemert, one of the older members of our church, shook her fist at me today and said, "Why didn't God answer our prayers for the healing of Clarice." I said, "Tilly, look at her three sons and you'll see the healing that God gave in answer to our prayers."

TEARS ARE HEALING

It was Saturday, August 18, 1984 and the end of Clarice's life was near. Her two sisters, Dot and Marilyn (called Mim by the family) had been there with us all week. They had been such a lift. They helped me go through all of her clothing. I was glad that much of her clothing could go to others who needed them, but it was still hard to see them go. It seemed so final.

Clarice had been in a coma for ten days, but that night the nurse said, "the end is near and she's slipping away quickly." Her pulse was 50/40. We had been holding vigil around her bed all day. We held her hands and stroked her arms and told her, over and over, how much we loved her. We sang some favorite hymns and prayed. Jesus was here and there was a sweet spirit in the room. Clarice seemed so peaceful.

At 9:15 p.m., we made a family circle around her bed and held hands as we thanked God for this beautiful life that He loaned to us for a little while. At 9:30p.m., after we had prayed, Clarice stopped breathing and the last breath of life left her lungs with a gushing sound. Mim sobbed, "She's gone." The nurse listened with the stethoscope. There was no pulse, no heartbeat. She said, "I'm so sorry" and I knew she really meant it, as she'd grown to love Clarice over these past months of caring for her.

The boys were all crying. One of them sobbed "Mommy, Mommy, don't leave us." Dot and Mim were both sobbing. But strangely, I felt the need to lift my arms toward heaven and release her spirit to the loving arms of her Heavenly Father. I claimed the words of St. Paul as I whispered, "Absent from this body is to be present with the Lord." It brought me peace and a sense of release to know that she was home in glory, healed and safe. "Lord, tell Clarice how much we love her. Take good care of her until we meet again." Then, I went to my room and wept alone in the darkness.

It's hard to understand the grip of grief. After nine years of living with the possibility of her death, my first reaction at her death was shock, utter shock. I could not believe that she was gone. It's so hard to let go of your lover.

"The anchor holds in the storm."

Later that night, I called Arv Anderson, the lay chairman of our congregation, to tell him of Clarice's death. At the end of our conversation I said, "Please tell the church tomorrow that the anchor holds in the storm." I heard a sob catch in his throat, as he thanked me for that word of hope.

The memorial service for Clarice was held at our church in Grand Rapids on Monday, August 20. Over 700 people crowded into the church sanctuary for the service which we called, "A Tribute to Clarice in Celebration of her New Life with Jesus Christ." And it was a powerful celebration. Though our grief was raw, our worship together was spirited and hopeful, as we claimed the words of St. Paul, "We grieve not as those who have no hope." (1 Thessalonians 4:13). The congregation sang boldly a great opening hymn of hope, by Martin Rinkart:

"Now thank we all our God, with heart and hands and voices,
Who wondrous things hath done, in whom His world rejoices;
Who from our mother's arms, hath blessed us on our way
With countless gifts of love, and still is ours today."

I wrote a tribute to Clarice, which I based on the Bible verse found in Proverbs 31:28, "Her children rise up and call her blessed, her husband also and he praises her." You could hear a pin drop as it was read.

The church choir sang the beautiful testimony song, "My Tribute," by Andrae Crouch. Clarice loved that song and it was her testimony that night:

> *"How can I say thanks for the things you have done for me?*
> *Things so undeserved, yet you give to prove your love for me?*
> *The voices of a million angels could not express my gratitude.*
> *All that I am, and ever hope to be, I owe it all to Thee.*
> *To God be the glory, to God be the glory, to God be the glory*
> *For the things, He has done."*

After our conference superintendent, Rev. David Dahlberg, preached a message of eternal hope, the church choir sang Handel's, "Hallelujah Chorus." It was a strong closing benediction to a beautiful life well lived in faith.

The next day, the boys and I flew to Minneapolis for another memorial service held in Clarice's home church in Dassel. Over 450 people attended as Pastor Wally Pratt brought a comforting homily and Mary Fall, who was also the soloist at our wedding, sang the same song at Clarice's funeral that she sang 19 years before at our marriage:

> *"Savior in Thy love abiding keep them in Thy tender care;*
> *Through Thy Spirit's gentle guiding,*
> *save them from each tempting snare."*

We lay Clarice to rest in the nearby Covenant cemetery. The plot is near to her parents. The boys and I linked arms at the close of the committal service and we sang, "We are one in the Spirit, we are one in the Lord. And we pray that our unity will one day be restored; And they'll know that we are Christian by our love, yes, they'll know that we are Christian by our love."

The boys stood in the receiving line, like young soldiers, greeting people and giving hugs to all who offered them. How proud Clarice was of her three sons. She must have been beaming with satisfaction that day to see these three young men, so grown and mature, at 17, 15 and 11 years, standing so tall in loyalty to their mom. Her six young nephews, whom she loved like sons, carried her casket to the grave site.

I read once that there is healing power in tears. We're often told that real men don't show emotion and "big boys don't cry." But Scientists have discovered that crying releases chemicals and hormones that are mood elevators into the blood stream. Tears release pain relievers that lighten the emotional pain. So, I began my grief work and I wept unashamedly. Tears came quickly as I talked with people and even weeks later when I was preaching in public. Grief work is hard work, but necessary for survival. And it's not only tears that brought some healing to my grief. I believe that God has given us other allies to bring healing from grief. I found a great healing balm in the promises of God's Word and in releasing the burden to God in prayer. And I found my pain lifted whenever I engaged in conversation with friends who patiently listened to my heartache. Words and friends too have healing power. I wrote in my journal on August 23:

> *"We returned to Grand Rapids today, following Clarice's funeral in Dassel. The boys and I were surprised to find ten of our church members at the airport to welcome us back. It was so great to see their loving faces. They said they just wanted us to be welcomed home by friends and not to return, all alone, to a cold empty city. I was overjoyed. But my first thought was, 'I can hardly wait to get home and tell Clarice about all these wonderful people who met us at the airport.' And then it hit me. She won't be there. I can't tell Clarice the news anymore. I wept, as I walked to my car in the parking lot. This begins my trail of tears."*

CHAPTER 8

MY THREE SONS

From the very start of our marriage, on August 14, 1965, Clarice and I were in total agreement about starting a family right after marriage. Because we were both in our late twenties and the biological clock was ticking, we didn't want to wait long before having our first baby. But in our first weeks of marriage we became alarmed when I, at age 27, came down with a full-blown case of mumps. Along with the swelling of my salivary glands and a high fever, I got the characteristic swollen face, which someone said made me look like a chipmunk with its cheeks full of nuts. Our doctor warned me to get plenty of rest and take it easy as mumps in an adult male could cause lifelong sterility. And while the mumps infection did pass, we remained concerned as we were not able to get pregnant for some time. Because my folks had struggled with the pain of infertility in their early years of marriage, we were especially nervous as we waited over a year with the fear of sterility hanging over our heads. But then, by the grace of God, it happened. We were pregnant! Hallelujah!

MY SON PAUL - AUGUST 4, 1967

After nine months of a very normal pregnancy, Clarice awakened a little after midnight on August 4 with stomach cramps. For over an hour she quietly struggled in bed with that discomfort, before awakening me around 1:00 a.m. We wondered if she had eaten something the night before that had upset her stomach. We laid, wide-awake, in bed until 2:00 a.m., when it suddenly dawned on me to read in our Baby and Child Care book by Dr. Spock (which every new parent read faithfully in those days) and look up the section called "Labor Pains." After reading that section together, we finally figured out that it was time to hurry up and get her to the hospital. She was in labor.

St Gabriel's Hospital in Little Falls, Minnesota was an old but well run Catholic hospital that was founded almost one hundred years before by the Franciscan Sisters of the Immaculate Conception. It was a very strict and very Roman Catholic Hospital. As soon as we arrived at the hospital, just after 4 a.m., the nuns quickly whisked me off to the father's waiting room, without even giving me a second to give Clarice a parting kiss. Fathers were not welcomed in delivery rooms at that time. So, here I sat and stood and paced the floor for the next 17 hours.

After that long and worrisome wait a nurse finally came to the waiting room at 9:30 p.m. and said that my wife was having some problems and was asking for me. When I entered the labor room, Clarice was crying and said, "Wes, I don't think I can go through with this delivery, the baby just isn't coming." She had been in hard labor for over 17 hours and was exhausted and discouraged. As I stroked her face we prayed together and then agreed to ask the doctor to break her water, in hopes that it would speed the delivery. Two hours later, at 11:34 p.m. our son was born and weighed in at 8 pounds and 10 ounces. As soon as I held him, I whispered in his ear the first human words I wanted him to hear, "Jesus loves you son and so do I."

We named our baby "Paul," after the great apostle of grace in the New Testament and we gave him the middle name of "Eric," after his great grandfather, Eric Olson, on his mother's side. Paul was a blue-eyed, red-haired bundle of Viking energy who was called, "Eric the Red," by one of his uncles. Nothing seemed to slow down his gusto for life.

Jesus loves you and so do I.

At four months of age he wore a brace, day and night, to correct his right foot from turning slightly in. I thought the brace would certainly hinder his ability to crawl or walk but it only seemed to speed up his ability to walk which he did at eight months. I was often late for work at church as I couldn't take my eyes off of this active and beautiful son of ours.

Paul was running at nine months and never stopped running throughout his whole childhood. From his earliest

Paul at 16 months of age in 1968.

days, Paul was always active, loved athletics and was an adventurous boy who enjoyed every day of life. He always woke up early and happy and raring to get going. In grade school, he enjoyed little-league football and baseball as well as Cub Scouts, swimming team, stamp collecting, playing the ukulele, Boy's Brigade at church and generally just horsing around.

In junior high school, Paul was involved in all the school sports programs as well as singing in the school chorus and serving on the student council. And he was always a great student. But he had to slow up just a little, at age 13, to heal up from surgery for torn cartilage in his knee, which he suffered while playing football and then again at age 14 to heal from surgery for a ruptured appendix. The same year that he suffered the ruptured appendix, he reached a high point in his spiritual life, with his confirmation and confession of faith before the Covenant Church in Grand Rapids. I was so privileged to be his teacher in the second year of confirmation study.

Paul continued to advance as a student at Union High School in Grand Rapids, being in honors math, as well as excelling on the school wrestling team, track team, golf team and playing center, offensive guard and defensive end on the varsity football team. Each summer he played in the community Senior League baseball team.

Paul's senior year could well have been a low point for him, as his mother was dying from cancer. But Paul continued to soar in all aspects of his life. He was honored that year by the Grand Rapids Optimist Club and the Board of Education as, "An outstanding student, recognized for his academic, athletic and leadership abilities."

Paul graduated from Union High School in June 1985, with four senior honor awards, including: The Physical Education Award, the Principal's Cup for Leadership, an Outstanding Service Award and the Principal's Service Award. I was so proud of my son and his exceptional accomplishments in education, sports and leadership.

That fall, Paul entered North Park College in Chicago, the same Christian college that I had graduated from 25 years before. Here he continued to sharpen his athletic abilities, playing Division III college football for all four years of his undergraduate studies despite the losing record of his Viking team throughout those years. But when they beat Elmhurst College in 1988, his hometown Grand Rapids paper ran this article about him:

"Paul Swanson made eight tackles as North Park College captured a 34-24 win over Elmhurst College. Swanson is a 1985 graduate of Union High School, who was honored this year by being selected to the All-

Conference Football Team of Illinois and Wisconsin."

By the time Paul entered his senior year of college, he stood 6'1" tall and weighed 240 pounds. He compiled a four-year record, as a defensive tackle, with 33 solo tackles, 12 assists, 1 fumble recovery and 2 quarterback sacks. He was named, "Male Athlete of the Year," by his classmates.

Paul graduated from North Park College in May 1989 with a Bachelor of Arts degree in Physical Education and a K-12 teaching certificate. In his senior year, he sent me the following letter of appreciation which humbled and blessed me:

Paul playing college football in 1985.

Dear Dad, I want to thank you for all you have done for me over the years. First of all, it's from your model and inspiration as my father, that I formed my value system, my morals, my spiritual relationship and a genuine love for my fellow man.

Those things were unique, compared to so many of my friends, because you instilled in me a deep Christian influence.

I want to also thank you for your encouragement over the years. So many times, during my college years, when something would go wrong, I would call you and your voice and counsel would make me feel better. You made me strong. Never once, did I think l to myself, I shouldn't bother him. I always knew that you would make my needs a priority and take care of me. I know that I don't say this enough, but I love you. Paul

The same spring that Paul graduated from college, he announced his engagement to Lyna Kristine Adamson, who graduated together with him from North Park, with a degree in psychology. They dated for four years in college, fell in love and set the date for their wedding on June 30, 1990, to be held at Lyna's home church in Trimont, Minnesota.

Their beautiful wedding was on a hot, sultry, day in June and I, with a lump in my throat, was privileged to perform the marriage ceremony.

His brother Mark was his best man while his younger brother Luke was a groomsman and my wife Sandy sang the solo, "Savior, like a Shepherd lead them." A single white rose on the alter was there in memory of his mother.

After five years of teaching and coaching at Niles West High School in Skokie, Illinois, Paul and Lyna announced that they were going to Quito, Ecuador for two years as short-term teachers at the Alliance Missionary Academy and as youth workers at La Florista Covenant Church in Quito. While serving those two exciting years, their first son was born on December 12, 1995, and named Noah Paul Swanson. He had dual citizenship in both Ecuador and the United States.

In 1996 this family, now a threesome, returned to the United States and settled in their home in Mount Prospect, Illinois. Paul continued his teaching and coaching career in nearby Skokie, Illinois. Their family was completed with the birth of two more sons, Seth Evert Swanson, born on April 10, 1998, and Caleb Adam Swanson, born on December 16, 2003. After raising three sons myself, I congratulated Paul with the caution that three sons are a handful, but a special joy for a father as well.

Paul and Lyna moved to a second home in Skokie, Illinois, to be closer to Paul's school where, over the past 26 years, he taught physical education, drivers training, football and boys track and field. In 2007, he was honored by being placed on the Coaches Wall of Honor for the Niles School District. In 2008, his leadership and administrative skills were recognized by the district when he was appointed as the first Administrative Director of Physical Education for the Niles School District. In 2017 the district again honored him by naming an indoor track event in his honor as the "Paul Swanson Relays." The award plaque stated that, "Paul Swanson is a "Coach" and "Administrator" who cares deeply for the people he teaches, for the people he works with and the student-athletes he leads. Coach Swanson has the unique gift to get his student-athletes to accomplish feats they thought were unobtainable. His legacy is not just defined by the championships and state place winners, but his unyielding integrity which he passes on to Niles North High School and the entire coaching profession."

Lyna has been a great partner for her husband's active athletic lifestyle and a wonderfully supportive mother for her three sons involvement in all types of school and community sports programs. She has been their chief cheerleader and family taxi driver to all the sports events in addition to pursuing a professional career in elementary education. Their sons have flourished in their studies and athletics with Noah spending a semester of his North Park University education in Sweden and Seth being the champion long snapper for the North Park Viking football team, while Caleb continues to excel as a quarterback on his community football team and the high scorer for his basketball team.

Throughout the years, Paul has continued to grow as a leader in his profession as well as in his community and church. After earning three master's degrees in the late 90's, with majors in Learning Disabilities, Behavioral Disabilities and Administration, he created a number of innovative physical education programs. He initiated the use of heart monitors for every student in P.E. and developed programs to mainstream students with disabilities by assigning each one to an able-bodied student to act as their legs, hands or eyes. With his mastery of the Spanish language he became a bridge-builder for Hispanic students in the school district and he has organized many mission work teams for building projects in Ecuador. Paul has served as the lay chairman of the Deer Grove Covenant Church where the entire family has worshiped and supported that congregation.

MY SON MARK – APRIL 25, 1969

It was on Friday, April 25, 1969, that a new voice was heard in the Swanson household when Paul's baby brother was born, just 20 months after his birth. We were surprised that morning, at about 8:30 a.m., when Clarice's contractions were suddenly very close. We had no time to get a babysitter for Paul, so we scooped him up, grabbed a suitcase and jumped into the car. We sped across town to St. Gabriel's Hospital in Little Falls, Minnesota for the birth of our second son.

Once again, the catholic sisters would not allow me to be in the delivery room with Clarice and they were insistent that our two-year-old son be taken immediately out of the hospital. After members of our church came and rescued Paul, I settled into the father's waiting room for what I hoped and prayed would not be another 18 hour wait, as it had been with our first child.

Our prayers were answered just two hours later when our second son was born at 12:33 a.m., weighing in at a healthy 8 pounds, 10 ounces. I loved him from the first moment I held him in my arms and whispered in his ear, as I had with his older brother, "Jesus loves you and so do I."

Our new baby son was a blond haired and blue-eyed little Swede, whom we named "Mark," after the Gospel writer in the New Testament. We gave him the middle name of "Donald," after Clarice's father, Oscar Donald Olson. Her father had passed away just three years before and it

Mark at age three in 1972.

meant a lot to Clarice that his name be carried on in the family.

Mark was a serene child who was content to be held and loved and to sit in his bouncy-chair just watching his active older brother entertain him. When he was just three months old he would laugh heartily whenever his brother would dance around or make funny noises. Mark also walked at 8 months, just like his older brother.

A year and two months after Mark's birth, we moved from Little Falls, Minnesota, to our new parish in Northbrook, Illinois. I thought that this would be a very difficult adjustment for our three-year-old son Paul and an easy adjustment for our one-year-old Mark. I was wrong. Paul loved his new home and the many new friends in the neighborhood, but Mark was uncomfortable with his new surroundings from day one. He was unhappy with his new home, didn't like to be left in his new bedroom and cried every time we left him in the church nursery. Mark wanted everything to be familiar, like his first home. It took him six months before he was comfortable in his new surroundings.

When Mark was four years old, he became an older brother to his new-born baby brother, Luke. Now Mark was the proverbial "middle child," with all the added pressure of birth order and sibling rivalries. But Mark always reflected the compassion of his mother and rose above feelings of insecurity or neglect, to become a very creative young man who was always our family peacemaker.

By the time that Mark was in kindergarten, he was flourishing in

My three sons at ages nine, seven and three.

his own personality. He loved school, learned fast and could rapidly read his first primers at age five. Mark especially loved his new puppy, named Pojke, which is Swedish for "boy." And he enjoyed being in a family of three boys. There was always excitement and adventure in his home. It was a happy time in our family.

But suddenly, everything changed. On August 5, 1975, our happy life caved-in, when the boy's mother suffered a grand mal seizure in their presence. It was especially traumatic for Mark. At first, the boys were all too scared to even talk about what was wrong with their mother. But when she came home from the hospital, it was especially in Mark's eyes that I saw fear. It took him many days before he even dared to enter her bedroom. In spite of our reassurances, he was afraid that his mother would have another seizure or even die. This was a very difficult time in Mark's life.

But kids are resilient and Mark began to flourish again as his mother's seizures were controlled by medication and she regained more strength. Still, I was especially concerned for Mark, almost two years later, when I was called to pastor a new church in Grand Rapids, Michigan after living for seven years in Illinois. We were on the move again and my main concern was how Mark would adjust this time.

Each of the boys had their own adjustment to make, but Mark especially surprised us by welcoming the move to Michigan. Perhaps it was just having a fresh start in a new home that didn't

Mark in his senior year in high school.

have all the negative memories of his mom's health crisis that he associated with our home in Illinois. Mark made a quick adjustment to his new neighborhood, school and church and made many new friends, who became "best friends," that have turned out to be lifelong friends.

By junior high school Mark had become our family "All Star." He became a very good athlete and at age 10 he won first place in the Ford sponsored, "West Michigan Punt, Pass and Kick Competition." He went on to win this competition two years in a row. Mark continued to excel in sports through his junior high and senior high school years, where he played varsity baseball and was co-captain of his football team. His recovery from surgery for a ruptured appendix (just like his mother and older brother's ruptured appendix – it seems to run in families), forced him to take a break from football in his senior year of high school.

Mark was always an exceptional student. In junior high, he was enrolled in both Honors English and Honors Math and at age 13, he was inducted into the National Honor Society. He kept up his "A" average throughout his high school years and graduated in 1987, with high honors, including the Academic Letter Award, which was given to only 41 students out of a student body of 1200.

Mark had become our family "All Star"

In the fall of 1987 Mark followed his brother Paul and was admitted to North Park College in Chicago. Here the two Swanson boys were teammates on the North Park Viking football team. In 1989, our local Grand Rapids paper carried this article about Mark on the sports page:

> *"Mark Swanson, a 1987 graduate of Union High School, is a sophomore on the varsity football team of North Park College in Chicago. The 6 foot, 201 pound, defensive end/linebacker has accumulated 41 solo tackles, 13 assists and 5 quarterback sacks."*

In 1990, Mark struggled with a difficult decision regarding his future career and he made the decision to switch from his business major to a history major, with a minor in elementary education. It meant that he would have to take a fifth year of college and as he struggled with that decision, he wrote to me concerning his confusion:

> *"I am very uncertain about my future vocation and confused about the direction that I am heading. I'm not sure that a business major is where I should be. Even though I feel confused and not exactly in control of my life, I welcome these feelings as my faith in Jesus is growing stronger in this time and I am letting God take control.*
> *Please pray for me, Dad, that the Lord will give my life new direction." Love, Mark*

Mark was well liked on the North Park campus, where he was elected to the homecoming court for three years in a row. When he graduated in 1992, he received the school's high honor, the Senior Par Excellence

Award for "academic achievement, for demonstrating interest in campus activities and for leadership in outreach to the homeless." He graduated Cum Laude, "with honors," and was listed in the Outstanding College Students of America for "academic excellence and extracurricular leadership." After his graduation from college, Mark moved back to Colorado where he got his Colorado Teaching Certificate and soon, thereafter he got a job teaching Math and Social Studies at Carmody Middle School in Lakewood, Colorado, a suburb of Denver.

With his move back to Colorado, Mark immediately became active in the singles group at Arvada Covenant Church. There he met Heather Rae Hahn, who had recently relocated to Denver where she was working as a graphic artist. Heather had graduated with a degree in Journalism from the University of Wisconsin. Mark and Heather fell deeply in love and announced their engagement in April 1995. On July 29, 1995, Mark and Heather were married in a beautiful outdoor wedding, held among the tall pine tree grove in her parent's yard in Manitowoc, Wisconsin. Mark's brother Paul served as his best man and his brother Luke as a groomsman, together with his college friends, Scott Thompson and John Love. I was again humbled and blessed to conduct the wedding ceremony for my son.

Ten months later, the happy couple welcomed the birth of their son, Christian Wesley Swanson, who was born on April 29, 1996. I was so honored to have my name given to one of my grandchildren. Mark and Heather were blessed again on April 2, 2000, with the birth of their beautiful daughter, Britta Grace Swanson, the first granddaughter born to the Swanson family. And their family was complete on December 26, 2002, with the birth of their third child, and second son, named Micah Roger Swanson. Micah was born just four days before my marriage to Carolyn Larson, but both he and his mother were able to be in the wedding party.

In 1999, Mark was awarded his Master's Degree in Educational Administration from the University of Colorado, together with certification as a school principal. He also continued to succeed in his career as was publicly acknowledged in the year 2000, when he was honored by the county as "Jefferson County Teacher of the Year." Mark is often cited for his effective and creative teaching style which includes student study tours of historical sites in both the United States and Europe.

In 1997 Mark and Heather purchased their home in Westminster, Colorado where they have raised their family for the past 20 years. Heather is a very gifted and creative woman who has risen remarkably in her profession as a graphic artist and now is the graphic designer for

O@P EDGE Magazine which is published for people with limb loss. She is such a caring and loving mother to her children and supports her husband in his professional vision of educational travel to augment his classroom teaching of history and geography. Their children too, have benefited from this vision with rich experiences of world-wide family travel to augment Christian's pre-med studies at North Park University and Britta and Micah's education at Standley Lake High School where Britta excels as a school athlete and pianist for the jazz band and Micah plays the cello in the school orchestra and is an outstanding student in the school honors programs.

In 1997, Mark and Heather purchased their home in Westminster, Colorado where they have lived and raised their family for the past 20 years. All three of their children grew up in that neighborhood and attended the Westminster Public Schools, including Witt Elementary, Wayne Carle Middle School and Standley Lake High School, where they all excelled academically.

Mark and Heather raised all three of their children in the spiritual nurturing and loving fellowship of the Arvada Covenant Church, a church I was privileged to pastor for nearly 14 years. Both of them are active in various ministries in the church and have been a wonderful Christian testimony to their children and neighbors.

MY SON LUKE – MAY 5, 1973

In the early 1960's, there was a situation comedy on ABC TV called "My Three Sons." In the show, Fred McMurray plays a single dad who raised his three sons alone, with all the comical situations of a house full of men. Little did I realize, as we watched the re-runs in the early 70's, that I would come to personify that long running TV show. But with the birth of my third son, on May 5, 1973, I was indeed the father of "my three sons." And I did, as well, come to raise them as a single dad.

It all started after midnight, on May 5 when Clarice awakened with strong labor pains. We realized we had to move fast as we had a fifty-minute trip from our home in Northbrook, to Swedish Covenant Hospital in Chicago. But first we had to call our friend Marilyn, a member of our church who had offered to come over and care for our two older boys whenever Clarice went into labor.

We arrived at the hospital sometime after 2 a.m. with Clarice in full labor and I in full panic, afraid that we were going to have this baby in the car. An hour later, at 3:27 a.m., our son was born and weighed in at a healthy 8 pounds and 4 ounces. We had made it just in time.

We named our third son, "Luke," after the "beloved physician" and gentile writer of the third gospel and the Book of Acts in the New Testament. Luke was given the middle name of "Ira," after his grandmother Madge's father, Norris Ira Lowry. I'm not sure that Luke has always appreciated his middle name, as it sounds like an IRA retirement plan in our day. But he always took it with good humor when his friends would call out, "here comes Ira."

The day after Luke's birth was Sunday. After being up all night in the hospital I tried to pull myself together, get the boys dressed for church and preach that morning to my congregation at Northbrook Covenant Church. But when I announced the birth of our third son, the congregation all groaned out loud. With two, active Swanson boys, already running around the church, I guess they were all hoping for a sweet and quiet little girl this time. To be honest, Clarice even thought that this easy pregnancy meant she was carrying a girl. But with the birth of Luke we became forever known as the couple with "my three sons."

As an infant, Luke loved to be held in our arms and cradled. His grandmother, Madge Olson, called him, "my little blondie" and would cuddle him and hold him for hours. His two older brothers also welcomed their towheaded and blue-eyed baby brother to our home with lots of squeezes and kisses and love. From somewhere our six-year-old son Paul had heard Elvis Presley sing, "You ain't nothing but a hound dog, cryin' all the time." So, one night at our dinner table prayer, as baby Luke was crying for his mother's milk, Paul prayed, "God bless our little hound dog, who's just crying all the time." We all broke out in laughter.

Raising three boys under one roof can be a challenge. Luke was the baby in our family and as such he had to learn from the get-go how to survive with his two older brothers. While the boys loved each-other and grew to be best friends, there

Luke at age two in Northbrook, Illinois.

were times when Luke took the brunt of being the youngest in the family order. Like the time we had hired a babysitter to watch the boys and they went wild and put Luke in the clothes dryer and turned it on with him inside. It was only for a few seconds. Luke survived, but our babysitter didn't. She refused to ever babysit at our home again. It added to the folklore of the preacher's wild kids.

In his early years, Luke was a very happy child, always so loving and compliant. And like his mother, Luke would wake up happy in the morning, eager and ready for the adventure of a new day and loving his family. But Luke, like his brothers, had to also face some very stressful experiences as a young child that could have negatively scarred his life:

- At age two, he experienced the trauma of his mother's grand mal seizure as she held him tightly throughout the ordeal.
- At age three, he went through the always stressful ordeal of a move and relocation to our new home in Michigan.
- At age five and six, he watched as his mother's health declined and as she went through serious surgery for a malignant brain tumor.
- At age 11, he experienced the painful crisis of his mother's death.
- At age 14, his father remarried and his new step-mother, Sandy moved into our home.
- In his Junior year in high school, he was again uprooted from his school and friends, as his family moved to Colorado.
- At age 20, his step-mother died from colon cancer.

How did Luke and his brothers survive all this stress without becoming angry and rebellious children? How does any family exist, much less thrive, when surrounded daily by terminal illness in the home? How did Luke grow up to be such a positive man of faith, who seeks to serve others who are suffering pain and injustice?

Early on in our struggle with cancer, Clarice and I made some basic decisions on how we could help our children to cope and even grow stronger in this tough time.

1. We agreed to never deceive the boys, but always tell them the truth about their mother's illness and in an age appropriate way to include them in the decisions, care and prayer for their mom. Because Luke was so young, at age two, he didn't need a lot of detailed information about cancer. He mainly needed to be held in our arms and hear us affirm that we would be there to love and care for him.

2. Even though our family spent a lot of time attending to Clarice's health concerns, we made it a priority to keep the boys' lives as stable and normal as possible. We encouraged the boys to keep up their regular involvement in school, sports, music lessons and church activities. We said it was Ok to laugh, have fun and always welcomed their friends into our home.

3. We believed that a child feels safest when their parents are consistent with family rules for things like a regular bedtime at night, homework before watching TV and always eating our evening meal together around our kitchen table. We would not eat with paper plates or TV trays, but we would eat complete meals at our table, which was set with real plates and silverware. This communicated to the boy's that our family time is special and the table became a sacred place for family conversation, time to affirm each boy's achievements and to support one another in prayer.

4. Clarice believed that a diagnosis of cancer was a teachable moment in a mother's life. While cancer had invaded her body, it had never diminished her heart of compassion or her faith. She wrote, "Out of the ordeal of fighting cancer has come real beauty to our love and faith and I wouldn't have missed this for anything." Her children were watching and they saw that their mother's walk matched her talk, and they caught their mother's faith.

Through all these stressful experiences, Luke grew into a young man who by age nine took first place in his fourth-grade reading contest and got the lead role of King Nebuchadnezzar in the church youth-choir drama. He loved building and racing his Pinewood Derby cars each year in Boy's Brigade. By age 11, the year of his mother's death, he was playing in the city baseball league and taking trumpet lessons at school, while learning at the same time to play the guitar from his grandma Helga. Luke made the same progress in junior high and senior high school where he played football with his Union Red Hawk's team and was active in free-style wrestling, the ski club and played trumpet in both the school band and the church orchestra.

Following his mother's death, Luke's major struggle became eating too much, which was his way of coping with his grief. He put on a great amount of weight, so much weight that he was embarrassed by his size. By his freshman year in high school he had finally reached the point of agreeing to join a medically supervised weight-loss program. We all went on the diet menu and celebrated, as in the first month Luke lost almost two pounds a day and one-half pound a day in the second month. He lost over 70 pounds in two months. He was immediately happy to fit into new clothes, but he also learned life-long dietary and exercise lessons that he has practiced into his lean adulthood.

Our family's move to Colorado in 1989, proved to be a difficult adjustment for Luke. It's really hard for a teenager to be uprooted from his school and friends in his junior year of high school. I know from personal experience. But Luke's adjustment to his new school was complicated by the cliquishness of the students. They were cold and unwelcoming to outsiders and his new football teammates seemed to shun new players. His adjustment to his new home in Colorado came slowly, but was greatly helped when skiing season arrived and he met a new girlfriend at our church youth group.

In June, 1991, Luke graduated from Pamona High School with honors and with his Pamona Panther's football letter. Like his brothers before him, he was admitted to North Park College in the fall, where he enjoyed reuniting with his Michigan friends as well as having his two brothers nearby.

By the end of his freshman year of college, Luke was sensing that God had a calling on his life. While his college majors were in Psychology and Elementary Education, he was now beginning to test his call to ministry by serving for two summers as a youth intern in our church in Colorado. And when I encouraged him to finish college with a degree in elementary education and at least begin a teaching career, if ministry in the church didn't prove to be his calling, he wrote to me:

> *"Dear Dad, After a lot of prayer and phone calls to our church, I have decided to take on the summer intern position in junior high ministry. At first I was reluctant, but now I'm certain that this is where God wants me. I know that you, Dad, were not gung-ho about the idea at first and neither was I. But I really feel now that this is where I should be. I feel I have matured a great deal in the last three years and have a lot of valuable insights to give to kids.*
>
> *Keep me in your prayers.*
> *Love in Christ, your son Luke."*

Luke graduated from North Park College in May, 1995, with his major in Psychology and a minor in Elementary Education. Following his successful application for teaching certification, he moved back to our home in Arvada, Colorado and got a job teaching at an elementary charter-school in the suburbs of Denver. He was an effective teacher and he was loved by his students and valued by the administration. But after two years of teaching, Luke resigned and entered Denver Seminary, while at the same time completing a seminary internship in youth ministry at Arvada Covenant Church.

In the summer of 1998, Luke sought to sharpen his ministry gifts by organizing a gospel team called, "Set Free." The four-member team toured Midwest churches and Bible camps with a program of music, dramas and teaching the gospel of freedom in Christ. In his promotional material, he wrote:

"Christianity is the one thing I thought would bring me bondage, but instead I found freedom in Christ. I desire for others to 'enter the narrow gate' and experience the same freedom."

In the fall of 1998, Luke transferred from Denver Seminary to North Park Theological Seminary in Chicago, where he got a tuition free Presidential Scholarship. It was the same seminary that his dad had graduated from, some 30 years before, only I didn't get the scholarship.

In December of 2000, through January of 2001, Luke and I traveled to Israel and Jordan where we studied together for six weeks at the Jerusalem University and College, which is located next to Zion's Gate at the old walled city of Jerusalem. It was a wonderful opportunity to study the ancient land in the light of Biblical revelation and to bond together as we walked were Jesus walked.

Luke graduated from seminary in May, 2002, and by fall accepted a call to help start a new Covenant Church in Novi, Michigan. Here he served as Pastor of Discipleship at Christ Covenant Church, but he soon realized that this church was not growing sufficiently to support their three full-time pastors, and thus, he offered to resign after one year of ministry.

Now, Luke was without a job and without a place to live. But he had a girlfriend, Sarah Lindquist, in Minneapolis and his Aunt Mim invited him to live temporarily with her in that same city. So, Luke made a big leap of faith and moved to the twin cities, where he found a part-time job teaching at Minnehaha Academy and a second part-time position at Bethlehem Covenant Church as their Junior High Youth Pastor. This arrangement became his platform for pursuing his relationship with Sarah and for seeking a pastoral position at churches in the twin-cities.

In the spring of 2003, Luke announced his engagement to Sarah Christine Lindquist and they set their wedding date for August 9, 2003.

Their wedding was held in the new chapel of Minnehaha Academy and Luke's childhood friend, Josh Cobbley, served as best man with his two brothers and fellow pastor Justin Saxton, serving as groomsmen. Sarah's parents walked her down the aisle and I was so blessed to help perform the ceremony of my third son. Luke's niece and nephews, Noah, Christian, Seth and Britta served as celebratory bell ringers.

By late summer, Luke accepted the call of Community Covenant Church in Minneapolis to be their lead pastor. This church is a historic, very diverse Covenant Church which has a majority of African American members. Luke said, "This is my dream church. This is what heaven is going to be like, with people from every nation, tribe, language and people standing before the throne of God in praise and adoration." On Sunday, October 26, 2003 he was installed as their pastor and I was privileged to share in his installation and bring the pastoral prayer. Before I prayed, I took off my suit coat and threw it around Luke's shoulders just as the prophet Elijah had set apart the young

Celebrating Luke's ordination to the ministry of Word and Sacrament in June 2004.

Elisha for God's service by throwing his prophets cloak around him and I prayed, "O God, may this symbol of the prophet's cloak be recorded in heaven. Set this young son apart for the service of our God and savior Jesus Christ."

Seven months later, in June 2004, I was again privileged as his father to lay hands of prayer and blessing on my son as he was ordained to the ministry of Word and Sacrament. Luke is called, together with his wife Sarah, to a Second Corinthians 5:18 ministry of reconciliation to God and neighbor. Sarah so beautifully complements Luke's call to city ministry by her passion in teaching other teachers for service in under-resourced area of the city and especially for early childhood education and kindergarten readiness.

Luke and Sarah have totally immersed themselves, for the past 15 years, in their church community in north Minneapolis. Here they bought a home, just three blocks form their church, and raised their three children, Adelaide Clarice Swanson, born on August 13, 2005; Elsa Joy Swanson, born on July,17, 2007 and Ezekiel Charles Swanson, born on June 4, 2009. Now all three of their children are enrolled at Minnehaha Academy in south Minneapolis, where their great-grandparents Clarence and Helga Swanson graduated from high school in 1927 and 1929 and where their mother graduated from in 1989, as well as their grandfather Steve Lindquist who graduated from Minnehaha around 1958. This outstanding Christian school has become a four-generation tradition in our family.

While we pray daily for the safety of their family, we admire so very much their dedication to making a physical and spiritual difference in the under-resourced areas of north Minneapolis. And, what Luke has learned from his ministry in north Minneapolis he brings to the national Covenant church, as he chairs the denominational commission on Christian action.

Sometimes a father doesn't realize the significant influence that he can have on his son. We men often focus on our mistakes as fathers and fail to see how we have blessed our children. But Luke humbled me and blessed me by writing, while he was in seminary, of my impact on him:

"Dear Dad, I want to begin by thanking you for everything that you have done for me. You have invested in my life more than any other person. Thanks, most of all for your love.

They once asked the great NFL running back, Berry Sanders, who his idols were and who he admired most. The reporters tried to suggest different legendary running backs, but Berry stopped them and said, 'None of these people have invested in my life.' He went on to say that it was his father who he admired the most because he had invested the most in him. I would have given the same response, I want to be like my dad. I admire you more than any other person, Dad. I not only admire you, but I consider you to be one of my best friends.

My prayer for you is that you never stop sharing your passion for Christ. You have touched so many lives and you have greatly influenced my life.
Love in Christ, your son Luke."

CHAPTER 9

FORTY YEARS OF PASTORAL MINISTRY

While serving my first church in Minnesota, I joined the local Kiwanis Club in order to get acquainted with business leaders and to expand my outreach into community service. It was here that I met and became friends with the county sheriff.

Early one morning, I received an urgent phone call from the sheriff asking me to come down to the county jail and minister to a young inmate by the name of Lance, who had just attempted suicide.

The jail was only five minutes from my home and when I arrived the young man was still lying on the cell floor, gasping for breath, with the crude noose that he had formed from a bed sheet, still beside him. A guard standing at the cell door, motioned me to go in.

I got down on my knees beside the young man and explained that I was a local pastor and I asked his permission to pray for him. He had injured his vocal cords in his suicide attempt and couldn't speak but he nodded, "Yes." I can't remember what I said in prayer, I only know that I cried out for God, in His mercy, to rescue this lost and broken young man, whom He loved. As I prayed he began to weep, in loud gasping sobs and like a drowning man grasping for a hand of rescue, he squeezed my hands so tightly that they hurt.

He squeezed my hands so tightly that they hurt.

After praying for him, I told him that God would never stop loving him and then I quoted from John 3:16, putting his name in the "whoever" of the verse saying, "God so loved Lance, that He gave His one and only Son, that if Lance believes in Him he will not perish but have eternal life." Just then, a medical doctor arrived and I had to leave Lance, having shared only that simple prayer and a Bible verse.

That next day I visited Lance again. He wept to see me come back. By this time his vocal cords had healed sufficiently so he could whisper his story to me. He had been arrested for stealing gas from a service station and had left his girlfriend and their two small children stranded in a motel room with no funds to pay for it. I explained more about God's love for him and his family and I promised to drive across the county to bring his girlfriend and their two children back to our city while he awaited trial. During the trip to bring them back, their little boy got sick and vomited all over the back seat of my car. Sometimes God's work gets messy but it's never boring!

God had begun a good work in Lance's life. Within a month, both Lance and his girlfriend prayed to receive Christ as Savior and Lord of their lives. Our little congregation reached out in love and provided shelter, food and clothing for the family until Lance was released from jail four months later. We then sent them off to their family in Oregon with our prayers and blessing and extra money for gas on their trip back.

That's the joy of pastoral ministry. For over 40 years of ministry I have been so privileged to see God working in the lives of people and to see lost people found. The term "Pastor" refers to the Biblical image of a shepherd caring for a flock of sheep. God wants His lost and straying sheep to be brought back into His fold where His under-shepherds can feed them, protect them and care for them spiritually. "Be shepherds of God's flock that is under your care," I Peter 5:2.

For over 40 years, I have been so privileged to be called "Pastor."

LITTLE FALLS, MINNESOTA – 1965 – 1970

My wife, Clarice and I had only been married for seven days, when we returned from our honeymoon to begin our first pastorate at Grace

Covenant Church in Little Falls, Minnesota.

I had grown-up in Little Falls when my dad served that congregation for a second time, from 1945-1948. So now, when I came to be their pastor in 1965, the congregation was both pleased to have the son of a former pastor come to serve them, but also somewhat cautious to have

My first church after seminary was Grace Covenant Church in Little Falls, Minnesota where we dedicated our new building in 1967.

me return as their young, untested and newly married pastor. Bill Holmquist, a leading member of the church, expressed that caution to my mom when he guardedly said, "I never dreamt that one day the little guy I had in my Sunday School Class in the 40's would someday be my pastor."

The congregation, which was celebrating its 75th Anniversary that year, had worshipped in the same old, timeworn church building for nearly all of those 75 years. The basement Sunday School rooms were dark and tiny, the fellowship room was inadequate and there was no off-street parking. The congregation listed 55 members on the roll in 1965, but 12 of them were in nursing homes and unable to attend. So, if we had 50 people in attendance on a Sunday morning, it was a great Sunday.

But a vision had been growing in our little congregation that one day they might build a new church on the two and a half acres of land they already owned in a new residential development, north of the city. So, amazingly, just three months into my first pastorate, the church board appointed both a building committee and a building finance committee to get the new church building on a fast track. I had my work cut out for me.

The church congregation then voted to put to the test the actual congregational support for a new, relocated church building by conducting a building fund drive, with a required goal of at least $20,000. The fund drive was set for Palm Sunday, April 1966 and that goal of $20,000 was an enormous leap of faith for a small church in 1966. But after much prayer, I, together with our leaders went out on that Palm Sunday afternoon and came back with many cash gifts and pledges. The total gifts were to be announced at the church service that evening.

When the congregation gathered back at our church that evening, our lay chairman had drawn the outline of a big thermometer on a large sheet of tag-board paper, which showed the results of the fund drive. He had colored in the thermometer with a bright red marker, to show how close we were to our goal. That night he covered the thermometer with a kitchen towel until the end of our worship service. With a big smile on his face he dramatically lifted off the towel covering to reveal that our little church family had *oversubscribed* the set goal. His drawing of a thermometer showed that it had blown its top off, like a Texas oil geyser and we had reached $24,000 in gifts and pledges. We formed a circle, held hands and sang the Doxology, "Praise God from whom all blessings flow." It was the best Palm Sunday celebration ever and there were many tears of joy.

It had blown its top off, like a Texas oil geyser.

But not everyone agreed with the church's relocation and building program. It wasn't all smooth sailing. Many of our older members had deep, sentimental ties to our present building. They had grown-up in that church, married and buried their loved-ones there and felt they needed to protect the old building. One elderly leader, on his death bed, begged me to never allow the church to be relocated. It was a stressful time for this young pastor.

In July 1966, when the congregation voted to proceed with the new building, a new swirl of activities began for me. In addition to writing my ordination paper and defending it in public ministerial examinations, I also preached at three services every week (Sunday a.m. and p.m., plus Wednesday evening Bible Study). Now I began endless, weekly meetings with our architect and building contractor and long hours with the church building committee. This all took place at the time of our first son's birth and combined to make me one busy young pastor. Our second son was born 20 months later.

And then something really extraordinary took place at our beautiful building site, located beside the Mississippi River. Out of the ground we watched in awe, as our vision of a new church became a reality. The new sanctuary seated 225 congregants with bright, spacious Sunday school rooms to accommodate 150 children, a large fellowship hall, a nursery, choir room, restrooms, a fireside lounge and a church office next to the pastor's study. A large canopy entrance provided a drop-off place for families and off-street parking for 52 cars.

With the new church dedication in November 1967 we saw the congregation take on new life with a 90% increase in membership by 1969 and a 230% increase in our stewardship and financial giving. It was a *miraculous* revival of a dying congregation that had been gradually wearing out. But not all the members were happy with the new location and growth, or the leadership of their young pastor.

A church building program can be one of the most divisive projects that any congregation can encounter and while we actually came through the experience as a united church family, we also were all exhausted by the project. We had tried, as a congregation, to save money by doing all of the interior finish work ourselves as well as the outside landscaping. It left the small congregation totally exhausted, with members asking to be left off of boards and committees for the next year. We couldn't even get enough Sunday school teachers for our now growing church. It was a discouraging time for me. And then, added to my dismay, I became aware that one of our leading, young families was telling people that they were leaving our church because of my "ecumenical activities" in the community.

This all happened after the assassination of Dr. Martin Luther King Jr. on April 4, 1968. I was chairman of our city Ministerial Association and I had actively worked to organize a community-wide, "Service of Concern and Dedication," in memory of Dr. King Jr. Hundreds of Little Falls residents joined the clergy (both protestant and Roman Catholic) to voice their concern and sorrow for the racial injustice and violence that was sweeping our nation. Our local paper, The Daily Transcript, reported that the community response to the service was, "Unprecedented in our city's history and the service made a positive call for racial justice in our nation." But the young couple in our church took issue with my participation in the gathering. And, while they said nothing to me personally, I learned that they were criticizing me behind my back saying I had compromised our faith by my being a part of the event.

I hate conflict and I especially dislike confronting fellow believers. But when I learned what they were saying to others behind my back, I knew I needed to meet with them quickly. The visit with the young couple did not go well. I listened carefully to their accusations against me and even asked forgiveness for anything I hadn't handled wisely. But when I would not back down on my pastoral, moral leadership at the King rally, they said I was a "compromiser" and they were leaving the church. I left heavy-hearted, but more convinced than ever that by taking a moral stand against racial injustice I was echoing my Masters longing, "That my house will be called a house of prayer for all nations," (Isaiah 56:7 and Matthew 21:13). I learned later, that the young couple had been negatively influenced by a religious group in our city that supported the ultra-conservative, anti-communist organization called, The John Birch Society. That local religious group had promised them a leadership role if they would leave our church. I was devastated and struggled for weeks with my old nemesis – fear of rejection.

I leaned more deeply on my "Good shepherd"

I learned through this experience, early on in ministry, that conflict is par-for-the-course in church leadership. It was for Jesus, as well as for the Apostles. But I also learned some valuable lessons in pastoral leadership and conflict management. I learned that I must always confront difficult situations in love and never in anger. Sometimes, I was the one who needed to cool off before confronting someone else. I learned that by listening carefully to others hurts and grievances, I could mitigate the conflict and find areas of agreement. I also learned that a vision that is high-handedly imposed, will be a vision that is strongly opposed. These were humbling lessons. But I also learned that there are times when a pastor must take a stand, provide strong leadership in difficult situations and thus shepherd and protect the flock. Most of all, these lessons in conflict management drove me to lean more deeply on my "Good Shepherd," Jesus Christ, "who laid down His life for the sheep," (John 10: 11).

Nevertheless, a year and a half later I resigned and accepted a call to the Evangelical Covenant Church of Northbrook, Illinois. I just couldn't get over the feeling that I'd had a vote of no confidence in my leadership and ministry at Little Falls. But, looking back, I realized that I did leave Grace Covenant Church too soon. We could have had many more productive years in ministry there, if I hadn't been so thin-skinned. Several members were very honest in their disapproval of my leaving after only five years saying, "You just have not stayed long enough." But with the strong encouragement of our denominational leaders and a growing sense of God's leading, we made the move to this growing Chicago suburb in June, 1970. The Little Falls congregation grieved as we said our fond farewells and left for Illinois.

NORTHBROOK, ILLINOIS – 1970-1977

We moved in 1970 from a small, Minnesota town of 7,000 people, to a rapidly growing Chicago suburb with a population of 26,000, surrounded by a metropolitan area of 5 and ½ million people. The city of Northbrook is on Chicago's affluent North Shore, at the northern end of Cook County and home to many

My second church was in Northbrook, Illinois where we dedicated the new facilities in 1975.

large pharmaceutical companies. Our family moved into a big, four-bedroom parsonage, located at 1884 Penfold Place, near the heart of Northbrook's old city. The city streets were lined with beautiful elm trees that provided our boys with lots of shade in our spacious back yard.

When we arrived in Northbrook, I was unaware of the fact that the previous pastor had been asked to leave the church. And while there had been a very effective interim ministry, under Dr. Burton Nelson, there was still a small group within the church that continued to be loyal to the previous pastor. It was to this former pastor that the group looked for ministry in times of sickness, crisis or death.

Three months after moving to our new parish, I accidentally discovered that the previous pastor had been driving down, daily, from Milwaukee to visit our hospitalized members in Chicago, while I had not even been informed that they were in the hospital. I determined that this was not a time for confrontation and that sometimes the best action is to take no action. I felt that time would be my ally and I determined to faithfully continue to reach out to the splinter group with love and respect. In time, I was able to win their trust and they became some of my most supportive members.

The Northbrook Church was part of a 60 acre, planned development by our denomination, in which our church was to be the spiritual center of a large Covenant Retirement Community with a city-wide vision. The retirement community had a "continuing care concept" of retirement living, which offered both independent living apartments or town homes as well as assisted living and nursing/rehabilitation care facilities. In addition, the center brought into the retirement complex a YMCA gym and pool for the recreational needs of the retirement residents but also for the church members as well as the entire community. This was an exciting concept and the expectations of denominational leaders were very high for immediate growth and expansion of the church.

With those expectations, we started our ministry that fall with a big bang. Our introductory days included a program of "35 days of Prayer and Preparation for Ministry Together." We called the congregation to a new level of vision and commitment. Within one year, we had outgrown our first worship facility and had appointed a building committee to study the raising of funds and the expansion needs of our sanctuary and Christian Education facilities as well as our outreach to the city.

By May of 1973, the congregation had voted to accept the building and expansion plans and we proceeded to raise $230,000 in an amazingly successful building fund drive. This fund drive was the green light to go ahead, one month later, with the ground-breaking ceremony for the expanded facility. All the children and youth of the church were invited to bring their spades and shovels to church on Ground-Breaking Sunday and participate in turning over the first shovels of dirt along with the president of our denomination, Rev. Milton Engebretson. The skilled workers then began transforming bare land into a beautiful edifice for worship, under our creative architect, Bruce Johnson and our skilled contractor and members of our church, Don Michealsen and Sons.

A year and a half after breaking-ground, we dedicated our expanded $750,000 church facility on April 20, 1975. The new worship center seated over 500 people with a large narthex that seated an additional 250 people. The expanded building included the tripling of our Christian education rooms and fellowship hall, together with a large choir rehearsal room and youth activity room. By this time, the church had grown to nearly 300 members with an additional 500 children and adult attenders.

The growth of the Northbrook Church was, for me, both exciting and unsettling. In our seven years of ministry there, it was definitely exciting to see the church grow by 77% in membership and the Sunday school grow by 114%. Our local church giving increased by an amazing 579%, while at the same time we took a big step of faith and sent out over a dozen of our most faithful leaders to help plant a new Covenant Church in Libertyville, Illinois.

I recognize that big numbers do not necessarily mean that lots of people were finding faith in Christ or growing in the discipleship of their lives. But in all this numerical growth, we especially rejoiced in the numbers of people who were coming to faith and growing in their service for God and His Kingdom. One of our young doctors wrote in our newsletter, "*Since attending Northbrook Covenant Church, I have had a spiritual rebirth in my life. A wonderful new sense of trust in our Lord Jesus Christ has come to me, which could only come through the Holy Spirit leading me along the path that God wants me on.*" Sometimes, the church altar was filled with people rededicating their lives, their marriages and their service to God. Added to that growth was the rich treasure of the mature and time-tested faith of our retired members from Covenant Village, who each week flooded into this young congregation with their joy and encouragement. It was definitely an exciting time and place to be in ministry.

The disquieting part of all this growth was for me an increasing sense of being overwhelmed by all the expectations and demands of that

Sometimes, the church altar was filled with people rededicating their lives.

growth. I felt, at times, that the "Peter Principle" of management theory applied to me and I had thus risen to the level of my incompetence. I had no building skills necessary to guide the church in the construction of new facilities. I had no training in fund raising or the amortization of loans, necessary for the leading of a church with a million-dollar budget. I began to feel that I was out of my league. But in spite of my limited abilities, God began to teach me some principles of His kingdom economy, in which He simply called me to faithfully use the talents He had given to me (Matthew 25: 4-5). He taught me that the fear of using my own given talents was often the root cause of poor stewardship and failure in ministry (Matthew 25:24-25). I also learned that God deliberately chooses to use what is weak and obscure to remind us that blessing and growth in ministry come from Him and not from our status, prestige or money (I Corinthians 1: 26-31). These principles would come to be severely tested in the months ahead.

 The Christian pastor and author A. W. Tozer said, "It is doubtful that God can use any man greatly until he's been hurt deeply." In August 1975, I was hurt deeply and brought to my knees with the devastating diagnosis of my wife's brain cancer. This was a time of intense soul-searching and struggle. But it was combined with one of the most demanding and time consuming assignments that any pastor could endure.

I was hurt deeply and brought to my knees.

That assignment came in the middle of our struggle with cancer, when after the dedication of our new church our denominational leaders pushed for our young congregation to host the entire 1976 Midwinter Pastor's Conference in our new facility. This meant hosting, housing and feeding some 500 pastors and church leaders, while at the same time meeting the expectations of dozens of committee members and denominational leaders as well as the needs of nationally recognized speakers such as Dr. Paul Reese and Pastor E. V. Hill of Los Angeles. All this fell on my desk just six months after my wife was diagnosed with a malignant brain tumor.

Additional stress was added the week before the Midwinter Conference, when a harsh February blizzard damaged the new flat roof of our sanctuary causing melted snow to leak into the sanctuary and drip directly onto the preaching pulpit. I had to place buckets beside the pulpit to collect the snow melt and then pray that the drips wouldn't hit the bald head of our distinguished speaker from Los Angeles. But he handled it well, by wiping the drips off his head and reminding us that all these earthly temples are only temporary. "TEMPORARY," he shouted, as he pounded the chancel brick wall with his hand. It was a sermon that pastors, who were in attendance, remembered and still remind me of these 40 years later.

But all of the strain of a rapidly growing church, the hosting of the huge Midwinter Conference and living daily with my dear wife's cancer diagnosis, combined to leave me exhausted and suffering from a stress related form of angina with its painful spasms in my chest and arms. I knew that I had to make some changes to relieve this high level of stress in my life.

So, in the fall of 1976 I resigned from the Northbrook Church and accepted a call to an older and well-established church in Grand Rapids, Michigan. David, our church lay chairman at that time, came to the church office and begged me with tears to reconsider my resignation. But I knew the Lord was calling me to this specific church when a month earlier, during my daily devotional time, I received a word of wisdom from the Spirit of God saying, "Pastor Clarence Winstedt, of the Grand Rapids church has resigned and you will be called to that church." I was totally shocked by that quiet voice of wisdom from God. I had never even been to Grand Rapids and had no information regarding the church's pastors or ministry. But three weeks later, the chairman of that church, Dr. Bill Tournell, called me and asked if I had heard that their pastor had resigned and would I be open to considering a call to their church. I knew this was *clearly* God's will for my ministry and it was time to obey His calling and move to Michigan.

After expanding our church building we planted three daughter churches from my third church in Grand Rapids, Michigan.

GRAND RAPIDS MICHIGAN 1977-1989

In January 1977, we moved our three sons and all our belongings to the "River City" of Grand Rapids, Michigan. Grand Rapids is the second largest city in Michigan with a population, at that time, of

183,000 people. The city is located about 30 miles east of Lake Michigan.

In the mid-nineteenth century, many Swedish immigrants had settled in that area where, with their wood-working skills, they often became part of the growing furniture manufacturing industry in the city. At that time, the city was actually called "Furniture City." Out of that large Scandinavian population a Swedish Mission Covenant Church was established in 1880. It was to this strong and vibrant church, with its 576 adult members, now called the Evangelical Covenant Church of Grand Rapids, that I began my ministry in 1977.

At the time of our call to Grand Rapids, some concern was expressed by the Pulpit Search Committee over Clarice's health. I could only tell them that her seizures had been under control for the past year-and-one-half and while she was taking life more slowly, she nevertheless was growing stronger each year and caring well for her family. This would all change in two years.

The move to Michigan went very well for both Clarice and the boys. The church had provided a beautiful, four-bedroom parsonage for our family at 36 Centennial Ave in northwest Grand Rapids, about five blocks from the church. After getting our home set up and the two older boys settled in their new school, we entered into ministry with this loving congregation. The church's ordained and commissioned staff worked so very co-operatively with me and came to include Garth Bolinder, Tom Cowger, Jeffrey Norman, John Larson, Walter Ribbi, Norman Johnson, Rich Murray, Carl Janson and Walter Anderson plus a wonderfully supportive paid staff.

In many ways, the Grand Rapids church was my dream church. The congregation was Christ-centered with a long history of being solidly evangelical and theologically conservative, but not rigid. They were well grounded in the authority of Scripture which was expressed beautifully in a strong, worldwide mission program. It was above all, a loving, family-centered church, with some families having four generations actively involved in the church each week.

The congregation expected Biblical, expository preaching each Sunday and they loyally supported our two Sunday morning services with nearly 500 coming back each Sunday evening for another gospel preaching service. The evening services always included glorious music from our church choir and orchestra, under the direction of Norman Johnson, our Minister of Music and a renowned Covenant composer. Our Wednesday evening family night brought hundreds of children, youth and adults back to church for an all-church meal in Fellowship Hall, followed by youth meetings and adult Bible studies.

While we were located in the heavily churched city of Grand Rapids, with all of its Reformed and Christian Reformed Churches, we were somewhat unique as a deeply committed Evangelical church that focused on salvation by grace alone, through faith alone, in Christ alone. So, under this Biblical preaching of the gospel of grace, together with the church's strong mission and family oriented ministries, the church grew even stronger. In our twelve-and-one-half years of ministry, the membership grew by 32%, to nearly 800. The Sunday School grew 74%, to 640 students and the church giving, to both local work and missions, increased by an amazing 302%. Once again, I became involved in another building program, this time to expand the church significantly with more classroom space, office space and a greatly enlarged entrance lobby.

In anticipation of our church's one-hundredth anniversary in 1980, I challenged the church and its leadership to consider this significant milestone as the appropriate time to plant a new daughter church within the Grand Rapids area. I said, "You should not come to your 100th birthday without a daughter to celebrate with you." They all agreed and when that vision was laid out before the congregation, it resulted in members from three distinct areas of the city committing themselves to plant daughter churches in their neighborhoods. Out of that anniversary vision, money was raised and members were commissioned and sent out to eventually form the following three daughter churches: Thornapple Evangelical Covenant Church in the south-east area of the city; Fellowship Covenant Church in nearby Hudsonville, and Redeemer Covenant Church in Caledonia. We were surprised by triplets.

In 1997, I received the Covenant's "Jimmy Award," given by James Persson, then Covenant Church Director of Church Growth and Evangelism, for being the pastor who, at that time, had started the most daughter churches. Altogether I had started five daughter

"I want my tombstone to read: 'Wes Swanson, Father of Three Sons and Five Daughter Churches.'"

churches in Illinois, Michigan and Colorado. On receiving the award, I said, "I want my tombstone to read: 'Wes Swanson, Father of Three Sons and Five Daughter Churches.'" The planting of the daughter churches in Grand Rapids was, arguably, the highlight of my ministry there.

In 1980 and again in1983 my precious wife Clarice underwent surgery for a malignant brain tumor. It was an agonizing time. Between February

1980 and August 1983, Clarice had five surgeries including two surgeries for removal of the brain cancer, a ruptured appendix, placement of a port for chemotherapy and then placement of a shunt for fluid to go directly from her brain to her stomach. Toward the end of her life, for 16 months, the boys and I cared for her in our home, together with a daytime nurse. For much of this time she could do nothing for herself. This greatly affected my normal ministry to the church, both positively and negatively.

The positive side was the devoted way that the church ministered to us and became the loving arms of Jesus, to carry us in our brokenness. It was in this dark time in my ministry that I learned how invaluable it is to have a support group of peers. My Covenant Pastor's Cluster Group met with me regularly to encourage and listen to my wounded heart. These regular meetings of our West Michigan Pastors Cluster, surrounded me with godly support in the midst of my tears. They were an invaluable part of my life for 12 years because they took time to listen, lay hands on me in prayer and love me. How rich is the body of Christ in the desert times of life.

The negative side of this period in ministry was dealing with my own guilt in having to delegate so many of my normal tasks to other staff members so I could devote more of my time to my wife's medical needs. And my sons also needed more of their father's love and attention in this tough time as they slowly lost their mother. It was important that I was at their sports events and that we share special times together at Detroit Tiger baseball games and fishing on Lake Michigan. We also built together a fish pond and garden in the back yard of our home so their mother could enjoy the flowers and fish from her wheelchair. But even here, I discovered that I was ministering significantly to the church as a wounded servant, by putting my marriage and family first.

In 1982, after five years of ministry in Grand Rapids, the church graciously granted me a three-month sabbatical for a period of study and travel. Clarice was in one of her times of cancer remission and this gave me a wonderful opportunity to recharge my batteries by taking some exegetical course-work at Reformed College and at Baptist Seminary in Grand Rapids, as well as preaching in and traveling to Covenant churches throughout Alaska. But the trip of a lifetime for our family of five, was when we made precious memories, traveling together while I "guest preached" for six weeks throughout Mexico. Two years later Clarice died.

After Clarice's death in 1984, I went through a dark period of soul-searching and despair. I hadn't lost my faith or my call to ministry, but for several months I struggled with depression. I had great difficulty sleeping at night, little interest in food and no energy for doing ministry at church or getting our home back up and running. It was a very dark and lonely period for me and for a brief time I felt like I had died too. I should really have had professional grief counseling, but I chose to just tough-it-out and carry on. My saving grace was my three sons, for whom life had to go on. They needed their dad to show the strength and faith that would help them recover from their own grief. Their active lifestyle was my grief therapy and soon the depression passed.

Another significant part of my recovery was ministering to others who were struggling with cancer in their own families. It seemed like people throughout the city who were faced with a cancer diagnosis came out of the woodwork and flooded my office with requests to talk and share their pain. They would always begin by saying, "I know you'll understand what we're going through." Out of those conversations, I organized a city-wide Cancer Support Group, which met at our church weekly. Eventually, we helped three other area churches set up similar programs that would include informative talks on cancer and its treatment by medical speakers, time to listen and encourage each other and time for group prayer.

But my real recovery of joy and love for life came two years later, when I made a mission trip to Japan and met again our Covenant Missionary, Sandy Tengwall. We began a long-distance relationship, between Michigan and Japan, through letters and phone calls, which resulted in a beautiful gift of love for us both and our marriage at Salem Covenant Church in New Brighton, Minnesota on July 11, 1987.

Our Grand Rapids congregation went all-out to celebrate our engagement and marriage, with receptions and showers and an over-the-top wedding gift of a new, 1987 Ford Crown Victoria. It was too much and I was uncomfortable with such an extravagant gift. But I soon realized that the congregation *needed* to celebrate as part of their own grief recovery from Clarice's death, and also from the death of the church's long term Minister of Music, Norman Johnson, who died just months before Clarice.

While Sandy had some challenging adjustments to American culture after 12 years of living in Japan, the next two years of our life in Grand Rapids were quite happy as Sandy and I ministered together in the church, as well as co-ministering in mission conferences held throughout the Midwest.

On one of these mission preaching trips to Loveland, Colorado, as we drove past the city of Arvada, the Spirit of God whispered to my heart, "Someday you'll serve me here." Two weeks later the chairman of the Arvada church called me to see if I would be willing to meet with members of their search committee, who would fly to Michigan to meet with us. We began conversations with the Arvada church, which culminated in my submitting my resignation to the Grand Rapids Church and accepting the call to become the lead pastor of the Arvada Covenant Church on June 25, 1989.

It was very difficult for our family to leave the Grand Rapids church. We had built deep ties of love and grief and faith that bound our lives together. So, after twelve-and-one-half years of a very fulfilling and expansive ministry, we wept as we bid farewell to this dear church family that had been such a privilege to serve.

ARVADA, COLORADO – 1989-2002

I always thought it was ironic that the first three churches I served had some reference to water in their city name. I should have been a

In 1999, we dedicated the new church facility at Arvada Covenant Church in Colorado which was my fourth congregation.

Baptist pastor with all that water in Little Falls, Northbrook and finally in the "River City" of Grand Rapids. But with our move to Arvada, Colorado, that all changed. When we arrived in this high desert city, I asked one of our church leaders what the word "Arvada" meant. I was thinking that it might mean "Bubbling Stream" or "Mountain River" and thus continue my water-themed churches in this new ministry. But this leader reflected the discouragement and exhaustion of the congregation at that time by saying, "I think Arvada means 'Dried-out Gourd.'"

The name Arvada, is actually a Danish word meaning "Eagle," but the Arvada Covenant Church had not been soaring like an eagle in their past few years. The city itself had been spiraling upward as a rapidly growing suburb of Denver with a population in 1989 of 90,000. Its rapid growth as a Colorado boom town had soared following the first Colorado gold strike, which was discovered in their city streams in 1850. But, the church itself had declined significantly when the previous pastor split the church in 1988, taking over 200 members to form a new congregation in the area. Furthermore, I discovered that an additional 100 discouraged members had left the church to attend other denominations, or they just stopped going to church at all. It's no wonder that the congregation was discouraged after losing over 300 members in the past two years. But, on our arrival in Arvada, I was shocked to discover the depth of grief and pain that the remaining 400 members felt as a result of the split between the two congregations. It was symbolized in the comment that a woman made after my first Sunday at the church, when she confronted me and with anger in her voice said, "After the last pastor, I'll never trust another pastor again." I knew then where I stood as pastor of this wounded church.

I knew then where I stood as pastor of this wounded church.

I was puzzled at first over how I might provide effective leadership and a renewed vision to the church. I could have taken a strong, authoritarian leadership role at that point, but that was the style of the previous pastor who had high-handedly forced his vision on the congregation. I remembered the lesson I had learned in my very first parish, that, "a vision imposed is a vision opposed," so I chose a "servant leadership" style that started with listening respectfully to both the pain and the dreams of this congregation.

To achieve that goal, my wife Sandy and I invited our church members and friends to visit our home in small groups. They all received a written invitation to come to the new parsonage and get acquainted with their pastor and his wife. In our first six months in Arvada we welcomed over 400 members and friends into our home. There we shared many afternoons and evenings telling our faith-story and then asking each of them to introduce themselves, explain how they came to the church and then, most importantly, share their vision and dream for the ministry of their church. Many people said, "We've never been asked to share our vision for the church. We've always *been told* what our vision should be." But it was out of those shared dreams that the congregation regained ownership of the church's vision and healing for the wounds experienced in the split.

I also set out to build an atmosphere of care and appreciation in the church. I tried to model an "attitude of gratitude" through public expressions of appreciation and letters of thanks which I sent weekly to our faithful leaders. I also created an opportunity each week, for the membership to use the, "Encourage-U-Gram" cards that I had printed in the weekly bulletin, to express thanks to a Sunday School teacher, board member or staff person. Our weekly staff meetings also included time to pray through our membership rolls and then send a card to those we had prayed for saying, "We remembered your family in prayer this week." Within a few months, the negative comments were replaced by positive words of appreciation. The church family was beginning to heal. I was also careful to build a consensus with our leadership by meeting often with them, over breakfast or lunch, to listen carefully to their concerns and to be certain that we were on the "same page" before bringing new matters to the entire congregation. I sought to be "high-touch" in an increasingly "high tech" world and I was especially alert to the needs of hospitalized and aged members.

This servant style of leadership worked well to bring healing, both to our congregation as well as to the split-off church. Within three years, the two churches were co-operating in various ministries. In addition, in 1994, our church called John Wenrich to join our staff for the express purpose of starting a daughter church in Golden, Colorado. To me, the enthusiastic support of our congregation for this new church plant was clear evidence that a new day, a new healing, had come to our church family.

Under my ministry as Lead Pastor and together with the dedicated partnership of our ordained and commissioned staff pastors including; Orville Sustad, Bruce Finfrock, Keith Hamilton, Bill Hector, John Wenrich, Lois Erickson, Ann E. Vining, Tammy Buchan, Betty Greenwood, Mary Cunningham, along with many other paid support staff, we saw the church take on new life. In my nearly 14 years of ministry in Arvada, we saw the membership grow 128% to 1,053 adult believers and reach an average Sunday morning attendance of over 1600, with holiday attendance running over 2500. Our Sunday school grew 163% to 1,132 students and by 2002, our financial giving to the church's general, missions and building fund, had increased to an amazing 335%, giving two and a quarter million dollars annually. We also added a mid-week Family Night ministry called "Oasis Night," which included a family meal and Bible studies for hundreds of children, youth and adults.

But in the spring of 1993, our faith was tried and tested once again, by a sudden and totally unexpected cancer diagnosis for my darling wife. How could this be happening again? What is this shadow of cancer that seems to hang over our home? Why us? Why me? Why? Why?

When Sandy died on April 14, 1994, just eleven months to the day from her diagnosis with colon cancer, it was again an unbelievably shocking and dark time for me, but it was also a difficult and soul-stretching time for the entire congregation which had grown to deeply love Sandy. But, by the fall of 1994 the congregation had rallied in their commitment and vision, which was seen in their enthusiastic support of the daughter church plant in Golden, Colorado. Within eight months of our commissioning and sending many members to be part of this new church, the Arvada congregation had rebounded in growth and were stretching our present facility and parking to the maximum. The congregation voted unanimously to relocate the church to a new site with plenty of room for future growth.

The search for a new site, with a minimum of ten acres of land, was met with many obstacles including state environmental laws, city tax codes and neighborhood associations who opposed a growing church in their neighborhood. After a discouraging year of searching for land and getting shot-down at 20 possible parcels of land, the search committee and the entire church, was frustrated by all these closed doors.

Suddenly, in early 1996, we became aware of a choice 15-acre piece of land which was located in the fast-growing West Arvada area, right next to the rolling hills of Van Bibber Park and just four miles from our present church. The land was spectacular with a fantastic view of the Rocky Mountains to the west and located right along-side the heavily trafficked Ward Road to the east. The committee knew of this choice piece of land but erroneously understood that it was either sold or under contract.

God had actually set aside this land for us.

I believe with all my heart, that God had actually set aside this land for us, 35 years before when in 1963, a newspaper editor form the Philippines, by the name of Jimmy Go, had purchased a large tract of land in Arvada as an investment. The Go family was a deeply committed Christian family in the Philippines, who had suffered greatly under Japanese occupation during the Second World War. But, following the war, when purchasing this land with reparation money from the Japanese government, it was Jimmy Go's prayer that part of that land would be developed for some type of Christian ministry. Over the following 35 years, the majority of the land was sold off for housing and commercial development and now with the last 15 acres available, Jimmy Go's prayer for a Christian ministry on that site still waited for God's answer.

Talk about being touched by a miracle! When our church became aware of the availability of the Go family land, it seemed too good to be true. God had waited until we had exhausted our feeble search for land and then placed in our hands a gift of the most valuable piece of property in the entire area. For thirty-five years this choice piece of land sat waiting for us to earnestly ask God to lead us to the relocation site that He had been saving for us.

The Go family, now living in Canada, was so thrilled that an evangelical church was interested in buying the last 15 acres of their father's property, that they reduced the price by $200,000 and pledged to give back to the church a tithe annually, from the interest we paid on the land payments. The family also gave our church significant gifts in memory of their father and for the answer to his prayer some 35 years before. But, this was only the beginning of our need to keep waiting on God for His direction and deliverance. No sooner had we purchased the land than we became aware of major road-blocks to any construction on that land. In the summer of 1997, we were informed by the Corps of Engineers that our land next to Van Bibber Creek, may be home to a mouse (the Preble's Jumping Mouse) that was on the endangered species list. This mouse, together with an endangered field orchid, could permanently shut down our entire project.

In James 5:16, the writer directs us to humble ourselves before God when we face impossible and perplexing situations. "The prayer of a righteous man," he wrote, "has great power in its effects." In a matter of days, God powerfully answered prayer, by leading us to a biologist who had just completed a thorough study of the entire Van Bibber Creek area. With her compiled evidence, after a year's effort to trap the mouse, she was prepared to demonstrate that the mouse and field orchid were not found in the area. The Corps of Engineers accepted her report and gave us the green light to proceed with construction.

But by early spring of 1998, following our groundbreaking and initial construction, we realized that evil forces were trying to take the land and our building project away from us and sow fear into the hearts of God's people. Repeatedly, throughout that spring, vandals struck the building site, causing thousands of dollars of damage. Soon, it became apparent that this vandalism was much more than youthful pranks and we were facing deliberate sabotage. Not only was there the theft of expensive equipment from the builders locked storage shed, but also the destruction of computer data and software systems, the cutting of telephone and electrical lines and alarm systems, the deliberate relocation of surveyor's stakes and the burning of wooden foundation forms. The vandals even broke into the construction trailer and set fire to all the contractor's blueprint documents. We realized that we were dealing with hate crimes of a frightening and evil proportion.

Once again, the leadership was driven to their knees in prayer. On June 28, 1998, I called the entire church to gather at the building site following our Sunday morning services and reclaim the land in prayer. That event became a turning point in the construction and in our faith. As we walked and prayed around the construction site, a bit like Joshua with the priests and the armies of Israel walking around the walls of Jericho, we reclaimed the land and the building for God's glory and believed God for His protection of the site and even the salvation of the vandals through the witness of our church. After that prayer service, the vandalism, which had occurred almost weekly, stopped for nearly four months. We had indeed seen that the power of our God is greater than the powers of darkness. And while, approximately four months later, the vandal made one more attempt at breaking into the construction trailer, he was apprehended by police and arrested. Sadly, he was a 17-year-old high- school student, with a radical environmental belief that he was saving the land from destruction by Christians. Once again, we realized that, "If God is for us, who can be against us," (Romans 8:31).

After that prayer service, the vandalism stopped.

The first service in our newly completed church, at 5555 Ward Road, was held on Palm Sunday, March 28, 1999 with our church youth carrying in the communion table, the pulpit, the baptismal font, the Bible and the church flags in a solemn, but joyful procession. An official dedication of this 55,000 square foot facility was held on May 2 with Rev. Glen Palmberg, President of the Covenant Church, speaking. These indeed were years that were touched by God's miracles and blessings.

In 1989, when Sandy, Luke and I moved to Colorado, the church did not have a parsonage for us to live in. Their former parsonage located next to the church had been remodeled into their church office called the Covenant House. The leadership of the church was hopeful that we would be able to qualify for a mortgage and buy our own home in the area. But I had taken a $10,000 reduction in salary by accepting the lead pastor position at the Arvada church and with my two older sons in college, I could not afford both a mortgage as well as the major costs of tuition, room and board for my college sons.

Throughout my years of ministry, God had always provided for us financially. I never once asked a church what my salary would be before accepting the call to a new church. I believed unquestioningly that if this was the church that God was calling me to serve, the Lord would provide for our needs. And He did. I was very prudent financially and always lived on the 10/10/80 principal in which I gave the first 10% of my income to God's work, saved the second 10% for investment in mutual funds and lived very carefully on the rest. It was out of that long-range financial commitment that I was able to save enough to pay the tuition/room and board for all three of my sons in a private Christian college and provide a nest-egg for our retirement. But my frugal financial plan did not allow for a major home mortgage at this point in my life. We needed a church parsonage to live in.

This situation called for prayer. Immediately a group of women, the church prayer warriors, began meeting for seasons of earnest prayer for a parsonage. They prayed specifically that the house next to the Covenant House would be put on the market and listed for sale. Within two weeks that specific house was put up for sale and the church, within a week, raised the money for its purchase. That June, we moved into that beautiful four-bedroom parsonage located right next to Covenant House at 8610 West 69th Place. It became known as the home that prayer purchased.

In 1998, with the relocation of the church and the sale of both the old church and the parsonage, I began looking for a fixer-upper house, near the new church site, that I could remodel and live in. I found an ideal house, located just three blocks from the new church, at 5392 Arbutus Street, that was definitely a fixer-upper and within my price range. Together with my son Luke who was living with me and serving at our church and Chris Williams who also lived in my home while serving as a youth intern, we began immediately remodeling the house. We gutted the kitchen and built a kitchen island, as well as finishing off the basement with six rooms, including a full bath and a study for me. It became my home for the next five years.

I love to preach. Throughout my years of ministry in Arvada, there were times that I had to preach to my congregation while going through my own personal tragedy, or in times of local or national crisis. In 1994, I was called upon to preach to our church just two weeks after my wife's death. It was Mother's Day and tears ran down my face as I spoke. There were times that I struggled to control my own feelings of sorrow as I preached at the funeral for a young mother who, in post-partum depression, had taken her own life, or the tragic funeral of a young, newly engaged couple in our church, who died together in a heartbreaking auto/truck accident. What is the word of hope and comfort that you bring to others, when your own life has just fallen apart?

And then there were the times of national crisis when, for example in 1999, the Columbine High School massacre left 13 students and a teacher dead in nearby Littleton Colorado. Or, when on September 11, 2001, America itself was under attack by Islamic Terrorists, who attacked the World Trade Center in New York and the Pentagon in Washington D. C., leaving thousands dead and injured. As hundreds of people overflowed our church for prayer and comfort on that day, what could a pastor say to bring hope when the very foundations of a nation are being destroyed?

What is the word of hope and comfort that you bring to others, when your own life has just fallen apart?

It's at crisis times like these that people are listening for a word from God like they've never listened before. It's a moment that calls for a pastoral response; a word from God that breaks through the gloom and offers an anchor in the storm. What a privilege it was, as a pastor, to stand before those great congregations and proclaim, "God is our refuge and strength, an ever-present help in trouble. Therefore, we will not fear, though the earth give way and the mountains fall into the heart of the sea." (Psalm 46: 1-2). I was always humbled to see the living God come to His people through His Word and see life and hope restored.

Following the dedication of our new church facilities, a flood of new people streamed into the church, with over 3000 people (both members and constituents) now calling Arvada Covenant Church their church home. In just two years we had more than doubled in size. This greatly challenged our staff, as I struggled to keep them working in harmony with each other and reconciled to one another. In addition, I became increasingly involved in cross-cultural pastoral ministries in Denver, serving on Governor Bill Owens prayer support team, working with Mile High Interchurch Ministries, supporting Heart to Honduras missions and the Promise Keepers organization. In addition, I was invited to minister to churches and Covenant missionaries in the Democratic Republic of Congo, Japan, Columbia, Mexico and Honduras. In my life, ministry was at a high point of activity, as well as excitement and exhaustion. Things would soon change.

In the spring of 2001, things changed radically and I was forced to slow down as I dealt with my own grave diagnosis of prostate cancer. Prostate cancer is the second leading cause of death among American men and with the death from cancer of my two much loved wives, I was devastated. With my PSA blood count rising monthly and following two biopsies, it was determined that my cancer was at stage II, which meant that while it was presently contained within my prostate gland, it was positioned near the edge of the gland and ready to move to stage III, spreading to other vital organs. I admit to moments of genuine fear. But, surrounded by the faithful prayers of God's people, I had a good measure of peace as I underwent radical prostatectomy surgery on May 17, 2001. I also was thankful for life, but recovery and strength came back slowly.

Months later, recognizing my continued exhaustion after surgery, I realized that I had to make some major decisions regarding the future of my ministry at this dynamic church in Arvada. One year after surgery, I submitted my resignation to the congregation and at 64 years-of-age, I announced my retirement. I would always be called to ministry, but now the form of that ministry would change greatly.

The congregation was so gracious in celebrating my nearly 14 years of ministry at Arvada Covenant Church. Over one thousand people filled the church for my farewell reception on Sunday evening, August 18,2002. The staff summarized my years of ministry at Arvada Church, reporting that I had delivered 1,621 sermons, attended 3,210 board or committee meetings, made 2,625 hospital or home visits, baptized 354 persons, dedicated 124 babies, conducted 116 weddings, confirmed 421 youth and conducted 184 funerals.

On that night, the congregation sang the hymn written by my friend Bryan Jeffery Leech, "*This is a time to remember the greatness of the Lord; He has so faithfully led us as promised in His Word; He has so bountifully given His grace like refreshing rain; He has so lovingly pardoned and made us whole again.*" Tears streamed down my face as I remembered how the Lord had so bountifully refreshed this precious congregation that it had been such a privilege for me to serve.

When I stood that night to respond to their loving words at my retirement, I became choked up at the sight of all the beautiful faces in this precious congregation. As I tried to regain my composure, I stood mute for several minutes as my mind raced back over the past 40 years that I had been privileged to touch the lives of thousands of individuals with the Word of God and loving pastoral care. Strangely, I thought that night of one young confirmation student named Evie who had probably been the most difficult student I ever had in 40 years of teaching classes and I shared her story. Evie was an angry and rebellious 13-year-old who often ran away from home and was defiantly dating older men. Her

"Evie, Jesus has a much better plan for your life."

parents were beside themselves with worry and unable to control their daughter's risky lifestyle choices. Many times, I would be called by her parents to come to their home and try to help counsel Evie. I remembered saying, "Evie, Jesus has a much better plan for your life than the one you have chosen." She would laugh at me. I thought I had totally failed her as a pastor. Twenty-one years later, I received an unexpected phone call from Evie saying, "Pastor, I don't know if you remember me, but you were my Confirmation teacher when I was a rebellious kid. My life has been a mess. One day, when I was homeless and nearly ready to give up, I stumbled into Pacific Garden Mission in Chicago with my three little children where I heard the same message of God's saving love that you taught me. I remembered that you always said, 'Evie, Jesus has a much better plan for your life.' I realized that you were right and I surrendered that night to Jesus. I never forgot the seeds of Jesus love that you sowed in my life as a young angry girl. I just wanted to call and say, Thank you Pastor." Tears streamed down my face as I remembered the privilege of investing my life in 40 years of Pastoral Ministry.

CHAPTER 10

FALLING IN LOVE AGAIN

When one loses a spouse it's a shattering experience. But men, especially have great difficulty grieving the death of a wife. Masculinity is equated with being strong and stoic, repressing your real feelings and throwing yourself immediately into your career, so as to distract yourself from painful grief. And I was no exception to that male pattern.

Following Clarice's death, I felt I had to put on a protective mask of strength and well-being to cover-up my painful feelings, especially for the sake of my three young sons. I was now their only parent and I felt

I put on a protective mask of strength.

I had to be strong to protect them from overwhelming grief. In addition to that, I was also a pastor and the church always looks to their pastor to be strong and comforting in times of crisis and death. And my personal time of crisis and grief was no exception. A man said to me at the time of Clarice's death, "I don't know how to help you in your loss, Pastor. You're the one we always look to for help

and comfort in our losses, so I figure you're ok." So, I put on a mask of strength believing that a grieving, struggling pastor would be an embarrassment to a church. But I wasn't OK.

The pain I went through in losing my wife was indescribable. I struggled silently with depression, withdrawal and I became a workaholic to avoid dealing with my grief. I was very lonely, but I felt I had no one, no "safe place," where I could honestly share my grief and mourn. Three years later, Sandra Joan Tengwall came into my life and I suddenly found the one who would listen to my grief and be the confidant that I could speak with openly about great loss.

SANDY, MY "SONG BIRD"

I had known Sandy for 20 years. She was part of our extended family as the double cousin of Howard Tengwall, my brother-in-law from my first marriage. But it was actually through her older sister Audrey Tengwall Skoglund, that her name came to my attention and, strange as it may seem, it was at the time of Clarice's funeral in Dassel, Minnesota. Audrey stood in line at the funeral waiting to express sympathy to me. At the end of our conversation, she said, almost as an afterthought, "You know my sister Sandy." I affirmed that I knew her through our extended family and that she was also one of our church's missionaries to Japan. Then Audrey said, with a smile and twinkle in her eye, "I think Sandy is about your age. You should get better acquainted with her." I didn't know how to respond to that obvious matchmaker's nudge, so I said nothing. But a thought had been planted in my mind that came back to me often in the next year, when struggling with loneliness and grief, "I should get to know Sandy better."

"You should get better acquainted with her."

Sandy was well-known in our family and the Covenant denomination as an outstanding soprano soloist. While completing her Master's Degree at Wheaton Graduate School, she had sung throughout the Midwest on concert tours and had even cut recordings of her singing with her dear Korean friend, Faith Kim. Now, as a missionary in Japan for the past 12 years, she had used her outstanding voice as a witness to the Gospel throughout that nation. As a matter of fact, early in her ministry she sang so much that she abused her voice and painful fibrous polyps (called "singer's nodes") formed on her vocal cords resulting in the necessity of her being silent for an entire year. She said, "The year of silence was a precious time of listening for the voice of God and learning to know Him intimately."

So, Sandy became my "Song Bird." The dictionary says that, "A Song Bird is a bird with a melodious song, that attracts other birds," and I was definitely attracted. At first, I thought that Sandy was out of my league. Her beautiful voice and her effective missionary service in Japan put her in another class altogether. There was no way that I thought she'd be interested in me. But it was the attraction of Sandy's beautiful voice that continually drew my heart toward hers. When I heard her sing at a mission conference I thought immediately of Audrey's advice, that I should get better acquainted with Sandy. So, in 1985 when I unexpectedly bumped into Sandy at the Covenant Annual Meeting in Minneapolis, I got up the nerve to ask her to have dinner with me. We talked for several hours about ministry and family and that's where I learned that she had returned from Japan to care for her sister Audrey, who was now dying from breast cancer. We understood each other's heart as we talked about living with painful grief. As a result of that dinner date in Minneapolis, we agreed to begin writing to each other as soon as she returned to Japan. Sometimes, when my busy schedule would prevent me from writing for a couple of weeks, she would write back saying, "Don't forget me here in Japan. I keep looking for your letters." It meant a lot to know that she enjoyed our correspondence, so I'd quickly get a letter off. I remember the first day that she started signing off her letters to me with the tender words, "Love Sandy." My heart raced with excitement and I began to express my growing feelings for her by closing my letters with, "Love Wes."

VISITING JAPAN - 1986

A year later, in the fall of 1986, missionary Marlan Enns and mission staff member, Ken Lundell, were leading a Covenant World Mission sponsored tour of our Covenant mission in Asia, including Japan. When I told Sandy that I was coming on that tour and I would be in Japan in October, she was so excited and said "We must spend some time together." I was certainly more than willing.

That fall mission tour of Christian work in South Korea, Taiwan, Hong Kong, Thailand, China and Japan, was more exciting and soul-stretching than I ever dreamt could be. I definitely thought the highlight of the trip came in Udon Thani, Thailand (about 350 miles NE of Bangkok) where we took a side trip to the village of Dong Samran, near the Mekong River. Here we worshipped with 400 Thai Christians and received Holy Communion, composed of red berry juice and balls of sticky rice. We sat together with our shoes off, on the dirt floor which they had covered with thatched mats, in their open-air church building that was located in-between pig pens and fish ponds. While it was a primitive setting, the Holy Spirit was powerfully present in their beautiful Thai style of worship, including expressive dance and native stringed instruments. At the close of the service the Thai Christians secured string around our wrists as they said, "I am bound to you in Christ." I was deeply moved. Tears rolled down my face as I shared communion with a Thai farmer and his young wife who was nursing their newborn baby. But the real highlight of this trip through Asia was still to come in Japan where Sandy waited for me.

After arriving in Tokyo, our group checked into the hotel where we were met by a number of Japanese church leaders and missionaries, including Sandy. I can still see Sandy's mischievous smile as she greeted me very formally in public, so as to give no hint that we'd been writing letters to each other for nearly a year. "Well, Pastor Swanson," she said, as she shook my hand very ceremoniously, "How good it is to meet you in Japan." I winked at her and she broke out in laughter.

We had a week of whirlwind tours to some of the most scenic and beautiful cities of Japan, including Tokyo, Kyoto, Nara, Kamakura, Miyajima Island and Hiroshima. We met many Japanese Christians at the Covenant Seminary in Tokyo, (the largest evangelical seminary in Japan) as well as at the Covenant's Odawara Christian Center. At the Meguro Covenant Church, we met Pastor Ishida who spoke to our group, saying, "Forty years-ago, we had a terrible war between our two nations. But today we stand together, united in love, all because of the forgiveness found in Jesus, our Lord and Savior."

It was at one of the worship services at the Odawara Christian Center that Sandy was asked to sing. I was again spellbound by her beautiful voice and her worshipful style of singing. She captured my heart that morning as she sang a Bill Gaither song which expressed so well my brokenness and grief, and I knew right then that I was really in love:

"Something beautiful, Something good
All my confusion He understood
All I had to offer Him was brokenness and strife
But He made something beautiful of my life."

On our second day in Japan, I had a tender reunion with Yumiko Kato and her husband Satoshi Kato-son. In the early 80's, Yumiko had lived in our home and served our church in Grand Rapids as the first missionary from Japan to America. Yumiko wept as she threw her arms around me in welcome to her tiny Japanese home. I think she wept both for joy at seeing me and also for Clarice, whom she had loved dearly. Then she served Sandy and me a delicious traditional Japanese meal of tempura with deep fried sea food and vegetables, all served in a beautiful presentation with Tentsuyo sauce.

Sandy and I spent so much time together throughout those scenic trips in Japan, that other group members were overheard complaining, "Why does the missionary always have to sit with Wes Swanson?" I guess our numerous and exclusive times together had blown our cover. But on one last trip, when Sandy was unable to go with me, I took a chance on Sandy's ring size and bought her a jade ring. That night I invited her out for dinner. I had walked many blocks alone in Tokyo, trying to find a little romantic restaurant, but I could only find a Shakey's Pizza Parlor – Japanese style. They served a strange blend of western pizza with raw sliced tomatoes, little corn cobs and seaweed on top. We talked together for hours and as we left I gave her the jade ring as a "promise ring," pledging that in my heart and prayers I would seek God's plan for our love and our lives. She accepted it affectionately, and it fit her perfectly. The next morning, our mission group left for our return trip to America.

Following our time together in Japan, Sandy and I wrote to each other weekly and occasionally spoke together through international long distance calls, which had to be short since they cost a lot. But it was always worth it to hear her voice. And as our love for one another grew we would talk about our future together and how open Sandy might be to leave missions in Japan, for a new mission in America.

A LONG DISTANCE WEDDING

Just before Christmas in December 1986, I made an international phone call to Sandy and asked her to marry me. Without hesitation,

she said "yes." We spent the next 30 minutes on the phone, expressing our love for one another and setting the date of our wedding for July 11, 1987. This would give us six months to make long distance wedding plans and notify our families and churches, both in Japan and America, of our engagement. Thirty years ago, that was an expensive phone call, costing me $25.66. But it was well worth it as it brought me instant benefits of joy and excitement in the knowledge that my love, my beautiful "Song Bird," would be with me soon.

Sandy and I announced our engagement in January 1987.

Immediately after the holidays, I called our church chairman,

Arv Anderson, and told him that I had some exciting news I wanted to share with him over lunch. He was all ears, as I told him of our engagement, but I asked him to keep it hush-hush until Sandy officially notified the Covenant Department of World Mission. In congratulating me, he jokingly said that he could keep this news confidential but he couldn't guarantee that his wife, Nancy, could keep it quiet very long without exploding.

After the first of the year, I notified the Grand Rapids congregation of our engagement. This began a period of further healing for our grief, as the congregation celebrated our engagement and officially adopted the following resolution at their annual meeting:

"Be it resolved: That the official minutes of January 19, 1987 Annual Meeting of this church, record the expression of joy and happiness of the Grand Rapids Evangelical Covenant Church regarding the engagement of our pastor, the Reverend Wesley Swanson to Miss Sandra Tengwall.
Further Resolved: That we joyfully support the Reverend Swanson and Miss Tengwall in their decision to be united in marriage. With love and prayers of thanksgiving, we encourage both of them as they continue in faithful service to God. We look forward, with great anticipation, to the years ahead as we all work together to share God's love and to further His Kingdom. May God richly bless you, Wes and Sandy.
Unanimously adopted,
January 19, 1987

Sandy left Japan in June and came to Grand Rapids where she was so graciously housed at the home of Eleanor Lego. The church went all-out with bridal showers, receptions and celebrations galore and we made final preparations for our wedding to be held at the Salem Covenant Church in New Brighton, Minnesota. We chose this church as it was near to her ailing father's residence, a nursing home in New Brighton.

With her brother, Arlan Tengwall walking Sandy down the aisle and the Executive Secretary of Covenant World Mission, Rev Ray Dahlberg performing the wedding ceremony, we were married with Sandy's three nieces and my three sons in the wedding party. Sandy's dear friends, Faith and David Kim sang a duet based on the Old Testament book of Ruth, "Whither thou goest, I will go" and Sandy sang a wonderful prayer solo by the Swedish pietist composer, Salma

Lagerstrom. It had been sung at my first wedding and was once again our wedding prayer:

"Savior in Thy Love abiding, keep us with Thy tender care;
Through Thy Spirit's gentle guiding, save us from each tempting snare.
On the unknown path before us, guide us with Thy mighty hand;
Should we faint and fall, restore us, through all perils help us stand."

My three sons stood up for us as Sandy and I were married on July 11, 1987.

The next day, we began our honeymoon trip by flying to Vermont for six glorious days at colonial inns in Dover and Grafton. We were so in love. But our honeymoon was cut short as I had a long-standing commitment to speak for a week at Pilgrim Pines Camp in New Hampshire. Sandy was so understanding, but pleased as well, that her missionary friends from Japan, Jay and Ellen Haworth, would also be at the camp. So, we made the best of our commitment to preach on our honeymoon and I felt a little like my parents who, 60 years before, had preached and ministered in little country churches on their honeymoon.

That fall, the Grand Rapids church blessed me again with a six-week sabbatical trip to the country of Israel. Three of those weeks we spent studying in the old city of Jerusalem at the American Institute of Holy Land Studies (now called Jerusalem University and College). The studies at the institute were exciting as each day we visited the Biblical sites that we were learning about. But our studies were also intense and exhausting as we hiked to many ancient sites, including the quarter-mile Snake Path to Masada, crawling into the Qumran Caves of the Dead Sea Scrolls, doing archaeological digs at the site of Solomon's summer palace in Gaza, swimming in both the Sea of Galilee and the Dead Sea and riding horseback into the ancient Nabatean capitol of Petra in Jordan. Sandy said jokingly, "We ran, where Jesus walked."

In addition to our sabbatical study time, Sandy and I had an extension of our honeymoon by sharing three amazing weeks of personal travel in Israel. This included an interesting stay at a Kibbutz in Shefayim, an invitation to a Bar Mitzvah ceremony and dinner in the home of a very kind Jewish family that we met at the market in Netanya, and a fantastic meal at a Palestinian home in the Muslim Quarter of the old city of Jerusalem. This meal had been pre-arranged by Art and Jean Anderson of our Grand Rapids Church, as they had housed a young Arab college student who lived with them in Michigan throughout his college study and whose family lived in old Jerusalem.

We got lost, trying to find the family home in the winding streets of the Muslim Quarter of Jerusalem, but we were treated like royalty when we finally found their house and all the relatives who had crowded into their small living- room to meet the Americans who had helped house their son in America. We were greeted with numerous hugs and kisses on each side of our face. In typical Middle Eastern hospitality, they rolled out a multi-course meal that included huge platters of rice and meats in delicious sauces, flavored rice wrapped in grape leaves, pita bread that we filled with salad, plus selections of olives, dates and various nuts, as well as sweets served with endless cups of Arabic coffee or soft drinks. We sat at this abundant table of fellowship all day, as they asked numerous questions about our life, family and our faith. It reminded me of the intimate fellowship that Jesus described in Revelation 3:20, "I stand at the door and knock. If anyone hears my voice and opens the door, I will come in and eat with him, and he with me."

One highlight of our Sabbatical travel came on a four-day trip that we took from Tel Aviv to Cairo, Egypt. Here we were intrigued by the wonders of the Museum of Egyptian Antiquities, shopping at the Kahn Al-Khalili Bazaar, climbing high inside the great pyramid at Giza, riding camels to the Great Sphinx and visiting the Alabaster Mosque in Cairo.

The spiritual high point of our Cairo trip came on Sunday, October 25 when we took a taxi from our hotel to the nearby St. Andrews United Church, an English-speaking church in downtown Cairo. When we walked into the large patio entrance, we found it filled with dozens of refugees from war-torn Eritrea, who had fled to Cairo from the war with Ethiopia. We had a personal interest in the Eritrean people as our Grand Rapids church had sponsored a dozen refugee families from Eritrea who had been placed in our city. It was a thrill to meet and speak with so many of these refugees in Cairo who spoke perfect English.

When the worship service started, we noted that the bulletin stated that the Eritrean choir would be singing that Sunday. We were so excited. But when it came time for the choir to sing, only one young man stood up to sing a song whose melody I immediately recognized. It was written by Nels Frykman, the American Swedish Pietist, and it came from our Mission Covenant revival history. The young man sang fervently in the Tigrinya language:

"I have a friend who loveth me, He gave His life on Calvary;
Upon the cross my sins He bore, and I am saved forever-more.
O hallelujah, He's my friend! He guides me to the journey's end;
He walks beside me all the way and will bestow a crown some day."

When the service was over, I made a beeline for that young man and asked him where he had learned that song. He replied that it was the Swedish Mission Friend missionaries who brought the gospel of salvation by grace, through faith in Christ, to Ethiopia over 75 years ago. He added that their favorite songs in the churches of Eritrea were all the Swedish revival songs like, "Day by Day and With Each Passing Moment" and "Children of the Heavenly Father," both written by the Swedish hymn writer, Lina Sandell. Here I was, 6000 miles from home and so humbled to discover in Cairo, Egypt brothers and sisters in Christ from Eritrea and Ethiopia who had come to faith in Jesus, the Messiah, through the Covenant worldwide witness.

Following our sabbatical travels, I was excited to get back to our home and ministry in Grand Rapids. But it was not as exciting for Sandy. After having lived outside of America for over a decade and having served twelve years as a missionary to Japan, it was an especially challenging time of adjustment for her. In those years of missionary service, Sandy had adapted very well to the Japanese language, Japanese culture and missionary lifestyle. She had, in many ways, adopted a mixture of both an American and a Japanese mindset. To be sure, there had been many cultural frustrations and obstacles for her in those 12 years in Japan. But there had also been many rewards, in the deep friendship she had formed with the Japanese people, the intimate fellowship of the church in Japan and the missionary staff who had become like family. Suddenly, she found herself uprooted from her missionary role with her Japanese friends and abruptly was now an American pastor's wife with three step-sons.

Not only was Sandy going through a tough transition to American culture, she was also confused about her role in the American church. In a country where only one percent of the Japanese population are Christian, she had become accustomed to very small and intimate Japanese congregations of less than 30 members. Now she found herself worshipping in a well-organized American church of 800 each Sunday, which left her confused as to her role and feeling out of the loop.

Early on, we sought out professional counseling for Sandy and while this was somewhat helpful, I could see that we both needed a fresh start in a new location where Sandy could once again find her calling and role in ministry. So, a year later, we saw the Lord's hand guiding us in our future ministry together, when after speaking at a mission conference in Colorado, the Lord clearly called us to a new church in Arvada, Colorado. I submitted my resignation to the Grand Rapids church in the early spring of 1989 and we began our new ministry at the Arvada Covenant Church on June 25, of that year.

Moving to this new church was especially difficult for me. The Grand Rapids church had been such a faithful support throughout my ministry, especially at the time of my grief in the loss of Clarice and then in my remarriage to Sandy. I even told the leadership that I would give back the car that they'd given us in celebration of our marriage, just two years before. I felt embarrassed to be leaving so soon after they had so beautifully affirmed and celebrated our marriage. And it was also a very tough time for Luke to be leaving all his friends and relocating to a new state and a new school, in his junior year of high school. But, the move for Sandy was like a breath of fresh air. In the Arvada church, she poured herself into the church's music ministry, was involved on the mission committee, became a Mentor Mom in the church MOP's program (Mothers of Pre-schoolers) and began teaching ESL classes as well as extensively teaching about Japanese Culture in numerous Denver area public schools and even in a private Jewish girl's school. She had recovered her role in ministry and was elated to be back in-the-groove again.

The move for Sandy was like a breath of fresh air.

In the spring of 1990 we ministered together in Mexico and then in the late summer we made a return trip to Japan. We preached together for a month in seven Japanese Covenant Churches and when I returned to the states on September 4, Sandy stayed for a second month of ministry and renewed fellowship with Japanese friends. When Sandy returned to Colorado, at the end of September, she was like a new person, happy to be back in America again. Sandy had seen that her Japanese friends and the Covenant Mission had successfully moved on without her and so she was content to leave Japan and happy to be back to her new mission in America. Through the next three years our lives were rich in love and vibrant in ministry, as we shared in an increasingly healthy and growing church.

A SHOCKING DIAGNOSIS

In the spring of 1993, while attending a meeting of our Midwest Covenant Conference in Salina, Kansas Sandy became alarmed over feelings of nausea and a sudden drastic change in her bowel habits. We left the conference immediately and returned to Denver, where our doctor ordered a colonoscopy. Generally, there would be a month wait for that exam, so we were amazed to get one scheduled for the very next day. Following the exam, the medical technician met with us and said there was a very large tumor in Sandy's colon and that after 24 years of screening for colorectal cancer, his professional opinion was that it was probably malignant.

We were numbed by this news and uncertain as to what to do. She had absolutely no symptoms until earlier that week. And now our life was suddenly turned upside-down. At the urging of our doctor, we met that same afternoon with Dr. Nelson Mozia, a gastroenterologist, who immediately scheduled colon surgery in two days.

The surgery was scheduled for 9:00 am on May 14, 1993 at Lutheran Medical Center in Wheat Ridge. At noon, Dr. Mozia came out to the waiting area and said, "I'm very sorry Pastor, I have some bad news concerning your wife's surgery. The cancer in her colon had already spread to other vital organs and her liver was entirely engulfed by cancer. Unfortunately, she has only a few months to live."

How could this be happening again?

I was in complete shock. We hadn't even been married for six years and now I'm hearing this devastating diagnosis of terminal cancer again. My mind raced back to the terrible diagnosis of my wife Clarice's terminal brain cancer. "No! No! No!", I gasped, "This can't be." How could this be happening again? "Oh, not my dear Sandy, my love. Oh God, help us," I cried.

I had to pull myself together, as this shocking news was complicated by the fact that I was committed that day to conduct a 2:00 pm funeral service at church for Bill Cobb, a prominent member of our church. Leaving Sandy in the recovery room, I drove my car to church and with all the windows rolled up, I yelled at the top of my lungs, "God, help me, I'm sinking." It was perhaps the darkest time in my life. I was numb with a broken heart as I read aloud at the funeral service Jesus' words of hope from John 11:25-26, "Jesus said to her, 'I am the resurrection and the life. He who believes in me will live, even though he dies; and whoever lives and believes in me will never die. Do you believe this?" I was stricken, but still I haltingly whispered to myself, "Yes, I do believe this. Even if everything is taken from me, even if Sandy is taken or you take my own life, I will still believe this." Tears ran down my face through the remainder of the service as I surrendered my entire life.

When I returned to the hospital following Bill's funeral, Sandy's room, as well as the hallway and the waiting area, were all filled with our church members who were there to support us. Many were clustered in small groups praying for us. The community of faith was surrounding us, like comforting angels, in this dark hour. I was so deeply grateful for this blessed company of faith that encircled us. We were not alone. I didn't want to cry publicly, but seeing all those dear people and seeing Sandy looking so ill and fragile in the hospital bed, the tears just streamed down my face. I shot a prayer upwards, like an arrow, "Oh God, you already know what we need, in your mercy, help us, oh help us." There was a sense in which my tears too were a form of prayer. And combined with the earnest prayers of God's people, the light of God's peace began to break through. How else do I understand this deep peace in life's darkest hour? Jesus promised, "Peace I leave with you; my peace I give to you, I do not give to you as the world gives. Do not let you heart be troubled and do not be afraid," John 14:27.

Within a week, we took Sandy home. But unfortunately, the wound did not heal, as a staph infection had invaded the surgical site as well as the area of the reconnected colon. I had to quickly learn how to be Sandy's home-nurse; daily cleaning and repacking the surgical site, as well as giving her daily injections of antibiotic medication to fight the infection. We were both physically and emotionally exhausted, but we claimed Psalm 73:26, "My heart and my flesh may fail, but God is the strength of my heart and my portion forever."

It took about a month for the wound to slowly heal and the infection to clear-up. Then we began the next phase of cancer treatment as we were introduced to Dr. Jennifer Caskey, our medical oncologist, who began weekly treatments of chemotherapy. She was a wonderful woman and a compassionate Oncologist. Just being in her office was calming and reassuring. I would bring a book with me to each treatment and as Sandy slept throughout the treatment, I would read and pray. I thanked God for the mind and skills that He had given to our doctors as well as the amazing gifts of God's creation that science harvests to treat disease. Sometimes as I prayed, I would visualize the chemo, this gift from our God, gobbling-up the cancer cells in Sandy's body and it would give me peace. Ultimately, all healing comes from God and His creation, "And the leaves of the tree are for the healing of the nations," Revelation 22:2.

The week we took Sandy home from the hospital, our daily inspirational reading said, "If God is going to do something wonderful, He starts with a problem. If God is going to do something spectacular, He starts with an impossibility." And so, after five months of chemotherapy, God did something spectacular and Sandy was declared *in complete remission* of cancer.

That November, at the church Thanksgiving service, we stood together as a couple and gave public thanksgiving for God's healing work in Sandy's life and for answering the prayers of our congregation. We read Psalm 107:2, "Give thanks to the Lord, for He is good; His love endures forever. Let the redeemed of the Lord say this – those he redeemed from the hand of the foe."

A medical doctor in our congregation wrote, "We can be sure that the healing which has come to Sandy is from God. Regression of liver metastasis in that type of tumor is almost never seen. There are many things that we as Physicians cannot do, but the power of God is unlimited." Those were good words. And they reminded us that each day was a gift and however long this remission lasted, it was a powerful gift from God. So, we lived one day at a time, prayerfully and gratefully.

On Valentine's Day 1994, we shared our traditional Chinese meal from Panda Express, sitting on the floor, dressed in our Kimonos, reclining beside our low coffee table, eating Japanese style. By this time, Sandy had lost all of her hair due to chemotherapy treatment. I wrote on my Valentine card, "You are more beautiful and precious to me with each passing day. And then I quoted from the Song of Solomon, "How beautiful you are my darling! Oh, how beautiful! Your eyes are doves." And Sandy, in her card to me said,

"My wonderful Wes, you are my special Valentine. How glad I am that you are mine and I am yours. Your love and patience these months are your special gift to me. I love you more than ever and

look forward to many more Valentine Days with you. All my love, Sandy." Neither of us could have known this was to be our last Valentine meal together.

On March 28, we had our regular appointment with our oncologist, Dr. Caskey. She gave us the results of Sandy's latest x-ray and blood work. In the last weeks, we had seen troubling signs in Sandy's health. She was weak and nauseous and had no appetite. Now we sat quietly and waiting in the doctor's office as she studied the x-ray. We held hands as we waited – mine were sweaty and Sandy's were cold. I was silently praying the ancient prayer of the Eastern Church, "Oh Lord Jesus Christ, Son of God, have mercy on me, a sinner." I prayed it over and over. It gave me peace. Sandy too was praying.

Finally, Dr. Caskey said, "I'm very sorry, but there's been a recurrence of the cancer and it's very aggressive.

We asked, "What about more chemo treatment?" and "What's the prognosis?"

She said, "At this point, the cancer has become resistant to the treatment and has spread to the lungs. There are no further treatments that we can offer and Sandy has very little time left."

Sandy was like a superwoman. She thanked the doctor for all she had done and hugged her and all the staff warmly. Sandy's sister Bonnie was with us from Minneapolis and heard the doctor's verdict. She was very quiet as we drove home and put Sandy to bed. I wrote in my journal:

> *"People react so differently to a terminal diagnosis. One family in our church left our congregation saying they could not remain in a church where the pastor's wife is being disciplined by God with cancer. They had a twisted religion in which God was a terrible judge who zapped imperfect people with cancer. They said that if we were really walking faithfully with the Lord, He would definitely answer the prayers of faithful people and bring healing to her. So, they left. But Sandy had such a totally different response saying, "I know my loving Lord is absolutely trustworthy so either way I win. Either He will heal me miraculously now, or He will heal me in glory. Either way I win!"*

The next Sunday, April 3, was Easter Sunday. Our kids, Paul, Lyna and Luke surprised us by coming home from Chicago to join Mark, who lived in Denver, in a wonderful family reunion over the holiday weekend. I knew they realized that time was short and they had come to say a tearful goodbye to their step-mother. Tears were brimming in everyone's eyes as Luke gave Sandy a beautiful card that spoke for them all;

> *"Dear Sandy, you are such an inspiration to me. Whenever I feel down I think of you and your spirit lifts me. You have meant so much to our family and I have confidence that God will allow you to continue to bless us. Thanks so much for the endless support that you and Dad give me. I pray for you daily. I love you, Luke."*

At the Easter service that Sunday, two men from the choir come down at the close of the service and helped Sandy walk up the chancel steps, so she could join the choir in singing the glorious "Hallelujah" chorus from George Frideric Handel's Messiah. Sandy looked so weak and frail, but she insisted that she needed to join our Easter choir as it was her rehearsal for the heavenly chorus she would soon join. The congregation was deeply moved by her painful effort to sing.

The next week Sandy was exhausted and slept much of the time. But she was also preparing me and others to say goodbye. On Wednesday of that week she, with great difficulty, had me help her go to the church to attend her last meeting of the MOPS women. She said, "I just need to say goodbye to my girls." On another day that week, she told a visiting friend, "I feel so bad for my dear Wes, that he has had to go through this sorrow twice." I would find little yellow sticky notes posted on my bedside Bible, written to help me accept that the end was near. One note was from Ecclesiastes 3:1-2, "There is a time for everything and a season for every activity under heaven: a time to be born and a time to die." On another sticky note was a verse from II Thessalonians 3:3, "But the Lord is faithful, and He will strengthen and protect you from the evil one." She closed all her notes to me saying, "Wes I love you so much." I was grief-stricken, but deeply moved and comforted that my precious wife, in the dire weakness of her last days, was concerned about me, praying for me, seeking to minister to me, helping me to let go. Oh, my love.

By the next Sunday, Sandy was getting weaker and weaker. Her brother and sister-in-law, Arlan and Dee Tengwall, together with her sister, Bonnie Crosby, all came that week to stay with us. Out-of-town friends, get-well cards and flowers flooded our home, including special visits from Ray and Nancy Dahlberg, her old boss at the Department of Covenant World Mission as well as her dear missionary friends from Japan, Leonard and Grace Peterson. By this time, Sandy couldn't even open her eyes and she had no strength to speak. An encouraging note to Sandy from one of our church members, caught the sentiment of so many, *"Dear Sandy, you are so very dear to our hearts. I'm so thankful for all you have taught us. I can still hear you singing, 'The King is Coming.' Thank you for showing me what it means to be a faithful servant of Jesus Christ."*

On Tuesday, April 12, our doctor informed us that Sandy had less than 24 hours to live. It was such *somber* and *stunning* news from her doctor. I felt almost paralyzed by this shocking turn of events. How could this be? My heart was physically hurting inside of me, like it's broken. I knelt beside her bed and told her that the doctor said there was very little time left for her here with us. I said, "It's likely that tonight you'll go to glory and be with the Lord." Though she hadn't been able to speak for several days, from some reservoir of strength, deep within her soul, she broke through the silence and spoke out loudly, "Yes, GLORY, I'm going to glory today." Like a little, six-year-old girl who was totally excited to go to her best friend's birthday party, Sandy *couldn't wait* for her first day in heaven to begin. I knelt beside her bed and wept. Oh, my wife, my love.

By Wednesday, April 13, we had moved Sandy into a hospital bed in Mark's former bedroom and we held vigil around her continually. We were all sitting beside her bed, holding her hands and telling her we loved her. I had some soft recorded music playing, mostly hymns that she loved and every-so-often we would all join in singing along with the hymns. Sandy was unresponsive and her breathing was very labored. The Hospice nurse arranged for oxygen to be administered, but it didn't seem to help her. She struggled for each breath. The cancer had filled her lungs.

I believed that she saw what we didn't see, that the King of Kings, Jesus himself, had entered the room.

Through that long night and into the wee hours of the next morning, it became sheer agony for all of us to watch her gasp for every breath. Bonnie cried out, "Oh God, take her home." And then suddenly, around 5:00 am on April 14, Sandy opened her eyes and smiled at us all. A big beautiful smile. Her breathing became as normal and natural as anyone's breathing. She looked toward our windows, to the mountains in the west and pointed toward something or someone that she saw. She burst into an enormous smile. I believed that she saw what we didn't see, that the King of Kings, Jesus himself, had entered the room. And He said, "Sandy, my daughter, it's time to come home with me." Moments later she closed her eyes, took her last breath and went home to be with her Lord. "…Away from the body and at home with the Lord." (II Corinthians 5:8)

The next Sunday afternoon, over 800 people filled our church and overflowed into the narthex and fellowship hall for Sandy's memorial service. Our conference superintendent, Wesley Olson, brought a powerful message and a massed choir sang Handel's "Hallelujah" chorus, the one Sandy had sung with them just two weeks before. As they sang, we caught a little bit of the glory that Sandy now experienced. Shivers swept down my back as the great choir soared in singing, "... *King of Kings and Lord of Lords and He shall reign forever and ever.*" Amen.

The boys and I left the next day and flew to Minnesota for a funeral service and burial for Sandy at her home church, Salem Mission Covenant Church in Pennock, Minnesota. Our friend, Ray Dahlberg, who was Sandy's pastor/mentor when she was a Director of Christian Education in Portland, Oregon was the preacher of God's healing word. We sang one of Sandy's favorite hymns by Fanny Crosby. It was her testimony:

"Blessed assurance, Jesus is mine! O What a foretaste of glory divine!
Heir of salvation, purchase of God,
born of His Spirit, washed in His blood.
This is my story, this is my song, praising my Savior all the day long;
This is my story, this is my song, praising my Savior all the day long."

THE DARK DAYS OF LOSS

I was first widowed at age 46 and now I was left alone again at age 55. What are the odds that one man would be plunged into the devastating loss of two much loved wives from cancer, before he finishes his 55th year? Twice in a lifetime seemed like grief overload. I wondered if I would ever really recover from grief, or would I just learn to live with the pain?

Some people thought that I would be angry with God and leave the ministry, even rejecting my faith. What does a pastor do with his broken heart? Where do people of faith go when bad things happen? How does a pastor survive when all the props are kicked out from under him as for the second time in ten years he lays his wife in a grave? Do you reject your faith? Do you abandon your call to ministry? Is that your only recourse?

When my faith is shaken and I sink into dark doubts, I have to go back to the basic foundations of life and faith. I don't know why bad things happen. Why the innocent and the godly suffer is such a mystery to me. There is so much that I don't understand about injustice and inhumanity and suffering. I cry out with Jesus, "My God WHY?" But there are some things, some basic things, *that I do understand* and I go back again and again to the basics of my faith:

- *I understand* that everything in the cosmos had a starting point at some time. With explosive force the universe came into being at a point in time.
- *I understand* that creation is full of beauty and design and laws that govern its life. I do understand that this did not happen by accident or random chance. Life testifies to a designer behind the beginning of all things.
- *I understand* that something like a snowflake, a flower, or a living cell cannot come from nothing. In the book of Hebrews 3:4, the writer says, "For every house is built by someone, but God is the builder of everything." It's the difference between having a gigantic pile of lumber, pipes, electrical wire and bricks all lying in a jumbled heap on the ground and a beautifully constructed home with all the plumbing, wiring and heating ducts perfectly in place. That perfect house did not construct itself from that jumbled pile of material. It took an architect, a builder and carpenters to build that beautiful house. "Every house was built by someone." Even so, I understand that the eternal God is the master designer, the builder of life and the universe. And the evidence of His master design is everywhere. (Psalm 19).

I hold onto what I learned in the sunshine in the dark night of my sorrow.

- *I understand* that the eternal creator God has reached out to Planet Earth in Jesus the Messiah with redeeming love, saving grace and eternal hope (Galatians 4:4-7). By faith, I make the choice to accept this evidence of God, even in the harshest storms of life. I hold on to these bed-rocks of faith with all the strength that my faith can muster. What I learned in the sunshine I hold onto in the dark night of my sorrow and it gives me peace. This is what *I do understand* and it gives me hope.

I held unto these basics of faith in the times of raging storms in my life. So actually, my faith grew deeper and stronger in this painful time. Without my faith in God and His promises I would be completely overwhelmed by grief and without hope. And I can't survive without hope. The Bible says, "And hope does not disappoint us, because God has poured out His love into our hearts by the Holy Spirit, whom He has given us," (Romans 5:5). My grief drove me to lean, ever more deeply, on the basics of my faith and on my Good Shepherd and His promise to lead me safely through "...the valley of the shadow of death," (Psalm 23:4). And since "faith comes from hearing...the Word of Christ" (Romans 10:17), I dug deeper into God's Word and fed my grieving heart on His nourishing spiritual food.

Surprisingly, my call to ministry became even more important in this time of painful loss, as I found that God prefers broken vessels to help mend other broken lives. The missionary D.T. Niles once said that a preacher "is just one beggar telling another beggar where to find bread." I had indeed been broken by sorrow, but I was not destroyed. The harsh lessons in life served to make me stronger in my calling to the ministry and made me point even more urgently to the only source of *eternal bread*. Jesus said, "I am the bread of life...come down from heaven, which a man may eat and not die," (John 6:48 & 50). People in my congregation listened, as never before, to this broken beggar tell of this bread of life. My friend Lee Snyder called me the "Thornbird Preacher," as one with a pierced heart who preached and sang the song of redemption like never before.

Someone said that "what defines us is how we rise after falling." And I rose, in my grief, to realize that I am such a blessed man. I began to see that the life and love I had shared with Clarice and Sandy was a gift, a beautiful gift from God. I had been so blessed to receive that gift from my Heavenly Father, but I didn't deserve that gift and I didn't own that gift or control its lifespan. We just were blessed to share that gift of love and life for a little while. And when the gift was withdrawn, I chose not to turn with bitterness at the Giver, but rather with great thanks to the Giver for the blessing of having been chosen to love and care for these two beautiful wives, for a little while. The choice for all of us is clear. We can rise from tragedy to be either bitter or blessed. I chose to be blessed.

Grief is one of life's most difficult journeys and everyone works through these stresses differently. You'd think that I would have learned some better ways of coping with grief this second time around, but I didn't. Maybe my personality is genetically programed to withdraw socially when overwhelmed by grief and to stay extremely busy so as to avoid thinking about my grief. It was not just to avoid thinking about grief, but mainly to avoid slipping into depression. For me, it's a slippery slope from grief to self-pity to depression. And I can't afford to wallow in that dark swamp of depression. Keeping busy wasn't the best way of dealing with grief, but I guess it's my way. It would have been better to seek out a Christian counselor, but I didn't and that decision delayed my grief recovery.

For the next eight years after Sandy's death, I poured myself into a wide range of busy activities, designed in part to avoid thinking about my grief. In the fall of 1994 I helped to facilitate the organization of our new daughter church in Golden, Colorado. In 1995 I was the preacher of the ordination message at the national Covenant Ordination Service held in Cincinnati, Ohio. From 1996 to 1999, I worked tirelessly on the land search, fundraising and construction of our new 55,000 square foot church building. It was also at this time that I bought a fixer-upper house, located just three blocks from the new church and I worked on my days off and late each evening on completely remodeling my new home.

In 1996, I was asked by the Covenant denomination to travel for three weeks to the Democratic Republic of the Congo, speaking in the CEUM (Covenant Churches of Congo), and bringing a series of messages to the Covenant missionary retreat held in Karawa, Congo. Here the Covenant has over 200,000 members in the CEUM churches and maintains five hospitals and 93 local clinics with over 80,000 students in their Christian schools.

While in Congo, I was privileged to visit our churches in Gemena on the day that the entire region gathered to dedicate the M'baka Bible, the first complete translation of the Bible, both the Old and New Testament, into the Ngbaka language. About 2,000 people from all over northwest Congo and the Central African Republic had gathered for this dedication, including representatives from Protestant, Roman Catholic and even Muslim religious groups. It was being celebrated by everyone like a national day of independence.

The entire assembly exploded with cheering and dancing and hugging and crying.

The celebration started out very formal and somber, with the Bibles being brought into this great assembly by young Congolese women, all dressed in white and carrying in the Bibles on silver trays. It was like a holy-hush swept over this great assembly of people as the women carrying in the Bibles walked slowly into the church, with a hesitation step, that created a suspenseful anticipation of the arrival of God's Word in their very own language.

After the Bibles had been carried to the front of the church, Pastor Duale Lengena, a leader of the CEUM, held two of the Bibles up, high above his head, and shouted, "THE WORD OF GOD!" With that triumphant announcement, the entire assembly exploded with cheering and dancing and hugging and crying. Older ladies, called "the Dancing Ladies," entered from the back of the church, shouting and dancing to drum beat. The celebration went on for hours with speeches and music and food. It was such a privilege to be in attendance on that historic day and to see how excited the M'baka people were to receive the Word of God in their own language.

Upon my return to the states, I continued my exhaustive schedule as I moved my mom to Colorado in 1998 so I could help care for her at her advanced age of 92; I organized the dedication of our new church facility in May 1999; I led mission/preaching trips to the countries of Columbia and Honduras, while continuing to lead our growing church and preach at numerous Covenant camps and retreats. Sometimes I would admit to myself that I was burning the candle at both ends, but I felt I was up to the task and could handle the stress.

Then suddenly, in the spring of 2001, I was stopped in my tracks with a diagnosis of prostate cancer. I was devastated with this diagnosis. After losing two precious wives from cancer, I struggled to grasp that now it had come to me. So, because of the aggressive stage of my cancer and the fact that it was about to spread to other vital organs, I submitted to radical prostatectomy surgery. Amazingly, I have remained cancer free following my surgery. But my recovery from surgery was slow and the strength needed for ministry did not return.

One year after surgery, I realized that I would probably never regain the strength necessary for continued ministry at this dynamic and growing church. It was a very difficult time in my life. I think I was actually struggling with burnout, complicated by my lack of energy following surgery and my unhealthy grief avoidance. The church had grown rapidly and I had not recovered the physical energy or emotional resources to deal with all that growth and the related stresses. Wracked by worry, I would wake up exhausted in the morning and feel tired all day. I felt frustrated with the petty quibbling of some staff members and I no longer had the patience to deal with these stresses or the passion for my work. So, in the spring of 2002, I made the hard decision to resign as Lead Pastor and wrote to the church family on May 28, saying:

"I am writing to inform you that I have submitted my resignation as the pastor of Arvada Covenant Church, effective September 1, 2002.... It was especially following cancer surgery, last year, that I realized it is time to consider retirement. It's hard for me to say goodbye to you. You have been a wonderful congregation to serve these past thirteen and one half years.

How can I ever express how much you have meant to me personally in my time of grief and loss. You truly have the gift of encouragement! But we have stepped out in faith together and built God's Kingdom. Your vibrant faith has inspired me, more often that I could hope to inspire yours. Thank you for being you!"

I truly loved this congregation. For 40 years of pastoral ministry, I held fast to the belief that when a pastor truly loves his people and longs to see lives transformed by the grace of God in Christ, there will be growth and progress and we will bear fruit. The Arvada church was a testimony to that transforming power of love and grace.

I have been so privileged these past 40 years to be just a broken man, pointing broken people and broken churches to Jesus, the healer of broken hearts.

Whatever I would do in the future, I would do it as a single man.

Following a great retirement celebration of my 40 years of pastoral ministry (of which nearly 14 years were invested at Arvada Covenant Church), I was, all of a sudden, no longer the pastor of a local church, and my future life and ministry was undefined as I eased into retirement. I thought, perhaps I'll travel in retirement. Perhaps I'II focus on my grandchildren. Perhaps I'll do interim ministry or volunteer missionary service. A two-week mission/evangelistic trip to Germany had whet my appetite for more international ministry, but I just didn't have the energy now to take on a new challenge. Whatever I would do in the future, one thing was certain, I would do it as a single man.

THE WALLS AROUND MY HEART

After Sandy's death, I built huge walls around my heart to protect myself from the risk of another heartbreak. I'd had my heart broken twice by the time I was 55 years old. So, for the next eight years I closed my heart to any further relationships in order to protect myself from getting hurt again.

There were people, especially women, who tried to break down my protective walls by phoning me or writing letters to me expressing their openness to being my "best friend," "a weekly dinner companion," or as one wrote, "Hey, cowboy, this cowgirl is looking for a date for next Saturday night. How about square dancing with me?" One lady, who I felt was actually stalking me, made an appointment with me at the church office and when I asked about the nature of her visit, she said, "I wanted to discuss when we should set the date."

"What date?" I said.

"God had revealed to her," she explained, "that we should be married and she wondered when we should set the date?"

I was utterly shocked and said, "God had definitely not revealed that to me and I would appreciate it if she would never raise the subject again."

I ran the other direction from all those invitations and built the walls around my heart even higher. I wanted to be certain that I was safe from the risk of more heartbreak and as a pastor I didn't want even the hint of impropriety to cloud my closing years of ministry. So, I focused all my energy on keeping my guard up and building my protective walls.

SURPRISED BY THE JOY OF CAROLYN

Around the first week of January, 2002 I was surprised to receive a letter from Carolyn Aley Larson, a college friend from way back in the early 60's that I had not seen in 40 years. Following her graduation from North Park College, Carolyn had married a fellow North Parker, David Larson and they had lived for 34 years on a farm near Princeton, Illinois. David was a farm manager and a pioneer in organic natural fertilizers. But everything changed suddenly for Carolyn, when in 1996 David died suddenly from a heart condition. One minute he was alive and talking with her and the next minute he was gone. It was an unbelievably shocking death and Carolyn and her family struggled with overwhelming grief.

I actually knew David better in college than I knew Carolyn, as he and I lived in the same campus dormitory and at one time we had been in a dorm Bible study together. While Carolyn and I knew each other casually, we had never dated in college or had any contact with each other over the 40 years following our graduation.

"Now there is a wonderful woman that I would like to get to know better."

In her letter to me, Carolyn wrote about her family, her church and her travels following David's death. She mentioned that she had recently visited with Ruthie Olson Fredrickson, my sister-in-law from my first marriage, who now lived in Edina, Minnesota and she also updated me on a number of mutual friends from our college years.

I remember how pleased I was to get Carolyn's letter. Everyone loved Carolyn in our college years together. She had been our Homecoming Queen in 1958 and voted "Most Ideal North Parker" in 1959. She was a 'social butterfly' on campus and very active in student government as well as in the college choir. But I also remembered that she was known on campus as a deeply committed Christian and I immediately thought to myself, "Now there is a wonderful woman that I would like to get to know better."

Following Dave's death, Carolyn sold their home near Princeton, Illinois and moved to Williams Bay, Wisconsin to be near her son, J. D. Larson and his family where he worked as program director of Covenant Harbor Bible Camp. While supporting her son's work at the camp and enjoying her two grandsons, Carolyn started hearing my name mentioned a number of times by mutual friends.

The first person to mention my name to Carolyn was my sister-in-law Ruthie Olson Fredrickson, whose husband Earl was related to Carolyn's side of the family. While visiting the Fredrickson's in Minnesota, Ruthie said to Carolyn, "I bet you know my brother-in-law from my first marriage?"

Carolyn said, "Who would that be?"

She said, "Wes Swanson," and then she hesitated for a moment before saying, "I think you two would be good together. But I don't know if he's interested in a relationship at this time. I'll pray about it."

Carolyn didn't know how to respond to that surprising conversation with Ruthie, so she said nothing. But in the next weeks, she had four other friends who unexpectedly mentioned my name to her. Two of these friends said that she should definitely write to me. But Carolyn shrugged off their suggestion saying, "women my age would never write to a man they hadn't seen in 40 years. I could never do that! It's just not proper!"

But after these repeated suggestions from friends, a seed had been planted in her mind and she began praying about writing a letter to me. One night she couldn't sleep so she got up, turned on her fireplace and started writing to me. After many drafts of possible letters, written on large legal-size yellow notepad paper, she felt that she had finally written an acceptable letter. But she only had frilly, girly stationary at home so she went first thing that morning to Walmart to get some plain paper. When she got home she realized that she didn't even have my full address in Colorado. So, on the sly, she called Doug Johnson, her pastor in Illinois and asked him to look up my name and address in the roster of Covenant pastors. She felt embarrassed to be asking her pastor for a single man's address. She felt just like a junior high girl all over again.

It was a cold, blustery day in Wisconsin when she went to mail the letter at the drive-up, outdoor mailbox. She silently prayed that if this letter was not in God's will, He would make a great wind blow it away as she reached out of the car window with the letter. But God didn't arrange to blow the letter away and it went quickly into the mailbox. That day events were set in motion that would change both of our lives.

After mailing the letter, Carolyn went home and immediately called both of her children to tell them what she had just done. First, she called her son J. D. and said, "Son, I've done something this morning that I've never done before and I don't know what you'd think about it?"

He said, "What did you do Mom, rob a bank?"

She replied, "No I didn't rob a bank, but I did send a letter to a college friend who lost his wife several years ago."

J.D. said, "Mom you've been grieving Dad for over six years now and it's time for you to get on with your life. I hope that guy writes back to you."

Then she called her daughter Deborah, in California and also told her that she had just written to a widowed Covenant pastor in Colorado who she had known back in college days.

Deborah also encouraged her mom saying, "Mom, I've been praying for several years that you would meet a Christian man. I'm glad you wrote to him."

Now the ball was in my court and while I wanted to write a letter back to Carolyn, there was this old battle raging in my heart and mind that said, "Don't open that door, it's too risky."

Following Sandy's death, I had built these walls around my heart to protect me from any risk of grief and heartbreak again. I was essentially controlled by fear; fear of risk and pain. After losing two precious wives from cancer I said, "Enough is enough." I knew only too well that when you take a risk to love, it's inevitable that at some point, you'll know loss. But Carolyn's letter had forced me to re-examine my fears.

I remember reading a quote from a book by C.S. Lewis, the Christian theologian, who said in The Four Loves: *"To love at all is to be vulnerable. Love anything and your heart will certainly be wrung and possibly broken. If you want to make sure of keeping it intact, you must give your heart to no one, not even to an animal. Wrap it carefully round with hobbies and little luxuries; avoid all entanglements; lock it up safe in the casket or coffin of your selfishness. But in that casket – safe, dark, motionless, airless - it will change. It will not be broken; it will become unbreakable, impenetrable, irredeemable. The alternative to tragedy, or at least the risk of tragedy, is damnation. The only place outside Heaven where you can be perfectly safe from all the dangers and perturbations of love is Hell."*

I knew that I didn't want my last years to be locked up in a 'casket of my selfishness,' so I looked carefully at the possibility of opening up a renewed friendship with Carolyn Larson. We had so much in common with our years at North Park College, our faith in Christ, our spiritual background and years of membership in the Evangelical Covenant Church as well as our many mutual friends around the country. And we also each understood what it was like to be broken by deep grief.

At some point in my struggle with fear I prayed, "Lord, if it's your will, make my heart willing to be willing to write back to Carolyn." And God answered that prayer. After eight years of building walls around my heart, the walls began to crack and I became open to the possibility of a new life, a new love, with all its inherent risks. But also with all its potential for happiness and joy.

Two weeks later, I wrote back to Carolyn thanking her for her letter and saying that if she was ever in Colorado, I'd love to see her. Unbeknownst to me, she already had plans to come to Colorado with a ski group from Iowa, but she hesitated to tell me, thinking she might appear too pushy. When she finally did tell me, I was delighted and arranged to meet her at the Village Inn Restaurant in Silverthorne, Colorado.

We had our first date in late March, 2002 as we rendezvoused one morning at the restaurant. We greeted each other at the front entrance with warm hugs and then I saw that we were not alone as she had brought two other gals with her for moral support. She was so nervous. After sliding into our booth, Carolyn was very quiet and allowed the other two ladies to quiz me with all kinds of questions about my background and ministry. I felt, at one point, that these gals were like her surrogate parents, sent to verify that this gentleman caller could be trusted with their friend.

I guess I passed muster, as an hour later they happily sent us off on our date which was to be a two-hour day trip to my mountain cabin. My sons and I had built the cabin, near Estes Park, Colorado some nine years before. Carolyn was again very quiet, all the way across the mountains and I felt that I dominated the entire conversation until she finally spoke up and said, "Wes, I would really like to use a restroom."

Now, finding a public restroom in the mountains is not that easy. And it wasn't until a half hour later that I finally remembered that the casinos in Central City had public restrooms. But when I pulled into the

Golden Gate Casino, I was shocked to learn that I had to pay top dollar to the valet parking guy for a quick pit-stop. When we came out of the casino five minutes later, the valet said, "You must have hit it rich quick." Little did he realize that I had just used up half of my available cash to pay him. It was not a good beginning to our first date. But after that stop, Carolyn became much more talkative and we both enjoyed the remainder of our mountain trip.

When we finally arrived at the cabin it had begun to snow and I began to worry that we might become stranded at the cabin in a blizzard. The ski group from Iowa had teased Carolyn the night before about being stranded in the snow at my cabin and they wondered if we would be kissing on our first date. Carolyn told them that she couldn't remember if she had ever kissed on a first date. They all laughed. I was definitely worried, both about being stranded in the blizzard and the kissing part. And since the snow on the road was getting too deep to continue driving, we had to park at the neighbor's home and walk the last quarter of a mile to the cabin. Walking in snow at an altitude of 9200 feet, Carolyn became totally out of breath and struggled to get up the road then, somehow, make it up the 18 steps to my cabin's front entrance. I felt I had blown our first date by bringing her to such a cold, remote area.

Carolyn had carried two shopping bags of homemade cookies with her up to the cabin. No wonder she was exhausted by the walk! So, when I discovered that I had no bread in the cabin freezer for our lunch, I knew that we at least had lots of cookies to eat. After a quick tour of the cabin and a quick lunch, I panicked as the snow began falling even heavier. We quickly drove down the mountain to my church, Arvada Covenant, and I gave her an equally quick tour of the church. Carolyn said later that it gave her the feeling that I was secretly rushing her along on the tour to avoid any of the staff members meeting her. The news that their pastor had a girlfriend was not out-of-the-bag yet. But it wasn't the staff inside the church that I was primarily concerned about, but the blizzard outside the church that made me wonder if I'd ever get her back up to her friends in the mountains. So, as the snow fall increased, I had to cancel our dinner plans and I rushed her back to Frisco, where she was staying with the ski group. I felt that the whole day must have been a big disappointment for her. And when I walked her to her condominium door, I apologized for all the cancellations, the snow and the difficult terrain that I had dragged her into. I thought I had blown our first date.

I did give her a parting kiss!

I did give her a parting kiss after walking her to her door and I said that I hoped we could get together again soon. She amazed me when she said that she really enjoyed the day and she would like to see me again. After saying goodbye, I sang out-loud in the car all the way down the mountain. My heart felt light again with the joy of a beautiful woman in my life. After eight years of grieving Sandy's death, the protective walls around my heart were finally breaking down. It was a wonderful expansion of my heart.

After saying goodbye, I sang out-loud in the car all the way down the mountain.

Over the next eight months, our love for one another grew by leaps and bounds as we wrote to each other weekly and traveled to be with each other monthly. These visits included time to just be alone with each other, as well as family times. In May, Carolyn attended Luke's graduation from Seminary with me. In June, she baked a chocolate cake in Wisconsin and flew to Denver, with the cake boxed up and held in her lap, to celebrate my birthday. In September, I flew out to California to meet her family and in October, she joined me at North Park College when I spoke at the college homecoming chapel.

By October of that year I knew that our love had grown to the point that I was seriously looking for a diamond ring. I found a beautifully cut, solitaire stone, without a setting, at the Mine Jewelry Store in Aurora, Colorado. The salesman told me that if I sent the stone immediately out of state, I could avoid state sales tax. So, I took a risk and put this valuable stone in an overnight express envelope marked, "DO NOT OPEN," and sent it to Carolyn through the U.S. Post Office. It occurred to me days later to call and tell her not to try and open the package I had sent to her address, or shake it or hold it up to the light. But she had already done all of the above before I called!

On November 8, I flew into O'Hare Airport in Chicago and drove up to Williams Bay, to celebrate Carolyn's birthday on November 12. I also intended to make that day really special by asking her to marry me. I stayed with her friends the Bassies,' so that everything would be on the up-and-up and each morning when I arrived at her home, I brought the padded express envelope that I had sent. She was so curious to see what was inside the envelope! But each day I whetted her curiosity by switching the diamond stone for another gift and pretending that this is what was in the package all along. One day I gave her a book called, "Devotions for Engaged Couples." On another day, I gave her a CD by Rod Stewart, "Love Songs my Parents Sang." On another day, it was jewelry. Each day she would say, "It sure didn't feel like that when I shook the package!"

Carolyn and I were engaged to be married on Carolyn's birthday, November 12, 2002.

On November 12, we celebrated Carolyn's birthday by sitting in front of her glowing fireplace, where all her letters to me had begun. She opened the envelope with the diamond stone inside and I got down on one knee and asked her to marry me. There were tears in her eyes as she responded with an enthusiastic, "Yes." We went that same day to a local jewelry store and picked out a setting for the stone and then celebrated our engagement at our favorite restaurant, the Grandview in Lake Geneva. My protective walls were gone, thank God, and I was in-love again and a happily engaged man.

We set December 31, 2002 as the date for our wedding and Carolyn flew to Denver for Thanksgiving week, where we busily addressed wedding announcements to over 500 family members and friends. Since our wedding ceremony was to be a small, family only celebration, we invited all our friends to come to four public receptions to be held after the wedding in Arvada, Colorado; Williams Bay, Wisconsin; Pasadena, California and Princeton, Illinois. We also asked our friends and family not to send us wedding gifts but if they chose to honor us, to consider sending a gift to Covenant World Missions. Nearly 800 friends and family attended our receptions and they gave over $5,000 to missions in our honor. We felt so blessed.

Carolyn and I were married in the Mountain View Chapel of Arvada Covenant Church on December 31, 2002. This was the church that I had loved and served for nearly 14 years. It was eleven o'clock on New Year's Eve morning and we were truly ringing out the old and bringing in the new.

The simple chapel, with its large westerly windows that looked out to the majestic Rocky Mountains, was the perfect setting for our intimate, family wedding ceremony. There were more people in the wedding party than there were in the audience. My mom, age 97, sat in the front row next to Marilyn Olson, my sister-in-law. They were the only two people in attendance who had been present at all three of my weddings. In addition, there were only eleven other seated guests at the wedding including

Carolyn's brother Paul, her brother-in-law Steve, her nephew Mark and their wives.

But the wedding party was something else. It was truly a big family affair with all of our children, their spouses and every one of our grandchildren participating, including baby Micah who was born just five days before. Our two Pastor sons, J.D. Larson and Luke Swanson, officiated at the ceremony with Carolyn's daughter Deborah standing up as matron of honor and my son Mark standing as best man. Our daughter-in-law's, Linda, Lyna and Heather were bridesmaids and my son Paul and son-in-law Tom were groomsmen. Carolyn's niece, Karna and Luke's fiancé, Sarah Lindquist both sang such meaningful solos and each of our grandchildren had a special assignment in the wedding. Noah and Christian both carried in the rings, Seth was the Bible bearer, Britta was the flower-girl and Jesse and C.J escorted their Nana down the aisle. New born baby Micah laid at his mother's feet in his infant car seat.

Carolyn wore a classically elegant sheath with matching jacket in a light fawn color and a short, shoulder length, veil. She carried a bouquet of white roses mixed with small hydrangeas. She was radiant as her two young grandsons walked her into the chapel that was aglow with large candelabras and bouquets of white roses mixed with large hydrangeas.

The Holy Spirit was present from the very start as our two sons led the ceremony so capably with the readings of our chosen Scriptures and prayers. Our entire family sang together of our bonding in the praise chorus, "We are One in the Bond of Love," followed by the children's chorus, "Jesus Loves Me."

Carolyn and I had each written our personal vows and we gazed deeply into each other's eyes as I first said, *"My dearest Carolyn, it is no accident that we met and fell in love at this time in our lives, for it is clearly God's gracious gift to us. I have sensed the presence of the Lord in our relationship since it began and I believe it is God's loving guidance that has brought us to this day. Now before God and our family I promise to be your loving and faithful husband. I will honor you, cherish you, respect you and seek daily to meet your needs. No matter how many years God may give to us, I offer my love to celebrate with you each day that we are given...."*

And Carolyn likewise said, *"My precious, wonderful Wes, it amazes me that out of this whole world I would find the one person who would make my life complete and that we met, at this right time in our lives, to fall in love. I realize that our love is truly meant to be and is God's gracious gift.... I give you all of my love, unconditionally, and look forward to many years of celebrating our lives together.... With God as the head of our home, I pray that we as a couple will be Christian role models for our entire family and that our grandchildren will love to be with us and help to keep us young."*

Our New Year's Eve wedding was a small family affair held in Colorado on December 31, 2002.

At the end of the ceremony we formed a large prayer circle in which many of our family members prayed for our future life and love together. Then we all went to our home at 5392 Arbutus Street for a meal of Swedish meatballs, Swedish rice pudding, fruit, cheeses and Carolyn's homemade Swedish rye bread. Following an afternoon of family fellowship, Carolyn and I left for a wonderful honeymoon night at the Westin Hotel in Westminster. We laughed when we arrived at the hotel, as the "T" in the name Westin had burned out and the large electric sign said, WES IN. They had unintentionally renamed the hotel for us on our wedding night.

The next day we celebrated New Year's Day with a happy wedding reception for over 300 guests at Arvada Covenant Church and then we left for a beautiful honeymoon in Maui, Hawaii, a generous wedding gift from Paul and Barb Aley. We stayed in a lovely apartment at Wailea Ekolu Village, overlooking Maui's neighboring islands. Here we had a beautiful first week together as husband and wife and we thoroughly enjoyed swimming, snorkeling and picnicking as well as driving the famous Road to Hana.

Upon our return from Hawaii, Carolyn and I settled into our new life together which became very busy with our three wedding receptions in various parts of the nation. Carolyn's birthday club friends (sometimes called "the church ladies" from Iowa and their husbands led by Carl and Sharon Johnson) cooked up a fantastic Swedish Smorgasbord for 350 guests at the Wisconsin reception and friends in Princeton, Illinois (headed by Kent and Joyce Johnson) also put on a beautiful wedding reception for over 200 guests. We also returned that spring to two engagement showers and a wedding reception for our son Luke and his fiancé, Sarah Lindquist, who were married on August 9, 2003 in Minneapolis.

Throughout our first year, I continued to keep busy with speaking engagements, including preaching at the Colorado/Nebraska/Wyoming/Kansas Gideon Retreat and the Colorado Covenant Men's Retreat at Covenant Heights Camp. Carolyn quickly found new avenues of ministry to women who had been recently widowed and opening our home to entertain many new friends. We also, this year, put my home in Arvada up for sale and after we had completed some upgrading work, we were able to sell the house in just two days.

In June of 2003, we traveled to the country of Romania with Dr. John and Barb Sexton of our Arvada church. There we worked with a team of 38 dental and medical personnel who had been trained and recruited to treat the teeth of some 5000 children who suffered with HIV/AIDS. Carolyn and I were the spiritual chaplains of the team and I was also privileged to preach in churches in Bucharest and Constanta. We spent our weeks in Romania, supporting the staff and praying and playing with these suffering children as they waited for their dental appointments. These children were very ill with AIDS and often terrified of having dental work done after a lifetime of no treatment. Many of the children had mouths full of cavities, abscesses' and other extreme oral disease which most American dentists had seen only in text books. Sadly, many of the children had to have every tooth pulled out of their mouth.

We prayed with staff and played with these suffering children.

This tragic health crisis arose under the brutal communist dictator, Nicolae Ceausescu who knowingly allowed AIDS tainted blood transfusions to be given to Romanian children after birth. Romanian mothers believed that a blood transfusion for newborn babies helped them thrive in their first year of life. So, under Ceausescu, 5000 babies were tragically given the AIDS virus through this tainted blood. The Dictator then offered to raise these ill children which he placed in huge warehouses where they slept five to a bed and received one meal a day with no medical or dental care. Romanian dentists and doctors were afraid to touch these AIDS infected little ones.

When Ceausescu was killed in the Romanian Revolution of 1989, it was the Evangelical churches of that country who rescued these sick children and brought them into their homes and orphanages. Through World Vision International, Dr. John Sexton was invited to care for the dental needs of these children and over a ten-year period of sacrificial service, he became known in Romania as "The Doctor of Hope." Several times a year, teams of dentists and medical staff under Dr. John's leadership would travel to the Romanian cities of Bucharest, Constanta, Cluj, Iasi and Brasov, treating these suffering children.

I've participated on many mission trips throughout my years of ministry, but this one was particularly difficult. We were surrounded each day by scores of suffering children and our hearts ached as we ministered to these young victims of the AIDS pandemic. There is nothing more difficult for us, as people of faith, than the suffering of innocent children. It was like a dagger driven into our hearts whenever we looked into their young faces, saw their unspeakable agony and heard their cries of pain. The powerful words of Jesus on the cross, "My God, my God, WHY?," were echoed on our lips. It's the same question people asked at Auschwitz and Dachau. Why?

Good News is the Living Savior for the wounded.

The Bible doesn't give us easy explanations as to why the innocent suffer. Oh yes, we can say that these children were the victims of evil men and other people's bad choices. And God will ultimately destroy evil. But that word of judgment on evil does nothing to relieve the children's pain. Is there any word of comfort or hope right now?

What we discover in the Bible is the Good News of a Living Savior for the wounded, the heartbroken and the lost. That's both the reason and the motivation for our traveling over 5,800 miles from Denver to Romania to tell them that there is hope and comfort and healing in Jesus. Our team's hands became the hands of Jesus to bring God's love and hope in this broken world. I was so proud of our medical team and their dedication to bring relief and healing to these suffering ones. I realized again that I've been so privileged to give my life, in this dark world, to point others to the light of Jesus. We, indeed, were blessed to, "comfort those in any trouble with the comfort we ourselves have received from God" (I Corinthians 1:4).

In December 2003 Carolyn and I celebrated our first Christmas as a married couple. I worked hard to make Carolyn the special Christmas gift of a shadow box that told our love story. It's been fun, over the years, to see that shadow box sitting on the shelf and remember the excitement and joy of our first love and our first year of married life together. Over the 15 years since that first Christmas, our love story has grown more beautiful with each passing year.

The English romantic poet, William Wordsworth wrote, "Come grow old with me, the best is yet to be." It certainly has been true for us as our married life and love has grown better, richer and deeper as we have grown older. But a happy marriage doesn't come without work. It takes active commitment on the part of both partners to make love grow. Here are some of the commitments that we've made in our 15 years of marriage that have helped our love grow richer as we've grown older.

Our love story has grown more beautiful with each passing year.

- **We've made faith in Jesus Christ the foundation of our home**. It all began for both of us with a personal faith in Jesus, the risen and living Christ. It's not just the rote observance of a church tradition or a religious ritual, but a personal faith in Jesus the Messiah and a commitment to follow in His steps. **This personal relationship with God gives us a solid foundation for marriage** in the midst of uncertain times and the challenges of aging.

- **Communication is the life-blood of a marriage.** If there is no communication in marriage it soon grows cold and dies. The same is true of faith in God. Prayer and worship is the way we communicate with God. But if we never communicate with our Heavenly Father, our faith relationship grows cold and distant. That's why we've agreed to begin each day by focusing on reading from the Bible, God's blueprint for life, and then spending time together communicating with God in prayer. This always helps our love to grow as it's hard to nurse a grudge when you're holding hands with your spouse in prayer. And what better place to grow in love as a couple than in a church with other believers who want to communicate with God. Growing together in faith helps us grow richer in our love and friendship and communication.

- **We have a weekly date night.** To keep our marriage fresh and add some pizzazz to our lives, we have a fun night-out together each week. It might be a movie followed by dinner in a favorite restaurant, a symphony concert, a theatre production at the Lamb's Players in Coronado or just a picnic and walk on the beach. This weekly commitment says our love is special and worth the effort.

- **We keep a focus on the family.** With five children and their spouses, plus twelve grandchildren spread all around the nation, it adds joy to our marriage to celebrate their lives, marriages, graduations and faith. We seek to be fair to all by taking each grandchild on a special trip after their eighth-grade graduation and taking each family, one at a time, to a special week of vacation together. We also built and maintain a cabin in the Colorado mountains for our summer family reunions. But **our primary goal in all of our times together is to hand over the baton of faith and service to the younger generations.**

What fun we've had on the thirteen cruises we've taken together.

• **We find meaning and purpose in a lifestyle of ministry.** All of our life is lived under the Lordship of Jesus Christ. The longer we live, the more we have opportunity to serve Him. So, throughout our retirement years we have welcomed new opportunities to serve our God. In 2003 and again in 2005 we ministered to children with HIV/AIDS in Romania and Uganda. In 2004 and again in 2007 we helped build churches in Ecuador. In 2006 to 2008 we served together as the interim pastoral team at the Covenant Church in Turlock, California. In addition, our retirement years have been filled with opportunities to preach and minister throughout the United States in churches, on prayer retreats, at mission conferences, women's Bible studies, on church prayer teams, church pulpit supply, 55 plus conferences and pastor/missionary retreats. These all give our marriage meaning and purpose and an abundance of new friends.

• **We believe that an open heart to people means an open door to our home.** Carolyn has the gift of hospitality and together we have welcomed hundreds of people each year into our homes. Whether it's welcoming groups of neighbors to our home for meals, celebrating Advent with Swedish pancake breakfasts or having church youth groups or adult groups in our home for Bible studies and fellowship, these all invigorate our marriage and the good conversation sharpens our minds and souls.

- **We have fun together.** Over our years of marriage, we've taken thirteen cruises together to places like Alaska, the Caribbean, the Scandinavian countries, the Norwegian Fjords, the Baltic countries, Mexico, Italy, Greece and a river cruise from St Petersburg to Moscow. And "love boats" go a long way to give us quality time together and stoke our love fires. We've kept fresh physically and challenged intellectually, during our travels to Hawaii and Spain. In London, we enjoyed a week of stimulating, live theatre each night. Many additional fun trips with grandchildren to Disneyland in California and Epcot in Florida add laughter and adventure to our lives that enriches the body, mind and soul.

- **We are building memories together.** Carolyn builds memories as she invests in people to whom she gives home-baked goodies and her personally knit blankets or prayer shawls. Years from now, hundreds of people will look at the blankets and scarves she's knitted and thank God for the blessing of her life. I build memories in my watercolor paintings and scrapbooks. For 52 years, I have kept scrapbooks in which I document our lives and loves and travels. By looking back over our years of marriage we can reflect on the good times we have shared and as Philippians 4:8 says we can fill our minds with the blessings that God has showered in our marriage. On cold winter nights, we enjoy opening up a scrapbook and remembering fun times and laughing over changing styles. We often shed tears over pictures of loved ones now gone from sight and at home with the Lord.

"Thanks for the memories."

It's been said that love is a verb and not just a feeling. Feelings will fluctuate, but real love is based on a couple's vows of commitment, whether it feels good or not. And it's our deep commitment to our marriage that helps us grow in love and respect for each other, despite our differences.

Carolyn is much more outgoing and extroverted than I am. She loves to meet friends for lunch or talk on the phone at length with family. She begins each day by praying, "Lord, who should I visit today to help and encourage." She's a great example of one who intentionally keeps in touch with friends from 50 years ago, while I generally enjoy a quiet day just reading a good book or working on a water color painting. But because of our marriage commitment, our differences only serve to push each other to grow our personalities in wonderful ways we would not have expected.

So, for these blessed 15 years we have kept our marriage at the top of our priority list. There are times that we need to redouble our commitment to our marriage and dedicate quality time, as well as some quantity time to each other. But the motivation and inspiration is always the awesome wonder that God has brought us together out of broken lives to a new love and life together.

BONDING WITH MY STEP CHILDREN

Carolyn blessed our marriage with my step son J. D. Larson and my step daughter Deborah Larson.

When Carolyn and I were married, we formed a new blended family that included adult children and grandchildren from our previous marriages. Suddenly our marriage was blessed with an expanded family of five children and their spouses, as well as eleven wonderful grandchildren, not to mention our extended families spread over the nation. While changes in family structure always require patience and adjustments for everyone involved, we were so very fortunate to have the blessing and support of all our children.

Carolyn's daughter Deborah is a massage therapist in Carmel/Monterey, California. After high-school, Deborah attended our college alma mater, North Park University. She then spent one year as a volunteer at the Covenant Mission radio station in Nome, Alaska and later worked as an administrative assistant at the Japanese Consulate in Anchorage, Alaska. For the past 15 years, Deborah has developed a remarkable massage therapy business in which she goes to her client's homes for their therapy session. She's had many of the same clients for all of those 15 years.

Her father's death was a terrible blow to Deborah and I believe it was the catalyst that propelled her on a journey to find new meaning, new purpose and a new direction in her life. I knew that I could never fill the void that she felt in losing her father. Nevertheless, when I came on the scene she went out of her way to make me feel welcome in the family. Early on, Deborah told her mother that she was puzzled as to what she should call me as she didn't feel comfortable calling me "Dad." While she was so glad that I had come into her mother's life, she wanted to refer to me by something less cumbersome than "my mother's husband" and something warmer than "Stepfather." She opted to call me "Wonderful Wes." Deborah is a remarkably caring and generous woman who is always reaching out compassionately to those who are wounded or weak; whether it be animals or people. My role in her life has primarily been to love her mother. She finds joy in our love story. But I also support her journey to faith by affirming her, being a good listener and simply telling my story of God's grace.

Carolyn's son Jonathan David is known to everyone as J.D. and was just in the process of taking a new pastoral position in California when I first met him in 2002. J.D. graduated Magna Cum Laud from Westmont College in Santa Barbara in 1988, where he had equipped himself for Camping Ministry, serving eventually as Program Director at both Mission Springs Camp in California and Covenant Harbor in Lake Geneva, Wisconsin.

J.D. was highly effective in growing youth camps and developing the Covenant camping ministry to be unmistakably evangelical and spiritually impacting for youth. His strong leadership skills made him widely known both within and without camping circles and resulted in his being sought by North Coast Church, a large evangelical church in Vista, California to be their Pastor of College Ministries. North Coast Church has five area campuses in San Diego County and averages about 12,000 attendees at their services each weekend with over 90% of those attenders involved in small group home Bible studies during the week.

After being called to North Coast Church in 2002, J.D. proved his ministry skills and in 2011 was asked by church leadership to be the lead-pastor in their new North Coast Church plant in Carlsbad, California. The new church plant had 750 in attendance on their first Sunday and has grown five years later to average 1500 on weekends.

J.D.'s wife Linda is a registered nurse and helped to start a home nursing franchise for Qualicare Family Home Care in Southern California. Linda has all the qualities of an outstanding nurse and I have personally experienced her care and thoughtfulness since the very first day I met her. They are the parents of two sons. Their oldest son, Jesse David Larson and his wife Katrina live and work in Bellingham, Washington where they both graduated from Western Washington University. Jesse graduated with honors in Organic Chemistry and Katrina's addition to our family now gives us 12 wonderful grandchildren. They are very active in their church where Jesse is a worship leader. J.D. and Linda's youngest son is Christian Jonathan, known as C.J., who is a youth pastor and worship leader at North Coast Church, Carlsbad. In 2016, he graduated from the North Coast School of Ministry and celebrated that achievement with a class trip to Israel. He is a spirit-filled young man who is powerfully effective in ministry.

Last Christmas, J.D. suggested that he, C.J. and I form a family preaching trio and preach at the Christmas Eve services together. He said that we were the only family on the entire North Coast Staff that has three generations in ministry. It was a great privilege to be asked to preach the joyous Christmas message with my step son and grandson. J.D. has been so generous in giving me opportunities to be part of his ministry and warmly welcomed me into the family.

Our 70's are our go-go years, our 80's will be our slow-go years and our 90's will probably be our no-go years.

Healthy step parenting is always a challenge. While Carolyn and I were especially blessed to have the love and support of all our children, it still takes work to discover how to bond successfully as a step family. So, we have agreed as a couple to do those positive family things that build acceptance and trust, like respecting family traditions for holiday celebrations and traveling around the country to spend quality time with each family. We build memories by watching Sunday afternoon football games together, taking family trips, worshipping God, eating meals together and making it clear that we love them in our phone calls, birthday greetings and graduation parties. We welcome every opportunity to be together with our kids and grandchildren. This will change as we age, but for now we have the health and strength to follow Carolyn's rule that our 70's are our go-go years, our 80's will be our slow-go years and our 90's will probably be our no-go years.

CHAPTER 11

OUR RETIREMENT JOURNEY

We've been retired now for 15 years and these have been good years, just like the tee shirt brand advertises, "Life is good." Of course, we have the same health challenges as everyone in our age group. I struggle with significant hearing loss and with glaucoma and kidney stone surgeries. Carolyn suffered for years with knee pain culminating in the need for full-knee replacement and she deals daily with pain from a torn rotator cuff. They say that, "getting old is not for sissies." But aging well involves a positive attitude, a thankful heart, a clear purpose and a sense of continued usefulness to the Lord in retirement.

After serving 40 years of pastoral ministry in churches, I was convinced from the start of retirement that I would never retire from serving God. In Titus chapter two, the Apostle Paul instructs the older men and women to have a purpose in old age by teaching younger people how to follow Jesus through their teaching and example. I've memorized Psalm 92:12-15 as my retirement prayer, "The righteous will …still bear fruit in old age, they will stay fresh and green, proclaiming the Lord is upright; He is my rock."

Aging well involves a positive attitude, a thankful heart, a clear purpose and a sense of continued usefulness to the Lord in retirement.

As long as we have breath God has a plan and a purpose for our lives. This purpose is, first of all, to continue to grow more intimate in our relationship with Him. And secondly, to bear fruit in old age by serving Him through serving others.

REUNION CABIN IN THE ROCKY MOUNTAINS

My sons and I built our cabin in the Colorado Rockies over 25 years-ago for the specific purpose of having a reunion place to be with my children, to make it a fun place to bond with our grandchildren, but also to have a retreat setting for continued ministry in my retirement. As a young boy, I had grown-up with such positive memories of my folk's lake cabin in Minnesota. I hoped that the mountain cabin would become the same type of family retreat where our love and example could impact our grandchildren. It has become a place of continued ministry over the years as we have opportunity to build friendships and encourage the faith of hundreds of other people who have come to stay with us at our mountain retreat. The cabin has fulfilled its purpose in our retirement beyond our fondest dreams. But, in its inception, it was just a wishful dream.

In the summer of 1992 I asked a real estate agent in our church, Tom Shoup, if he would keep his eyes open for a piece of mountain property on which I could someday build a cabin. I jokingly said it would be nice if the property had a trout stream and if it was a being offered at a low price. Three weeks later, Tom called to say that he had found my piece of mountain property. Very shortly after his call, my wife Sandy and I, together with our sons Mark and Paul, joined our realtor friend and traveled the 40 miles up to the mountains to see this piece of property. We were disappointed. This small piece of land was right next to a busy mountain highway and was totally dominated by a soaring mountain hillside that made this property unbuildable.

My boys suggested that as long as we'd made the trip up to the mountains, we shouldn't waste the opportunity to do some mountain climbing. So, we climbed that rugged mountain hillside to the top where we discovered a dirt road encircling a small mountain lake, called Hidden Lake, with a sign next to a lot that read "FOR SALE." While the land didn't have a trout stream, it did have a small lake that I learned was full of trout. I became really interested in buying this lot.

I spent the fall and winter negotiating with a realtor over the sale of this one and one-half acre piece of mountain property, but the asking price of $15,000 was more than I could afford. The realtor said that I should offer whatever I could, as the owner in Florida was struggling with the economic recession and would lose the land if he couldn't sell it soon. I had saved $8,000 for a possible purchase of mountain property and when I offered it to the owner in early spring of 1993, he immediately accepted my offer.

Now this beautiful mountain land was our land. But my boys said that the lot next to our land was a more buildable site for a cabin as it gave a stunning view of the snow-capped Rocky Mountains. So, in contacting the same Boulder real estate agent who sold us the first lot, I learned that the next lot was owned by a man in California who was in the same financial crisis as the Florida owner. When I told the owner in California that I had purchased the lot next to his for $8,000 he immediately accepted my offer of the same amount and suddenly, by the summer of 1993, we now owned three acres of beautiful mountain property. I feel that God arranged this purchase at the right time as today each lot would sell for over $100,000.

I made sketches and floor plan designs of a possible cabin and then hired a Colorado architect, Ed Abyta, to draw up plans and blueprints. We were all set to begin construction when suddenly everything changed with the diagnosis of my wife's colon cancer and her subsequent death in April 1994. This devastating turn of events left me totally uninterested in working on any future cabin and I actually considered selling the land. It was my boys who said, "Dad, building the cabin in Sandy's memory is going to be our grief therapy. Let's start immediately." By June of that year we were plunging head-long into the project and already hiring subcontractors. And it did become our grief therapy.

"Dad, building the cabin in Sandy's memory is going to be our grief therapy."

Because I needed to be realistic about the high costs of building in the mountains, I determined that I would save at least 25% of the total cost by being my own general contractor. While I had no experience being a general contractor or even much hands-on construction experience, I did have a lot of construction knowledge from watching and helping in the building of four new church facilities over the course of my ministry. I also figured that we had time on our side and we could work slowly, correcting our mistakes as we learned on the job. It took us four years to build the cabin and we learned a lot from our mistakes.

My most important responsibility was finding and hiring the best subcontractors who would be willing to work in the mountains at 9,200 feet altitude. By asking a lot of questions and making a lot of phone calls, I was finally able to hire some very good subs for excavation, well-digging, footings and foundations, percolation tests and septic systems, carpenters, plumbers, electricians and engineers. It was especially challenging to work with the Boulder County Building and Land Use Development department for the permits and fees needed, as well as getting everything figured correctly with the building supply company. But, with God's provision of insight and the help of my sons, plus some knowledgeable carpenter friends and the brothers from my men's Bible study group who pitched in to help me, I was able to get everything rough framed by late August 1994.

But not without some sleepless nights and some dramatic challenges that were to come.

By September 1, I realized that winter snow was fast approaching the mountains and I was running out of time for more construction. We still needed to get the cabin closed up for winter, including permanently securing all the rafters, columns and beams, get the roof shingled as well as covering all the exterior walls with a weather-resistant wrap. I couldn't get all this done by myself or even with volunteer help, so I hired two young carpenters who said that they would do all of those projects if I would pay them in advance for working in the high country. Since our cabin is located at 9,200 feet elevation, I figured that their request was reasonable and since they came with satisfactory references, I paid them $7,000 to get the cabin enclosed and secure for winter. After two weeks of doing very little work, those young guys abandoned my project, left everything unsecured and took off with all the money I had paid them in advance. Even though I won a claim against them in Small Claims Court, I was not able to locate the young men as they had apparently taken-off for some other state. I lost my $7,000 and my cabin was left exposed to strong mountain winds and unprotected.

A week later, after they left my job site, we had an 85 mile-an-hour wind and snow storm in the mountains which blew the entire second floor of the cabin down to the ground, including all the unsecured rafters and the main column and beam. It was a major set-back and very costly, but fortunately, I had taken out a construction insurance policy that paid for about 80% of my loss. I was able, by God's intervention, to hire two Christian guys who were master carpenters and they were able, in the next few weeks with some unusually warm weather, to get everything rebuilt and secured for winter. Everything, that is, except the asphalt shingles on the roof which didn't have time to bond before another major storm blew them all off. Twenty years later, I still find some of those shingles stuck in rock crevices around the property. That spring, I took out another bank loan and subcontracted to have a metal roof put on the entire cabin.

Over the course of the next three years, together with the help of my boys and friends from church, I was able to get the cabin finished, including all the interior insulation, the dry wall, the oak-wood and ceramic-tile floors, the finish wood- work and trim, the kitchen cupboards and all the interior and exterior painting. I hired two local mountain men, Fuzzy Bob and Peter Lawrence, to install my soffit and fascia around the roof and to build my wrap-around deck.

For 25 years our family has celebrated reunions at our mountain cabin in Colorado.

In 1995, I bought a third lot at a local sheriff's auction at which I was the only bidder. I paid $10,000 for the lot, which became the site for our septic field and garage and gave us a total of five acres of mountain property. Over time and with many helping hands, we were finally able to complete the construction of the cabin. And while there were many frustrations and scheduling hassles along the way, through it all God led us to the day in late 1996 when we finally got our occupancy permit. Tears of joy ran down my face that day.

For twenty-five years God has blessed our mountain retreat as a place of both physical and spiritual refreshment. Hundreds of people and events have been held there including many pastor's retreats, church staff and Christian college faculty retreats, prayer retreats, youth group retreats, cousin reunions, life celebrations, family reunions, fishing, hiking and skiing trips and our own family gatherings. Since

Our grandchildren Addy, Britta and Micah helping Nana make Swedish Pancakes at the cabin.

191

our property is located in the high Rockies there is always the threat of destructive winds, crushing snowfalls and wildfire dangers. We realize that we could lose the cabin in a flash. Nevertheless, for twenty-five years, our mountain home has given us an outlet for significant ministry and it has given us purpose and meaning in our senior years. I stand in awe of this gift that God gave us.

WORLDWIDE TRAVEL WITH A PURPOSE

Some of our greatest experiences in retirement have come in our world-wide travels on short-term mission trips. What a privilege to serve others around the world and work shoulder to shoulder with local Christians. Together we built churches and homes in Ecuador, helped to conduct evangelistic crusades in the former communist East Germany and brought dental and medical teams to the AIDS stricken children of Romania and Uganda. These trips brought significant purpose and ministry to our retirement years, as well as pushing us out of our comfort zone and stretching us in ways we never would have imagined possible. We were blessed and received so much more than we gave.

One of these retirement mission trips was to El Chaco, Ecuador which is a city of some 6,000 people, living in the Amazon rainforest Northeast of Quito and is the capitol city of the Napo Provence. We served for two weeks in July, 2004 with 30 members of the Northbrook Illinois Covenant Church under the leadership of my Spanish speaking son Paul, who together with his wife, had served two years teaching in Ecuador.

Because the city is located in the Amazon rainforest with its abundance of rivers, huge waterfalls and lush tropical forests, the first purchases that we all made were tall rubber boots and plastic ponchos to help us keep dry in all the rain and mud. Some days we would have a heavy rain shower about every half-hour. And the old, primitive, Hostel de Yumbos hotel, where we stayed and ate, wasn't much dryer! Everything was damp and snakes, spiders and a plethora of birds and other animals surrounded our cottage.

Mixing cement and hauling rocks from the river to build a church in El Chaco, Ecuador.

We were warmly welcomed to the Chanta Loma Covenant Church of El Chaco by Pastor Obed and his congregation. Together we worked for these weeks on building a church, a home and a four-foot rock wall around the church, with rocks and gravel that we hauled up from the nearby river. We also conducted a children's Bible school for over 100 young children of the community.

Preaching in Ecuador with my son Paul translating into Spanish.

I was privileged to preach at that church, with my son translating into Spanish, as well as bringing a devotional message for the mission team each morning. But for both Carolyn and I, the greatest privilege was traveling in our retirement with the purpose of serving others.

Another mission trip in our retirement years, was traveling in January and February of 2005 to Kampala, Uganda in equatorial Africa. We went with a dental/medical team from Colorado under Dr. John Sexton and Dr. Paul Musherure of Uganda to provide dental work to children with HIV/AIDS. Our team treated over 300 children, ages 18 and younger, during those busy weeks.

Carolyn serving as post-op nurse with HIV/AIDS children in Uganda.

The AIDS crisis in Uganda reached epidemic proportions in the 1970's under the ruthless, eight-year regime of the dictator Idi Amin, who massacred an estimated 400,000 civilians and allowed the spread of AIDS to be unchecked. At the time that we were in Uganda, there were 84,000 children diagnosed with AIDS and one million AIDS orphans. It had overwhelmed their health care system and our team was a God-send to the nation.

We worked near the capitol city of Kempala at the Mildmay Centre for Health Care and Training on Entebbe Road. Most of the children had to wait in line for at least two days before seeing a dentist and our job was to entertain them while they nervously waited. We used puppets and flannelgraph to tell Bible stories and each morning the children and their caregivers would line up early, waiting for Carolyn and I to lay hands on them and pray for them. Sometimes we had to help hold kicking, screaming, children as the dentists worked on them. Carolyn also acted as the post-op nurse after the children's treatment. Since they were all infected with AIDS and their mouths were bloody from treatment, she had to be very careful.

Weekends would include special trips like a safari to the Queen Elizabeth National Park where elephants and roaring lions surrounded our cabin at night. We never ventured out after dark! On our return trip home from the park we stopped at Dr. Paul Musherusre's family home and were royally entertained. His father, who was a deeply committed Christian and had been Secretary of State for the government after Idi Amin's tyrannical regime, greeted us so warmly to their home saying, "Velcome, ve are aull born-again Christians in this home and your visit here has elevated us." We immediately loved this man and his family and then we heard, with heavy hearts, the heartbreaking stories of their suffering under Idi Amin.

While our lives were 'elevated' and changed by these cross-cultural experiences, we were especially happy to know that the lives of scores of Ugandan children and their caregivers were also changed and blessed by our team's ministry. As one Ugandan health worker told us, "You could have stayed in America and prayed for us or just sent us some money, but we can tell that you really cared for us by coming yourself."

INTERIM MINISTRY IN TURLOCK, CA.
2006 – 2008

One of the most rewarding experiences of our retirement years was serving a two-year interim pastorate at the Turlock Covenant Church in Turlock, California. This great, historic church was originally known as Beulah Covenant Church and, now in its 105th year, was struggling with an aged and declining membership. We were excited to be called by the Holy Spirit to serve this church, as it gave us an opening for continued ministry in our retirement years and it gave Carolyn her first opportunity to be a pastor's wife.

An interim pastor is one who serves a congregation between a regularly called, permanent pastor and usually serves for a short period of time. But our Conference Superintendent, Evelyn M.R. Johnson, had asked us to consider going to Turlock for at least six months to minister to the church and to help the conference determine the future viability of the congregation. To accomplish this assignment, we ended up staying at the church for nearly two years, from 2006 to 2008.

Interim pastors do not usually live in the community that they are temporarily serving. Rather they will drive in from out of town to preach on Sundays and may stay one extra day to visit the hospitalized members, or to be a consultant for the Pastoral Search Committee. But in our case, we were living at that time in Wisconsin and so took up residence, full time, in the Turlock church parsonage, with every intention of seeing if we could help to revitalize this aging congregation.

We had come to serve this church with nothing but our clothing and my Bible. This wonderful church family supplied the parsonage with all the furnishings, linens and cookware we needed to live in their home, next to the church campus. The mismatched furnishings all came from their attics or garages and included five 'retro' pink stuffed chairs which Carolyn amazingly arranged into a bright and inviting living space.

They were living in the middle of a mission-field in their own community.

Early on in our ministry we realized that the congregation needed to be reminded that they were here to serve and not only to be served, as they were living in the middle of a mission-field in their own community. A mission field that was crying out for ministry and hope.

The neighborhood surrounding the church had changed dramatically over the 100 plus years of the church's existence. Now, in place of well cared-for, middle class homes, the church was now surrounded by hundreds of homeless people who often slept and defecated on church property, violent street gangs and drug dealers who did their deals on the church steps and thousands of migrant and undocumented fieldworkers who, together with their families, lived around the church in desperate conditions.

But many of our church members were unaware of the critical needs of the surrounding neighborhood, as they would drive into the church from outlying areas on Sunday mornings and then leave the neighborhood immediately after services. We were an island of religious serenity in an ocean of poverty and chaos.

And for that matter, the people in the neighborhood had no idea that we were a community church that was there to serve them. One neighbor who had lived next to us for 18 years mistook our name, "Turlock Covenant" for "convent" and thought we were some kind of religious school run by nuns. Neither the church nor the neighborhood knew each other. They were like ships passing in the night. The future of this church depended on a recovery of their neighborhood mission.

After getting acquainted with this loving congregation, I challenged them to recover a renewed sense of mission by accepting their surrounding neighborhood as their primary mission field. They had been so faithful over the decades to send missionaries and mission funds to Africa and Asia, but they had essentially missed the mission field in their own backyard.

At first, I invited the church to just get acquainted with some of the people in our neighborhood. To do that, we sent teams of members into the neighborhood each month, two by two, to get acquainted with the community and introduce the church to them. Each team would generally include a Spanish and an English speaker and we would visit around 800 homes each month. Later on, our teams would ask neighbors how our church could help make this neighborhood safer for their children and asked if there were any prayer requests that we could share with our praying church. Neighbors started opening up to our visits and began realizing that this church really cared for them, with some neighbors actually attending our Spanish or English Sunday services. I will never forget the day that Edwardo and Selene Garcia responded to the invitation to receive Christ into their lives and home. Suddenly we had new babes in Christ in this aging church.

But, we really got acquainted with our community when our monthly visitation teams invited neighbors to a free dinner at our church every Wednesday evening, at which we would discuss our community's needs and struggles. Soon we had 50 to 75 neighbors in our church each week who had never before walked through the church doors.

Out of those weekly meals and discussions, we organized a periodic neighborhood health-clinic after learning that 80% of the migrant workers had no health insurance. We had as many as 600 neighbors flooding our church-grounds at these health-fairs. We also added to our staff a dynamic youth worker, Tim Hawkinson, who reached out to community youth at skate parks and organized after school tutoring for neighborhood youth. Our Associate Pastor, Linda Weiss Buie was an effective music and children's leader among both Spanish and English speaking families. We organized alley cleanups on Saturdays when we found that neighborhood decay was linked to trash-filled alleys. We asked the Turlock Police Department to help us organize a Neighborhood Watch Program to address the growing drug violence, crime and arson in the community.

We helped to organize the city churches for a homeless ministry and the church intentionally made our worship services and ministries more welcoming to the Hispanic culture, with monthly bilingual services held together with Pastor Samuel Galdamez of our Spanish congregation.

Through all these efforts we began to make inroads into the community and saw neighbors coming to a personal faith in Jesus Christ and join the church. One member commented, "With all this new life, I guess we are not dead yet! This church seems now to have a future."

Carolyn became the most outstanding pastor's wife and added significantly to the church's new life. She flung open the parsonage doors to welcome hundreds of members into fellowship dinners, youth celebrations, neighborhood Bible studies, women's coffee parties, Advent open houses and a community knitting group for abused and battered women. In our first three months in Turlock she had welcomed over 300 people into our home for fellowship, good conversation and prayer. When we left the church in 2008, one of the members said to us, "Pastor, we can accept that it's time for you to leave us, but we're keeping Carolyn here!" She had become deeply loved by the church and community.

"With all this new life, I guess we are not dead yet!

Another spark of new life came to the church when Carolyn and I led a team of 12 members and youth on a mission trip to a slum/squatter's village outside of Guayaquil, Ecuador. We combined our team with another team from Illinois and spent two weeks mixing cement in the street, shoulder to shoulder with Pastor Juan Carlos and his flock. We completed building the Flor de Bastion Covenant Church and also conducted a summer Bible School and sport's camp for 200 impoverished and neglected children. This destitute congregation had waited seven years for a team to come and help them build their church. Our youth returned home to Turlock totally fired-up to reach out to our own community mission field with the love of Christ.

Henry Ford said, "Anyone who stops learning is old, whether at twenty or eighty. Anyone who keeps learning stays young." Serving those two years of our retirement in the Turlock Covenant Church gave us purpose in life, joy in ministry and kept us young at heart. It was an important part of our serving God, through serving others, in our retirement.

LEAVING A LEGACY FOR MY GRANDCHILDREN

This book of my life journey is my legacy to my grandchildren. It's a gift to you of "me." I write this for Noah, Seth and Caleb Swanson, for Christian, Britta and Micah Swanson, for Adelaide, Elsa and Ezekiel Swanson, and for my step-grandchildren Jesse and his wife Katrina Shelman Larson and C.J. Larson. I want my grandchildren and perhaps future generations of great-grandchildren to know who I was and how God in His grace has set me free to become the man I am. This book of memories is my legacy to you.

I also leave each of you with the legacy of my love. Even though we may have lived hundreds of miles apart from each other, you have never been out of my heart or away from my love. We prayed for you before you were born and our love has followed you every day of your life as Grandma and I have daily lifted your name before God in earnest prayer.

Though separated by miles, we have been intentional in reaching out to you in love through our celebration cards, e-mails, Facebook messages and phone calls. And then there were the special times when we could be with you in person and wrap our arms of love around you. We wanted to create an oasis of love for you in our home or at the mountain cabin where you and your friends were always welcome. In those special times of celebrating your life and accomplishments we wanted to leave you with memories of fun, adventure and laughter as we hiked together in the mountains or played table games of dominoes, while eating Grandma's fresh baked cookies and drinking her chocolate milkshakes. We leave you this legacy of our unconditional love.

But, the greatest legacy that I long to leave you is the gift of faith. I've tried to share with each of you in person and now through this book, how Jesus Christ has made a difference in my life. I'm a lover of Jesus and He has given me peace and hope when I felt lost and abandoned in the storms of life. I have, throughout my lifetime practiced the ancient spiritual disciplines of walking in His footsteps and growing in friendship with God through listening to Him in His Word, communicating with Him in prayer and worshipping with His faith-family. It's like any friendship you may have. If you never speak to your friend or you never have any contact with each other, your friendship soon grows cold and distant. The same is true of your faith and friendship with God. If you never listen for His voice or spend time speaking with Him in worship or prayer, your faith friendship will grow cold and distant. But, when you spend time listening for God's voice and speaking with Him in prayer you'll grow in friendship with God and be changed and made new from the inside-out. I long to pass the baton of faith and Christian service to you. Here is my legacy of faith.

As I reach my 80th year, I realize that time is running out on my life lived here with you. I may not be with you in all the important seasons of your life. I hope I am privileged to share in each of your graduations from school, your finding a career you love, your mate selections and marriage, your future children and your faith commitment to service for God and mankind. But, if I'm not here physically, I look forward to seeing you in heaven. I together with your wonderful grandmothers Clarice, Sandy and Carolyn; leave you with these memories of grandparents who loved you unconditionally and walked before you in faith.

THE HOPE OF HEAVEN

In the early 90's, when I was the pastor of Arvada Covenant Church, the evangelist Franklin Graham, Billy Graham's son, held an evangelistic crusade in the northern suburbs of Denver. We enthusiastically supported the crusade as did most of the Protestant, Evangelical and even some of the Roman Catholic Churches. Everyone, that is, except the pastor of a large mainline Protestant church in the Denver area. I remember my surprise when this pastor circulated a letter among his congregation in which he adamantly opposed any support for the crusade.

Our deepest desire is to leave a legacy of Christian love for our children and grandchildren.

In his letter, asking his members not to attend the crusade, this progressive pastor said, "The Graham crusade will say that Jesus is the way to God and no one comes to God the Father but by faith in Jesus Christ." He then went on to state, "As far as I'm concerned, Mahatma Gandhi is more the way to God than Jesus Christ ever was." He also said that Graham will focus on the need for forgiveness of sin by faith in Jesus. He went on to remind his liberal congregation that he teaches that the concept of sin is obsolete and that he emphasizes the power of positive thinking, not the forgiveness of sin. And finally, this pastor said, "Graham will say that it is only by faith in Jesus that you will receive the gift of eternal life." Then, this pastor made a stunning statement to his congregation, "If there ever was such a place as heaven, I'd be bored out of my skull to be there."

I was saddened to receive this pastor's letter. He was a leader among the mainline denominations in Colorado and a board member of a large liberal school of theology. I couldn't imagine being a Christian minister and not having a word of hope for eternal life in heaven. To stand beside the casket of a church member and offer no hope of life beyond the grave, no certain word of resurrection to life eternal, no eternal promise of Jesus who said, "I am the resurrection and the life. He who believes in me will live, even though he dies" (John 11:25). If you have nothing to offer but a self-reliant message of positive thinking in this life, you become just an echo of the words of the Apostle Paul, "If only for this life we have hope in Christ, we are to be pitied more than all men" (1 Corinthians 15:19).

I believe in heaven because I believe the Bible. I bank my eternal life on John 3:16, "For God so loved the world that He gave His one and only Son, that whoever believes in Him shall not perish but have eternal life." The Bible makes it plain that the primary purpose of Christ's coming to this world was to save us and give us *eternal life.* The Bible says that God's people, "Have peace with God through our Lord Jesus Christ," and through Jesus, "We rejoice in the hope of the glory of God," (Romans 5:1-2). In the New Testament, Christian hope and heaven go together and rest on Christ's incarnation, death, resurrection and ascension into heaven. Heaven is the place where God's presence uniquely dwells. Jesus taught us to pray, "Our Father in heaven," (Matthew 6:9). Heaven is a real location, (John 14:2-3). It's the place of our treasure and pearl of great value, (Matthew 13:44-46). It's the place of our citizenship, (Philippians 3:20). It's the place where my hope is stored up for me in heaven, (Colossians 1:5). It's the place where, "Moth or rust do not destroy, and where thieves do not break in and steal," (Matthew 6:20). It's my forever home. (Psalm 23:6).

This hope doesn't in any way blind us to Jesus' command to feed the hungry, clothe the naked or visit the prisoner, (Matthew 25:35-40). The Christian is foremost among those who give the cup of cold water in Jesus' name, Mark 9:41). And as those who live for God's glory, the Christian will be chief among those who work earnestly

Work earnestly for compassion, mercy and justice.

for compassion, mercy and justice and long to bring Christ's healing to both body and soul.

Just days after burying my wife Clarice and then again, ten years later, after the funeral for my wife Sandy, I stood in the pulpit of my church and testified to the hope of heaven as, "An anchor for the soul, firm and secure," (Hebrews 6:19). I could never have survived the loss of my parents, my dear wives and numerous other friends and family members without the absolute assurance that when I die I'll "…be away from the body and at home with the Lord" (2 Corinthians 5:8).

Many years ago, I heard an old saint say, "I long to go home to my Jesus, I'm homesick for heaven." My heart echoes that longing. I have such awesome treasures in heaven. Clarice and Sandy are there and my folks and my birth mother and an uncountable company of believers who have gone before me. When disease, pain and death did its worst to them, Jesus did His best and brought them, in that instant, into His glory. They all wait there for me. The Bible describes them as, "A great multitude that no one could count, from every nation, tribe, people and language, standing before the throne and in front of the Lamb. They are wearing white robes and are holding palm branches in their hands. And they cry out in a loud voice:

'Salvation belongs to our God, who sits on the throne, and to the Lamb," (Revelation 7:9-10).*

Yes, I'm homesick for heaven. There *definitely* is a heaven waiting for us and we'll certainly never be bored to be there. Heaven is that awesome home that's filled with glory and grace and Jesus. The Bible says, "No eye has seen, no ear has heard, no mind has conceived what God has prepared for those who love Him," (1 Corinthians 2:9). I'm homesick for heaven.

I began my life abandoned and without a home. I come now to the closing years of my life, blessed by my adoptive home and confident in the hope of my heavenly home. The only reason I have this certainty of going to heaven is because God left heaven to rescue me. In the person of Jesus, the Messiah, God came for you and me. He lived the perfect life we've failed to live, He died the death for sin that we deserved to die and He rose again so that all who believe in Him will have the gift of eternal life and enjoy Him forever. This has been my peace in the storms of life and my hope for all eternity. I hope that you can say "amen" to that.

My life story ends with great peace in my heart, the absence of fear and hope for eternity, all because of God's saving action in Jesus Christ. The Apostle Paul sums-up this action in Ephesians 1:3-5, "Praise be to the God and Father of our Lord Jesus Christ who…predestined us to be *adopted as His sons* through Jesus Christ.

That's an amazing promise! It sums-up my story. By faith in Christ we are God's adopted children. This promise of our adoption by God into His faith family is a great trumpet blast of the Christian faith and the healing for my troubled heart. By nature, we are not children of God. While God is the great creator of all humankind, we are by nature and birth sinful people and the Bible says that sin separates us from God. The Apostle Paul says, "As for you, you were dead in your transgressions and sins, in which you used to live…But because of His great love for us, God who is rich in mercy, made us alive in Christ even when we were dead in transgressions - it is by grace you have been saved" (Ephesians 2:1, 4-5). Not only has God in His mercy, "made us alive in Christ," but He has also adopted us into the family of God and given us all the full rights as sons and daughters of the Heavenly Father. To top it all off, He has made us His heir with our final inheritance being prepared for us in heaven.

I was adopted into the Swanson family nearly 80 years ago. It was a gift from God who led my birth mother to the Swanson home. But I haven't words to describe the greatness of the gift from God when I was by faith adopted 60 years ago into the family of God. Through the past 2000 years, Christians have turned the world upside down with this life-changing message. We stand in awe before God's great plan for all humanity. Herein lies my peace.

The ancient church expressed their praise for our adoption into God's family in the great doxology called, "Gloria Patri." As the doorstep child, now twice adopted, it is my song of praise for all eternity:

"Glory be to the Father, and to the Son,
And to the Holy Ghost;
As it was in the beginning, is now
And ever shall be, world without end. Amen, Amen."

THE END